Peruvian Street Lives

▸ ▸ ▸ ▸ *Interpretations of Culture in the New Millennium*
Norman E. Whitten Jr., General Editor

Peruvian Street Lives

Culture, Power, and Economy among
Market Women of Cuzco

Linda J. Seligmann

University of Illinois Press · Urbana and Chicago

Unless otherwise noted, the photographs in this book were
taken by the author.

Library of Congress Cataloging-in-Publication Data
Seligmann, Linda J., 1954–
Peruvian street lives: culture, power, and economy among
market women of Cuzco / Linda J. Seligmann.
p.   cm. — (Interpretations of culture in the new
millennium)
Includes bibliographical references and index.
ISBN 0-252-02901-1 (cloth : alk. paper)
ISBN 0-252-07167-0 (pbk. : alk. paper)
1. Women—Peru—Cuzco—Social conditions. 2. Women—
Peru—Cuzco—Economic conditions. 3. Peddlers and ped-
dling—Peru—Cuzco. 4. Poor women—Peru—Cuzco.
5. Markets—Peru—Cuzco. 6. Women merchants—Peru—
Cuzco. I. Title. II. Series.
HQ1575.C89S45   2004
305.42'0985'37—dc21   2003014290

Contents

Acknowledgments

In an interview in *The New Yorker* with John Lahr, film director Mira Nair commented that she follows the dictum of André Gide—Tyranny is the absence of complexity—in crafting her films about life in India. She added that she keeps alert her "eye and ear for paradox." I had just seen *Monsoon Wedding* and, indeed, it was as Nair described it: "crammed with the contrasting textures of sight, sound, and sociology" (Lahr 2002:100). This book represents a modest effort to bring alive the world that the women who work in the markets of Cuzco inhabit, a world that moves from the daily doldrums of making ends meet to unexpected dramas that unfold in households and on the streets. It is a world in flux, yet it has its comforting rhythms. In the pages that follow, I touch on the major domains through which these women's lifelines flow. Surely, there is more, and will be more, to the story, but I could never have crafted this canvas of complexity without the help of the many women, and some of the men, in Cuzco's markets. For their interest in my work, their patience in guiding me, their insights and humor, their tolerance of my blunders, the flashes of anger that made me think twice, their willingness to be associated with someone who didn't exactly fit and sometimes affected their ability to make sales, and the protection they offered me when the markets became dangerous, I thank all of them, including those who looked on curiously but fearfully as I interviewed their companions. They include Luz Marina Pumalloqlla Huayllani, Eutrofia Qorihuaman, Lucila Chawar Ronda, Susanna Farfán, Justina Aparicio de Paliza, Eulalia Gonzáles Castro, Sebastiana Farfán Cinguna, Teodora Cárdenas Sierra, Doris Cerda López, Luisa Aguirre, Pascuala Huamani, Magdalena Puma de Raymi, Juana Huaman, Serafina Lorayku, Gregoria Quispe Yucra, Teófila Carpio, Jacinta López Quispe, Doris Palma, Doris Amachi, Rosa Quispe, Baudelia Cataldo, Nanci Salazar, Doris Argondoña Martínez, Eva Carhuarupay, Enriqueta Sana, María Cuba, Martínez Suárez, Melchora Rayo, Margarita Juru, Wilma Hinajosa, Marina

Ordoña, Marta Hernández, Hilda Villafuerte Toledo, Felícitas Lucrecia Cardona Ríos, Alejandrina Wayka, Domérica Hermoza, Zoraida Sálazar, Josefina Solorzano Cárdenas, Juana Calvo Córdova, Flora Pompiya, Leonarda Rimachi, Julia Chacón, Ofelia Tingo Arias, Natalia Linares, Marina Condori, Janet Aragón Olivos, Ruperta Gamarra, Claudia Futuri, Lucho Galdos, Virginia Lenes Tacuri, Alejo Gutierrez, Juan Roa Apasa, Aidé Tito Romero, Victoria Quispe, María Inés Caballero Huachaca, Pablo Apasa, Santisa Juanca Huayta, Bernice Alvarez, Liberata Condori, Jovita Arampa Puma, Elizabeth Anchaya, Laura Carwarupay, Lucre Carwarupay, Aidé Garces, Amilcar Huarez, Elizabeth Layqa, Agustín Mamani, Susanna Mora, Eutrofia Qorimaña, and Elena Vega. This work would not have been possible without help from Teófila Huaman Tito, my research assistant, who managed a fruit stall with her father, mother, and sister. Teófila was old and wise before her time. She was funny and smart, she had plenty of gumption, and I learned so much from her. She kept me going when I became disheartened by closed doors, broken promises, and the difficulty of making sense of things. In 1991, Edgar Galdos Enríquez, the son of a husband-wife team who sold clothes in the Tupac Amaru market, also helped me conduct interviews in the market. Vicki Galiano Blanco taught me a great deal as she energetically and meticulously assisted me in making my way through the archives of regional newspapers and periodicals in Cuzco, searching for information on the history of markets and marketing.

Cuzco is a departmental capital, but it is simultaneously a little village in which people cluster and inhabit the same haunts from day to day. I taught a class at the Colegio Andino of the Centro de Estudios Regionales Andinos "Bartolomé de Las Casas" on gender, class, and ethnicity in the Andes. My students came from different parts of Latin America, Europe, and the United States, and I benefited from my dialogs with them, especially Alexandra de Mesones and Agustina Roca. Miguel Ayala and Silvia León offered me a sense of family in Cuzco that made me less lonely, and they shared with me their knowledge of and experiences in the markets where they did their shopping. Carolyn Dean, Nada Hughes, Kathryn Burns, Marta Zegarra, Julia Rodriguez, and Jean-Jacques Decoster understood well the art of combining lively and sometimes wry conversation with laughter and a good meal now and then. I was glad to be in their company in Cuzco.

Kathleen Fine-Dare listened, commented, and offered suggestions with kindness, intelligence, and the trust born of friendship that lasts. I owe Steve and Sally Herman a special acknowledgment. I value greatly their open-mindedness and pleasure in intellectual engagement. They have more to do with this book seeing the light of day than they realize. Florence Babb has been a pioneer in explaining the unique position and activities of women who worked in Peru's markets and the organization and functions of informal economies. Her contributions have inspired me and led me to delve deeper into these subjects. Over the years, she has always been a generous mentor. Her careful and thoughtful review of this manuscript challenged me to achieve greater clarity and precision in my thinking.

I find it rewarding that the University of Illinois Press is bringing out this book as the first in the Interpretations of Culture in the New Millennium series. When I did my graduate training at Illinois, its anthropology faculty was intense, contradictory, talented, and passionate about their subjects of research. I think it was precisely the clashes between them that allowed me to forge my own path, taking what I thought was the best from each. All of them were committed to doing field research. It was in Norman Whitten's seminar "Ritual and Power in Social Life" that I began to think about the material I had gathered between 1974 and 1981 on Carnival festivities in different villages and market towns of the southern Peruvian highlands and Bolivia. It was at that moment that I linked ethnicity, religiosity, and power and began exploring, with Whitten's encouragement, the position and representation of *cholas,* women of mixed indigenous and Hispanic ethnicity, many of whom work in the markets. My subsequent field research alerted me to the dynamism between Andean peoples and their physical environment. The cultural and political knowledge and economic rationality of Quechua people in both city and countryside continue to remind me today to avoid jumping to conclusions, to listen, and to look at old practices and situations with new eyes. There is always more to learn.

I appreciate the commitment that George Mason University's College of Arts and Science and the Provost's Office have made to supporting research at a time of serious fiscal constraints and am grateful to them for awarding me a faculty study leave grant and a subsidy for the preparation of the book index. I owe a special thanks to Laura Kaplan, my graduate research assistant. She helped me systematically organize my interview data and took a genuine interest in the subject matter of this book. The Wenner-Gren Foundation remains one of very few foundations that generously supports anthropological field research. This book would not have been possible without a grant (#6313) from them in 1998.

The University of Illinois Press staff, particularly Joan Catapano, Theresa L. Sears, and Carol Anne Peschke, have made the preparation of this book a pleasure rather than a headache. I am impressed by how smoothly everything has gone each step of the way.

I am immensely grateful to my husband, John R. Cooper, who has put up with "the book," traveled to watch it in the making, and read it with close care and encouragement. My mother, Barbara B. Seligmann, provided childcare every Wednesday morning, giving me precious time to think, write, and re-write. My father, Albert L. Seligmann, took his blue pencil to almost every page, once again demonstrating that small things make big differences. At the beginning of the new millennium, my own household structure underwent a transformation with the addition of our daughter. This book is dedicated to Mina Mei Li Cooper, now age four, who jolted me into awareness that life is short, surprising, and full of searching questions.

Peruvian Street Lives

Introduction

Cuzco, a city of movement. Thousands pour through the streets, all seemingly with a destination. Others huddle on the sidewalk. If one moves along with the current and picks different currents, one gradually realizes that there are rhythms: times for setting up shop and closing down, eating, taking a siesta, gossiping with friends, working, etc. This all takes place basically outside. Some señoras quietly hide behind their cloth dress-length aprons, slurping their soup with hunks of meat from enormous caldrons; others snooze under makeshift tents. The number of products for sale in multiple places is staggering and almost defies belief. When I close my eyes, what I see is flows of people but not exactly chaos. These complex flows really and truly don't seem to be a "stage" in any kind of modernization process. (field journal notes, July 1998)

Cuzco's markets resemble many others around the world.[1] Walking through them, one finds oneself in the core of the city, surrounded by agitated movement, cacophonous noise, stenches, people bearing hundreds of pounds on their backs, rumbling lorries, beckoning and wheedling vendors, and the lurking presence of pickpockets. It is almost impossible not to delight in the remarkable variety of merchandise for sale, ranging from fresh bread, vegetables, fruit, and dry goods needed to fill one's daily shopping basket, to newfangled hair baubles and dachshund-shaped porcelain teapots from China, to practical items such as luggage, underwear, and stockings, to exotic objects, incense, and herbs that Quechua people use to prepare ritual offerings. Traditional open air markets that date from colonial times meet with visions of modernity and postmodern mass media images in odd ways. Women sit on the sidewalks in front of their woven cloths on which medicinal herbs are heaped while young girls at their permanent market stalls don white nurse's uniforms and stand behind shiny stainless steel containers of the very same herbs. Rap and *chicha* music blare out from alleyways, and it is easy to get caught up in the movement and rhythm of market life.[2]

Many of us do our shopping not in places like these but rather in supermarkets, price club warehouses, or fancy gourmet boutiques. A few of us have the good fortune to shop weekly at outdoor Saturday farmers' markets, taking in the smell of fresh bread and flowers and meeting people who seem to come from a healthier, organic land. As we shop, we may keep in mind the pennies we want to spend or the quality of the produce. Depending on our schedules, we may dally at the supermarket, trying to choose among the dizzying variety of brands and products available to the average consumer. More likely, though, we monitor our time, organizing our grocery shopping as efficiently as possible. Some of us religiously save coupons, and others throw caution to the wind, attracted to a new product by television commercials or simply by the way the product tickles our fancy and sense of need or desire to consume. With hungry children, limited time, a mortgage, and a budget, we may decide to drive the distance to a warehouse where we can buy in bulk. Regardless of our shopping habits and needs, the places we go to are strategically well organized. Our immediate sense is that they are clean and the produce is carefully washed and processed. Usually, employees stock the shelves, work the cash registers, and load the groceries. Carefully instructed by their company employer, they greet every customer and encourage them to have a nice day.

What a contrast, then, to enter the shopping world of open air markets, bazaars, and street vendors the world over. These sites are flooded by people selling and trading things. Nothing is refrigerated, the noise of bargaining is almost deafening, and the smells are overpowering. On my very first trip to Peru in 1974, we left Peru's capital, Lima, and traveled by train during the rainy season into the southern highlands, finally reaching our destination, a gray-looking large town called Sicuani at about 12,000 feet above sea level, some fourteen hours later. The first place we visited was *el mercado,* the market, where stalls built out of metal stakes and sometimes wooden platforms, informally roofed with flapping cobalt blue plastic, stretched on for miles. The sheer diversity and density of products available for purchase or barter—agricultural implements, baby chicks, padlocks, weavings, medicinal herbs, potatoes, rubber tire sandals—fascinated me. At the time, I scarcely thought about how strange we, in our enormous hiking boots, down jackets, and curious gazes, looked to the peddlers. They stared back at us quietly, with some hostility.

Now, after some twenty-five years of wandering the markets of southern Peru, I am more intrigued than ever by them. I've come to realize some of the reasons for my fascination, not least of which is that the markets I've come to know in Peru have their own logic. Even though some of the same rules apply equally to shopping in Peru and my home town in the United States, others are distinctive. Even when the goals are similar—to buy food to put on the table or to sell enough to continue selling and maybe even make a profit—the goals are reached in different ways. These differences matter. They tell us something about the cultural values and meanings that shape people's economic activities, and they dramatically reveal the constraints within which buying and selling take place in conditions of uneven development.

Anthropologist Sidney Mintz, who writes marvelously about markets and food and its meanings, tells a story, probably apocryphal, about the social side of how markets and market women operate in Haiti:

> [A] female market trader [was] trudging to market on a dusty road with a heavy sack of produce on her head. A foreigner met her and offered a relatively enormous amount of money for the entire sack. She refused and continued on her way. Frustrated, the foreigner complained about the lack of economic sense in her behavior (and by extension, the behavior of all petty market traders): "They are more interested in socializing with their friends at market than they are in making a profit." The truth is that it would have been foolish for a trader to sacrifice a long-run business relationship (by disappointing a regular customer) for a one-time killing—assuming that in fact such a partner were waiting at the market. (cited in Plattner 1989:213)

After only a few visits to the markets of southern Peru, I was a little perplexed by the lack of competition between vendors, all of whom were selling exactly the same product. How could they stay in business or make a profit? I also wondered about the range of prices the same vendor quoted to different customers. These prices seemed to have nothing to do with competition, scale, or quality. Even more inexplicable in the economic framework with which I was familiar was the peculiar phenomenon that took place when a person demanded fifty rather than ten of something when conditions of scarcity did not prevail and, instead of going down, the unit cost of each went up.

Often, Westerners who have the pleasure of encountering the ingenuity of Peruvian vendors, the charm of their personalities, and the beauty of some of their wares cannot help but ask why they don't capitalize on their skills and the quality of their products. These queries occasionally become fiercely judgmental in tone as foreigners and the Peruvian elite assume without delving further into the matter that street vendors must be ignorant, lazy, uncivilized, or content with their standard of living. I hope that this foray into the markets of Peru offers a better sense of who these vendors are, the stories and the logic of their economic ventures, and the complex webs of social ties and political pressures and possibilities in which their lives are situated. Buying and selling in the highland markets of Cuzco, Peru has a poignant and courageous human face. Almost every market woman has an apprenticeship story akin to one of suffering without redemption. Market women keep on keeping on in astonishingly adversarial conditions, I think, but they might tell it differently, seeing their life activities as mundane, a job that provides them with food for their families, punctuated by occasional challenges, harassment from police and politicians, and welcome sociability.

Truck Manners

I have many reasons for writing this book. I first started working in the Andes when I was eighteen years old and a junior in college. I went not to the city but to the countryside, where many of Peru's Quechua-speaking *campesinos* (peasants) lived. Travel was arduous. Most of the villages I worked in were located at more than 12,000 feet above sea level and to get to them from the market town of Sicuani, I either had to hike four or five hours up and down and then up again or take a truck from there before cock's crow.

Trucklife has its own system of etiquette, but if you don't know what it is, then you are subjected to early morning roughhousing without much to guide you as you try to figure out the right way to do things. If I was very lucky, I might be able to reserve the truck cab for some protection from the freezing morning air and the fine dust, but unless I had something more than the fare to offer to the driver, it was far more likely that a local official or wholesaler would gain that coveted refuge. The usual alternative for me was to do what everyone else did: find a place in the bed of the truck and prepare for many hours of scrunched discomfort and tension. In my case, the discomfort was offset by raucous interludes, almost always at my expense. Dressed in pants instead of a skirt, I was not wearing the right clothes, and I made the rest of the travelers feel self-conscious. I suspect they had some inkling of how self-conscious they made me feel.

Riding in the back of trucks several layers deep with people and their produce, saturated in the early morning aroma of 80 proof pure grain alcohol, coca leaves, and unwashed wool, I gradually learned some important survival rules.[3] The women who work in the markets taught me many of those rules, which I have never forgotten. Rule one: Occupy as much space as possible by spreading out your body, multiple layers of skirts, and bundles. Rule two: If encroachment seems imminent, prod and push, using any angular part of your anatomy, but do so subtly and try to give the semblance of innocence, disinterest, and nonchalance. Rule three: Share your food and drink with the people around you. Rule four: Look resolute but be lighthearted. Prepare to laugh at others' bumbling efforts to find a seat. Rule five: Have patience. Rule six: Do not argue with the driver, or you may be left behind the next time if the truck is full or you have too many bundles.

Women are treated somewhat better than men in truck-riding etiquette, but because I usually dressed in slacks rather than skirts, I was not necessarily accorded preferential treatment. In between the sudden lurches when I was able to keep my balance, I took in the appearance and behavior of the women of the market. Tough but not impassive, at the ready with raunchy jokes, quick to help their companions, shrewd and alert to potential deals, these women impressed and frightened me. They stood up for themselves, unlike many *campesinas* (peasant women) who tended to speak in whispers and sometimes withdrew into themselves at any sign of trouble, injustice, or aggression.

Gender, ethnic, and racial relations in Peru, as anywhere, are complicated, and scholars have argued about whether the relationship between Quechua couples was a balanced and complementary one, as many of the chronicles and early colonial narratives suggest, or whether it was simply an ideal that was not borne out in practice. It is probably the case that the inequalities between Quechua men and women had their origin in the implantation of Spanish mores and the transformation of existing regimes of labor. Whatever the situation was before the arrival of the Spanish conquistadors in the early sixteenth century, contemporary relationships between couples in the city and countryside are fraught with imbalances and inequalities. Many women in the countryside are subjected to double or triple days of labor, physical abuse, and subordination, despite the respect their impressive skills in domains such as curing, herding, cooking, and weaving and their knowledge of seeds command from both men and women. Nevertheless, they do voice their opinions, and, like any social relationship, theirs is a dynamic one. Over the last fifteen years, gradually more women from the countryside have begun speaking up publicly, and a few have occupied leadership positions in formal political hierarchies.

Even though the women of the urban markets experience similar conditions as their counterparts in the countryside and many of them began their journey in their natal highland village, the kind of work they do and the collective locus of their labor appear to have bolstered their morale and permitted them to struggle against these conditions. Their strength and their ability to defy existing ideals and categories on those long uncomfortable truck rides attracted me, and this book constitutes my effort to set out to try to understand their world.

In the course of making sense of their world, I learned a great deal from others who have also studied and written about the lives of market women from a variety of perspectives. Sidney Mintz (1964), Margo Smith (1973), and

Ximena Bunster and Elsa Chaney (1985) provided many of us with our first glimpse of the lives of women who worked as domestic servants and vendors in the urban setting of Lima, Peru. Florence Babb (1989) wrote a classic study of women vendors, now issued in a revised edition (1998), examining them in light of the political and economic challenges they faced. The setting for her work, as is true of mine, was the markets of a departmental capital, located in the Andean highlands, originally home to the majority of Peru's indigenous inhabitants. I was greatly influenced by Babb's study. Based on my own fieldwork, I began to delve into the cultural, economic, and political dimensions of the lives of market women in Cuzco, Peru, considering the tensions between the occupational category to which they belonged as economic brokers and the ways they were perceived and self-identified as cultural and political intermediaries (1989, 1993, 1998, 2000). An edited volume prepared by Larson, Harris, and Tandeter (1995) and a book by de la Cadena (2000) gave these earlier analyses a rich and detailed depth through their use of oral histories and archival resources. Weismantel (2001) and Albro (1997, 2000) have further complicated our understanding of the subject of market women by demonstrating the ways in which they become cultural images and icons in a context of intersecting and overlapping global, national, and local media currents and practices. And Colloredo-Mansfeld (1999), in his work on the weavers of Otavalo, Ecuador, provided a rich portrait of how culture and class fuse to create class cultures, a concept that illuminates and explains the ways in which market women may powerfully come together around some issues but splinter around others. All of these works have helped to shape my thinking about Peru's market women.

Key Moments: Conquest, Reform, and Civil War

Sidney Mintz tells us that in trying to understand "meaning," it is important to distinguish between "inside" and "outside" meanings. By "outside" meanings, he "refers to the wider social significance of changes effectuated by institutions and groups whose reach and power transcend both individuals and local communities: those who staff and manage larger economic and political institutions and who make them operate." He notes that "those who create . . . *inside* meaning do so by imparting significance to their own acts and the acts of those around them, in the fashion in which human beings have been giving their behavior social significance as long as they have been human" (1996:22, 23). Neither inside nor outside meanings are homogeneous, but like Sidney Mintz, I think it is important to consider how the life of these markets—the forms they have taken, their history, the labor relationships within them, and the views that people have of them and the people who work in them—are shaped by fairly abstract and distant phenomena such as economic globalization. I think it equally important to discern what these phenomena mean to different people and how and under what circumstances they may come to share these meanings. Therefore, in the chapters that follow I move back and forth between how distant yet enormously powerful conditions interact with the ways in which people live and try to make sense of these conditions.

Many conditions from afar have affected the lives of Peruvians.[4] Here let me mention four major events, cataclysmic in their own right, that have had a tremendous impact on the worldview and livelihood of Peruvians. The first, which I explore in greater depth in chapter 1, is the Spanish invasion and conquest of 1532, which radically uprooted people, decimated the native population, and wreaked havoc with indigenous gender relations, political hierarchies and organizations, and economic regimes.

The second is the agrarian reform of 1969. One consequence of four centuries of colonialism was a dramatic inequity in land tenure in which the Quechua-speaking rural population, generally known as *campesinos,* lost most of their land, becoming either permanent laborers on Spanish estates (*haciendas*) or sharecroppers. In the face of unrest among peasants in the countryside and a desire for national modernization, a left-wing military coup took place in 1968. The head of the military junta, General Juan Velasco Alvarado, expropriated and nationalized oil companies and major coastal agroindustries, such as sugar plantations. He also dramatically restructured the legal and political apparatus governing land tenure and labor relations in the Andean highlands and legitimized the urban squatter settlements that had sprung up around Lima and major provincial cities. Estate lands were expropriated and turned over to workers organized into cooperatives. Perhaps most importantly, the Quechua people were finally recognized as citizens, and they were able to use the law and courts to defend their land and labor rights. They were also expected to abandon their indigenous identities and practices and become integrated into the nation as Peruvians rather than Quechua peasants. Eventually, the reform measures were abandoned after another military coup, and twelve years of authoritarian governance without democratic representation ensued. (See Seligmann 1995 for a fuller analysis of the agrarian reform.) The story of Peru's agrarian reform, its mixed successes and failures, is a long and complicated one, but among the consequences were far greater numbers of rural inhabitants who flocked to the cities, using the markets, gaining an education, and challenging the status quo of racial discrimination. Among these urban sojourners and permanent residents were the women of the markets and their children.

In 1980, Peru experienced a third cataclysmic moment, perhaps its most somber epoch since the Spanish conquest, the inception of armed struggle: the civil war, which lasted more than a decade, resulted in at least 60,000 deaths and more than 7,000 disappearances, and ravaged the countryside and cities (*The New York Times,* Aug. 29, 2003). The majority of those who died were Quechua. Battles pitted approximately 5,000 Shining Path guerrillas (the movement is known in Spanish as Sendero Luminoso) and their sympathizers against military and paramilitary forces. Members of the Shining Path movement, dissatisfied with reformist measures, sought to dismantle the existing political and economic infrastructure of the nation. The climate of terror created systematic mistrust among Peruvians and exacerbated the currents of racial discrimination simmering just below the surface. Many of those who worked in markets, especially their children, were targets of attack, and not a few, disenchanted with the failure of the government to honor its promises to working people, were members or sympathizers of Sendero Luminoso.

When the 1990 presidential election took place, traditional political parties in Peru had been wholly debilitated. An independent, Alberto Fujimori, a Japanese-Peruvian known as "El Chino," was elected president. Many market women initially were taken with his embrace of Quechua traditions and his status as an immigrant and as a person of mixed ethnicity. He immediately abolished the Constituent Assembly and judiciary, and the measures he took over the next two terms in office (1990–95, 1995–2000) became ever more authoritarian and corrupt. However, he ushered in a more peaceful era because he ended the violence of the civil war by finding and arresting most of the leaders of the Shining Path guerrilla movement, including Abimael Guzman, gaining him the initial support of many Peruvians. Nevertheless, in an effort to restore Peru's economic health and attract foreign investment, Fujimori agreed to impose austerity measures and structural adjustment policies as recommended by the International Monetary Fund. These policies caused the standard of living of many Peruvians to decline precipitously. He also sought to strengthen the central government and its revenues by crafting a comprehensive and regressive tax law.[5] Many informal vendors operating at different scales found themselves paying taxes that they considered out of proportion to their meager earnings and living in fear of the tax collectors who roamed the streets of Cuzco. The tax law consequently became a lightning rod for mobilizing discontent and protest against the Fujimori regime by market women. Fujimori resigned from office, and he and his intelligence chief, Vladimiro Montesinos, eventually fled in disgrace from Peru in the wake of the discovery of widespread corruption, an international arms deal scandal, and blackmail.[6]

Ethnographic Undertakings: Research and Writing

Most readers appreciate a bird's-eye view of what they are about to peruse. The chapters that follow are built around issues that I found to be of central importance to the lives of Andean market women. Just as participant observation—getting to know the women in the markets and spending time with them at work and in their space—gave me valuable insights into why they organized their lives and work as they did, it was equally important for me to connect the dots, so to speak. I discovered that what was visible and audible was only part of the story. I had to track historical processes, government policies, ideas and ideologies, and connections between seemingly unrelated activities and individuals to construct a framework that adequately explained the links between the place of market women in Andean society, the behavior of people in markets, how they felt about their lives, and the opinions others held of market women. I also had to make an effort to discern whether the accounts and explanations that people gave me were truthful. It is understandable that many people I encountered would resort to lying or that their memories would not serve them well. Fear, shame, mistrust, resentment, the differences in power between the women in the markets and me, and the simple fact that at the beginning of my research, people did not know me and I did not know what were the right questions to ask contributed to ambivalent sentiments toward me and my research.

To get a sense of the validity of the narratives I gathered, I had to track things down. If some of the market women told me of incidents they had had with municipal agents, then I interviewed municipal agents about the same subject matter. Complaints among vendors about wholesaler or loan shark practices led me to wholesalers and loan sharks and the environment in which they operated. Discussions among vendors about how to strategically locate themselves encouraged me to spend time in many different kinds of markets in rural and urban areas. Because religiosity seemed central to the economic philosophy and social relationships of many vendors, I tried to join in festivals and quietly absorb the proselytizing of Evangelical Protestants. The many years I had worked in rural areas helped me understand yet another kind of religiosity among market women. I talked to grocery store owners, politicians, nongovernmental organization personnel, tax collectors, and bank loan officers. And I spent long hours reading accounts relevant to the markets in the municipal archives of Cuzco and then discussing these accounts with women in the markets and with government officials. George Marcus (1998:79–104) calls this kind of research "multi-sited" because it does not resemble the traditional case study. I would call it exhaustive field research that all ethnographers should aspire to because it is the only way to challenge our preconceptions and to comprehend more fully the deeper meaning of the words we hear and the activities and interactions we document. Part of the reason Marcus brings forth this concept is to call our attention to the artificiality with which we have often limited what constitutes our field site. In his vision of ethnographic study, the notion of the "local" is an artificial construction that can be understood differently if, in the course of our studies, we take account of a far broader set of interconnected sprawling and open-ended relationships and flows that impinge on what transpires in our initial research site. Even a partial effort to accomplish this will shift how we make sense of what we formerly thought were "local" settings and activities.

Over time, people did get to know me. The emphasis I placed on sharing with them what I was learning from them helped to bridge power gaps between us. Also of great help were the friendships and research relationships I forged with people in the market who themselves were viewed by other vendors as experienced and knowledgeable mentors. Finally, the sheer amount of time I spent day after day in the markets established me as a fixture. As the day's business and social interactions wore on with their own rhythms, I became less of an oddball and was able to catch glimpses of key moments that shed light on the backdrop of the everyday lives of women's work in the markets. Here I think of conversations with customers, the small tokens of assistance that women provided to one another, the shady visits from loan sharks, the brittle and sometimes brutal abuse by municipal agents, moments of hilarity, children coming to their mothers' stalls after school and helping out, and quiet interludes when a vendor picked up a magazine to read.

Two final aspects of the methods I used in my research deserve comment. With some trepidation, given my subject matter, I have chosen not to use pseudonyms unless someone requested anonymity or made it clear to me that they wished to hide their identity. The reasons for this are manifold. The women I worked with almost always wanted their stories told, they wanted their voices heard and the conditions of their lives understood, and they were quite passionate about the efforts they were making on behalf of their families and the obstacles that were placed in their way. Some of the people I talked to already appear in the public record as officeholders and political leaders. In all cases, I asked for their permission before using my tape recorder, conducting open-ended interviews, or taking their photographs. I use their names knowing that some will accuse me of violating a key ethical principle in anthropology: Do no harm. I must counterbalance that important cautionary note with my conviction that by using their names, I acknowledge the value of their lives as individuals and I also hope to convey to readers my willingness to have others contest or enrich this initial research. These are real people; others can talk to them, and they can talk back. We live in the same world.

Finally, I must address the question of reciprocity, a subject that is central to the pages that follow. What could I share without hypocrisy with the women in the markets, given the chasm between us? Words matter. It may seem feeble to suggest that some of the women who were in great economic need benefited from our exchange of words, our conversations, but indeed we shared fresh perspectives and opened up avenues of inquiry and knowledge. We learned from each other. And most of the women I spoke with shared my eagerness for learning even though their immediate concerns were far more pragmatic. Some of our dialogs made those pragmatic concerns central: alternative ways of establishing credit for vendors, making markets less dangerous places, establishing daycare facilities, dealing with familial abuse, using media channels to make their case known when their livelihoods were under attack, interpreting legislation that affected them, and sharing what I knew about how informal vendors in the United States lived and worked. Occasionally, I helped vendors meet their debt obligations by giving them bridge loans when they asked. I also felt happy contributing to festivals, buying a little of this and that on my daily trips to the markets, and bringing modest presents to some of my friends in the market: a pair of reading glasses, a colorful scarf, a notebook, a box of chocolates. In the end, though, the scales were tipped, and they have given more than I in this exchange. This book may offer us a different way of looking at the lives of women who work in open air markets and bazaars. However, I will not forget that almost every single day that I went to the markets, with tape recorder, notebook, and camera in my shopping bag, I returned with my shopping bag replete with apples, fresh bread, an avocado, some coca leaves, and tiny plastic bags of aromatic spices—gifts from the women I had visited—in addition to the photos, notes, and recorded conversations that furthered my research.

In organizing the chapters of this ethnography, I found myself creating a structure that reflected my own growing understanding of market life and replicated roughly the rhythms of everyday life for the women themselves. In chapter 1 I offer an overview of the history of the establishment of markets in Cuzco and the struggles over where they should be located and why.

Chapter 2 begins to draw us into why women become vendors and what skills and practices they rely on to establish themselves as vendors in the market. In an important article, Viviana Zelizer (in press) discusses the tendency of social scientists, theoretically and methodologically, to regard dualities that intermingle (hence dissolving the very notion of dualities) as "dangerous." Social scientists may also believe that hostile worlds—the world of capitalist and the world of noncapitalist economies, for example—should remain exactly that. What I found is that the models of reciprocity that market women deploy to establish themselves and gain loyal customers dissolve these dualities and hostile worlds into a stew. This very stew creates discomfort sometimes, but it is precisely what allows market women to establish and maintain a niche for themselves.

In chapter 3 I focus more intently on the ways in which gender ideologies and the structuring of households over time have had an impact on the work that these women are either forced into or choose to undertake.

In chapter 4, I address the world of wholesalers and how they obtain their goods, which they then distribute to retail vendors. Wholesalers play a critical role in market life, yet they are almost always hidden from the customer's view. There are many different kinds of wholesalers, and how they are regarded by women vendors at the retail level is more nuanced than usually thought. Producers and retail vendors do not necessarily generalize that all wholesalers are exploitive and deserve the negative reputation they have the world over. Instead, they make it clear that they recognize the necessity of wholesalers and that it is important to weigh the content of the social relationships they have with them, the risks that market women would otherwise have to take, and the nature and sources of the profit that wholesalers make.

In chapter 5, as I untangle the "chain of marketing," I trace how formal and informal markets are intertwined. I also show how consumers view the economic behavior of intermediaries in general, why they are so hostile to both retailers and wholesalers, the steps (and transgressions) that the municipality takes to respond to consumer complaints, and the impact these perceptions have on the livelihood of vendors.

In chapter 6, we enter the more hidden world of credit and loan relationships—the risky, sometimes threatening, and unstable nature of loan contracts that are forged with women vendors—and the impact of transnational capital on the availability of credit.

In chapters 7 and 8 I open several windows onto race relations. A close analysis of conversation in the markets reveals how language exchanges serve as a medium for socializing, negotiating, and exchanging information but occasionally become the vehicle for communicating racial and gender ideologies. Chapter 8 moves from conversation to other domains in which race is central to understanding how vendors perceive themselves and the ways they are viewed by others. I discuss the history of race relations in Peru and the reasons that women vendors of the markets, in particular, seem to suffer so deeply from racial discrimination. That they explode "dangerous dualities" and interpenetrate "hostile worlds" in their behavior and activities in a public space while providing valuable economic services and goods contributes to the ambivalence with which many Peruvians view them.

There is a celebratory and devotional dimension to the lives of most Andean market women. In chapter 9, the signs and symbols of market life take a different turn, represented by market women performatively through celebration and devotion. Through their participation in fiestas—sponsorships, dance and music groups, drinking and eating, and costumed mascots—their personal reading of the Bible, healing, and their faith in miracles, they have contributed to a popular religiosity that is central to their identities, allowing them to challenge the status quo, nurture ties of solidarity among themselves, express and take advantage of commonalities in their economic and devotional practices, and enhance their well-being through acts of faith.

In chapter 10, politics and political mobilization take central stage as I attempt to understand the political consciousness of vendors, the ties they forge with other classes and sectors of society, the conditions and causes that lead them to organize and mobilize, the tactics they use, and the reasons for their successes and failures.

Narrative Threads

A few common threads run through this volume. One is the importance of what I call spatial relations in understanding the lives of market women. We have tended to take space for granted and give primacy to history in which one event follows another and to narratives in which one word follows another sequentially. Yet to understand these events and narratives, we need to step out of our linearity and realize the simultaneity of forces that create the space for these events and narratives, what Edward Soja (1989:1) calls "a geography of simultaneous relations and meanings." Therefore, I have organized the chapters as vignettes. At another level, the organization of space intervenes substantially, if not dramatically, in almost all dimensions of the lives of Andean market women. How are the markets of Cuzco constituted as locales? What is their relationship to the region in which they are located? How does their

location contribute to the ways in which labor, social interactions, and access
to resources are organized? What makes community possible within markets,
and what forms does it take? I also keep in mind how the control and structuring of space matter in both the exercise of and challenges to political power.

In my work in markets, I found that behind the often heated political
conflicts that involved the markets and the women who worked in the markets lurked ideologies about what was considered an appropriate use of space.
People held very different ideas about the organization and uses of space. The
source of these ideas interested me. Social theorist Anthony Giddens has tried
to arrive at a general explanation for how space intervenes in the structuring
of society. His explanation of "locale," paraphrased by Edward Soja (1989:148–
49), fits well with my understanding of Cuzco markets as places that do not
solely serve the function of supplying consumer goods to the public:

> The evocative concept of locale, a bounded region, . . . concentrates action
> and brings together in social life the unique and particular as well as the
> general and nomothetic. As Giddens notes, it is a notion somewhat akin
> to "place.". . . For Giddens, locales refer to "the use of space to provide the
> *settings* of interaction, the settings of interaction in turn being essential to
> specifying its *contextuality*" (1984:188). These settings may be a room in a
> house, a street corner, the shop floor of a factory, a prison, an asylum, a
> hospital, a definable neighborhood/town/city/region, the territorially de-
> marcated areas occupied by nation-states, indeed to occupied earth as a
> whole. Locales are nested at many different scales and this multilayered
> hierarchy of locales is recognizable as both a social construct and a vital part
> of being-in-the-world.

Markets have distinctive identities. We need to travel back in time to begin
to understand their particular formation. We also need to move through the
markets to understand what takes place in them, the interactions between
people, how and where they work and live, where they come from, and what
they think. And we need to travel outward from the market to understand how
Cuzco's markets fit into other contexts, what Giddens calls "a multilayered
hierarchy." This hierarchy ranges from the agrarian countryside, to the capital
of Lima, to the circuits of industrial and finance capital moving within Peru
and between Peru and other parts of the world. These movements, anchored
in work and geography, create uneven and complex relationships between
multiple nodes.

The second thread that winds its way through these vignettes is the emphasis
I place on women as the primary subjects of this story. They take center stage
because they are the traders of the markets, the ones at the lowest level of the

marketing hierarchy: By the thousands they make things move from whole-saler to buyer. Some of what they experience as intermediaries is hardly sur-prising and can be generalized to all others who broker sales at the retail level. Some of their experiences are unique to them as women in Peru who are nei-ther Quechua Indian nor resolutely Hispanic mestiza. They are often the mainstay of the household economy and have figured out how to defend them-selves in a nation built on the reproductive powers of women and the aggres-sive bravado of machismo.

Market women have the reputation of being sexually promiscuous, aggres-sive, and a social irritant. Although they sometimes deliberately represent themselves as defying appropriate comportment, many researchers have shown how these perceptions derive directly from phenomena linked to racial and class discrimination, such as the temptation of forbidden fruit (crossing sta-tus, class, and racial boundaries), and the relentless discomfort that many Pe-ruvians experience because of the gap between their ideological commitment to racial mixing as representing the future well-being of the nation and their aversion to it on the ground, particularly as women symbolize most power-fully social reproduction.[7]

Although men are important to this story, they take a back seat. I tried sev-eral times to interview as many men as possible working at the retail level, but my interviews constituted a paltry six or seven at the central market. At the same time, gender relations and sexuality, the locale of the household and the family, the partnerships between men and women in the market, and the way fathers and husbands view their wives' and daughters' work in the markets and its effects on them are important aspects of the lives of these women.

Finally, what lies in store for their children, more than anything else, pre-occupies most of the women with whom I talked. It is always on their mind. Felicitas Lucrecia Cardona Ríos de Mamani, a respected political leader among the market women, became my close friend and introduced me to many other women in the market. She spent hours telling me about her life, and toward the end of her reminiscences about her life in the market, she sat back and explained,

> I have excelled in everything, I have educated my children, I have given them careers. My other daughter . . . Emperatríz, she is an accountant. My other son is an engineer. Well, some of them didn't want to study, but they got an old-fashioned education. So, I have suffered a great deal in my life but yes, I have educated my ten children. . . . The only thing that I lack is to go and establish a savings account for my children. Because, in reality, my hus-band has never provided for me. I've always supported the family with my

own earnings. . . . I continue defending my companions. I continue struggling, but not like before. I don't have that will power any longer. I only
wait for my children to call me and visit me. When they call me, I'm happy,
content, it seems like, something, as they say, has fallen from heaven. . . . I
live for my children. I don't live for my husband. My children remember
me. "My mother, how is she?" "Mother, take this, take this." "We have to
go visit mother." "Mama Lucrecia, what are you doing, Mamá?"

The third and final thread woven into this volume is that of voice. The preceding paragraphs evince perhaps all too clearly that Cuzco's markets cannot
be reduced to an abstract analysis of spatial or gender relationships. To such
an analysis, we must stir in the voices of the people who live in Cuzco and
work, buy, and sell in the markets. The paths they have taken, their opinions,
and their occupational and life histories provide the crucial ingredients of
experience and dynamism. Their lives are hardly set in stone; their voices do
not form a chorus. They alone cannot change the course of advanced capital-

*Felicitas Lucrecia Cardona Ríos de Mamani, political leader and vendor of manioc and
vegetables, 1998.*

ism, but however constrained they are by the difficult conditions in which they work and live, some of them find ways to be innovative and to challenge their being-in-the-world. Some of them pierce through the racist ideologies that prevail in Peru; others embrace them. I have decided to use vignettes because they point up the disjunctures and the discordant qualities that can be found among the women of the markets and because, to a degree, the vignettes are homologous to the way my understanding of market life came about.

Voices are also important to this story because it is easy for anthropologists to turn their subject matter into objects of study. I have sometimes done that because there was too much between us and because I was indeed engaged in a study. At the same time, some market women permanently changed the way I look at the world: I found myself laughing and crying together with so many of them at one thing or another. Therefore, I have tried to infuse the vignettes with my voice. I could not directly change the life conditions of the market women: the beatings they suffered, the thefts, the deaths of their children, sexual harassment, the bleakness of the day, and their spitefulness and jealousy toward each other. Nor could I easily cross the chasm between their reality and mine. Yet, surprisingly often, we found common ground. I have written this book not because it will change the lives of the women I met in the markets but so that next time you walk through the gaudy displays and raucous alleys of an open air market—or the shining sterile aisles of your supermarket—the voices of some of these women will recall to you the richness and grit of their street lives.

Notes

1. Cuzco, located in the southern highlands of Peru, in the Department of Cuzco at about 11,000 feet above sea level, was once the capital of the Inca empire, and it is surrounded by numerous ceremonial sites. Both the city itself and the mountains that rise up from its outskirts and then give way to valleys are home to many Quechua people. The Quechua people are descendants of the Incas. They were once distinguished by both language and culture, but 500 years of intermarriage and colonialism have created great heterogeneity among them. Nevertheless, at least 10 million people speak one of the four variants of Quechua, and they inhabit parts of Bolivia, Peru, Ecuador, northwestern Argentina, and small areas of Chile and Colombia.

2. *Chicha* music, a mixture of African, traditional Quechua highland, and *criollo* coastal rhythms, is associated with markets and with urban migrants in Peru. José Matos Mar (1988:85–86), a long-time researcher of urban life in Peru, dates its inception from 1968 and describes it "as a musical fusion of Colombian *cumbias*, Cuban *guarachas*, and Andean highland *waynos* in which traditional Andean music becomes 'tropicalized' and is played with electric guitars, organs, and drums. It is an urban creation . . . that

has gone beyond Andean regional traditions and achieved a national homogeneity. . . . One band alone has succeeded in selling more than one million records of 'Aguajal' in three years."

3. Native inhabitants of the Andean highlands have chewed coca leaves for centuries. The leaves are tucked into the side of the cheek and chewed together with a lime alkaloid, which helps to release the juices from the leaves, much as tobacco is chewed. Coca chewing increases stamina, staves off fatigue, prevents altitude sickness, and, because it is often chewed in a group setting, provides a warmth and sociability. Coca is also a key ingredient in ceremonial offerings, ritual prayers to the mountain and earth spirits, and medicinal poultices and teas. Cocaine is made from coca leaves, but it takes huge amounts of coca leaves to make an ounce of cocaine. Chewing coca leaves has always been associated with being Indian, and although it is central to the cultural identity of many Quechua people, it also has a very negative connotation, causing many native inhabitants to reject this part of their identity in order to avoid racial discrimination. Pure grain alcohol was introduced by the Spanish when they invaded Peru in the sixteenth century. It was often used in forced labor situations. The Quechua also consider it to have medicinal properties, and people drink small amounts of it while riding in the open air to protect themselves from "evil winds." Unfortunately, alcohol is abused, and there have been serious problems among highlanders with alcoholism. See Allen (1988) for a comprehensive look at how Quechua inhabitants use and view coca.

4. Peter Klarén (2000) offers one of the best overviews of Peru's sociocultural and political history that I have encountered.

5. The tax law (Decreto Supremo #055-99), issued April 15, 1999, is extremely complex. Initially, those earning more than 18,000 soles per month and occupying differing amounts of space for their businesses were required to pay taxes higher than 18 percent. This subsequently changed to 15 percent or more depending on monthly income. Those earning less than 2,200 soles per month paid nothing, and those earning between 2,200 and 18,000 soles per month would pay between 9 percent and 15 percent per month on a graduated scale. All vendors are expected to provide documentation in the form of sales receipts. I am not an expert on Peruvian tax law, but in noting when this decree was issued, I wonder how much influence the U.S. tax law had on the structure of Peru's revised law, despite the latter's very different economic and political conditions.

6. Fujimori remains in Japan and has not been extradited to Peru; Montesinos was arrested and tried and is now in prison in Peru. The current president of Peru is Alejandro Toledo, elected in 2001. He is a former World Bank economist who is married to a Belgian anthropologist; his mother is Quechua, and his father works as a shoemaker.

7. See Stephenson (1999, especially 1–58) and Weismantel (2001). For a more general discussion of how racial discrimination animates not only the metaphors we mistake for the real state of affairs but also how the use of the metaphors themselves reinforces a distorted understanding of the reality of race relations, see Guss (2000), Stepan (1990), Shanklin (1998), and Whitten (1981).

1

Market Spaces and Market Places

*The two reached Tacora boulevard, the area known as Manzanilla.
They had already begun selling things that had been thrown out
from the better-off residential districts of the city—old bottles, used
magazines, nails rescued from some demolition, chairs with worn
out upholstery, extras after the dining room had been redone.*

*There were also boxes of rusty tacks. The residents of the nearby
working class neighborhood of La Victoria bought them to ensure the
success of their strikes. Sowing the roads with tacks, they halted
traffic.*

*Tacora was not the enormous street market it would become
twenty years later, a plethora of every kind of recycled object imag-
inable, the huge Lima market where the motto of informal production reigned: nothing is created, nothing is destroyed, all is transformed.*

*But Tacora had already begun the transformation into an enor-
mous process of commercialization that almost always began with
rickety tricycles that were used to recover seemingly useless objects
from the Limeñan middle class. (Salcedo 1993:72)*

This quote comes from a wonderful little piece of literature that I found in
one of Cuzco's markets. It is a rags-to-riches account called *The Boss: From
Itinerant Vendor to Magnate,* by novelist José María Salcedo. Although it is
unclear whether it is fact or fiction, the book has generated enthusiasm among
many workers, and I saw more than one vendor poring over the book, which
is written in two columns, like a newspaper. It is the story of the members of
one family who come to Lima from the countryside and must figure out how
to make a living. One of the sons eventually becomes a magnate, a Peruvian
Horatio Alger. The street lives Salcedo describes with such humor and precision approximate those of so many of the vendors I talked with, except that
they are far from becoming rich, despite their best efforts.

In this chapter, using a wide-angle lens, I explore how the market women of Cuzco come to make sense of the city in order to make a living. In the first part, I offer readers an overview of how the current layout of markets in Cuzco has emerged and some of the significant debates and variables that have intervened in determining the location of urban markets in Cuzco. Although many urban residents have been most concerned about the image their city projects and the availability and price of foodstuffs and other necessities, vendors, in organizing their livelihoods, have depended greatly on their knowledge of spatial relationships, some of which has been refined from their experience of rural agricultural conditions and regimes. They have adapted that knowledge to an urban setting, and their use of space as a strategic means and a code of communication has assisted them in establishing themselves as vendors and in gaining an advantage in the marketplace. In addition, the ability of market women to survive as vendors depends less on individual competition than on household cooperation and how household members pool their diverse labor.

From Llamas to Volvos

A locus of contention and social conviviality, Cuzco's central market (known today as the Mercado Central or sometimes as San Pedro), was originally in the heart of the city, the Plaza de Armas. The plaza, a palimpsest constructed on the ceremonial ritual center of the Inca empire, was first divided into two parts, each with specific ritual functions. Images of deities from distant ethnic polities (with their human representatives) were brought to Cuzco, the center of the empire, and specifically to the plaza, to receive the blessings of the Incas and demonstrate the obeisance of their ethnic lords to these new rulers. The Incas did an impressive job laying out the infrastructure that in large part made possible the control of their burgeoning empire. By the end of the fifteenth century, in less than a hundred years, they had constructed a complex road system, bureaucratic apparatus, canal networks, and an imperial religious cosmology in a far-flung array extending from Ecuador to Chile. Many imperial rites began and ended in what is now the Plaza de Armas. Although doubts remain about whether large regular markets were a part of the Inca economy, there is enough evidence to argue that markets (called *qatu* in Quechua), when they did take place, tended to coincide with ceremonial imperial rites, bringing together representatives of many distant ethnic polities. These markets were not permanent structures but rather were enacted by the people who participated in them. As suddenly as they appeared, they vanished, periodically shifting the boundaries that defined who were insiders and outsiders, who were strangers and familiars.

Smaller local markets also periodically took place in different highland valleys. Peru's remarkable geography is structured by multiple vertical axes that permit cultivation of or access to particular resources at altitudes that range from sea level along the coast to more than 14,000 feet above sea level in the high sierra. Along the Andean slopes alone, ecological zones rise from the deep jungle to barren plateaus where llamas and alpacas graze and only one or two kinds of potatoes can be cultivated. In addition, Peru itself is often described as "three nations"—the coast, jungle, and highlands—thus creating yet another vertical gradient.

The Inca economy was primarily a redistributive one. Goods from different zones were gathered together by the Inca bureaucracy as tribute from local populations and then redivided according to the needs of different polities (with a portion siphoned off for the Incas). Yet it has been documented that long-distance trade of highly specialized luxury goods occurred alongside this redistributive economy, and at least from the colonial period onward and almost certainly from before that time, domestic trade took place as a subsidiary, and more local, activity.[1]

In 1532, the Spanish invaded what became known as Peru. Afterward, the population of Cuzco began to grow slowly. The majority of the indigenous Quechua population continued to reside in the countryside. The Spanish newcomers, although initially few in number, were accustomed to a European market system, and they needed food and clothing. Informal markets began to spring up in Cuzco. The markets were first operated by the Spaniards themselves as well as some impoverished *criollos* (those of Spanish descent but born in the colony). The structure of the Plaza de Armas reveals the centrality of marketing from the earliest days of colonial society. The portals that surround the plaza retain the names they were given according to the goods and services that were traded or sold there: bread, flour, sweets, fodder, ironworks, used clothes, and meat. At the center of the cobblestone plaza stood a massive stone fountain. The stockyards and the llamas, burros, and horses that transported goods from villages were concentrated in or near the plaza, and urban residents complained about the resulting filth and stench. Spanish authorities tolerated the activities of these merchants. Toward the end of the seventeenth century, mestizos, blacks, mulattoes, and Indians began to imitate these vendors. With the change in the color of skin and sex of the street vendors and the increase in their numbers, the initial tolerance of the municipal authorities gave way in many cases to repression. Well-to-do urban residents began to make denigrating remarks about the women who sold their wares in the plaza and portals, seated on the ground.

Convents and monasteries played a central role in commerce (Burns 1999). They acquired large numbers of stores from which they received rents. In the eighteenth century, for example, the Convent of La Merced alone owned fifty-eight stores and a number of small stands called *cajones,* similar to corner grocers, which operated from houses in different parts of the city. Some families also owned large pieces of property that they used for commercial purposes. In the late seventeenth century, one nobleman, Pancorbo-Seliorigo, counted as part of his property seventy-seven stores and residences in Cuzco.[2]

Smaller markets developed in plazas adjacent to the Central Plaza (Limaq Pampa, Pampa del Castillo, and Santa Teresa); vendors lined one of Cuzco's principal streets, Mutuchaca; and on Saturdays, an open air market, attracting a number of itinerant vendors, was held in the Plaza of San Francisco called *Sábado baratillo* (the Saturday flea market). Nevertheless, some conditions worked against the growth of markets. Cuzco's colonial population remained small yet powerful, and local ethnic groups and populations were prohibited from traveling far from their place of origin except for purposes of forced labor, thus inhibiting the development of regional markets. Certain colonial policies also stifled market growth. Forced to work in the silver mines of Potosí and textile sweatshops, native men were dramatically curbed in their ability to produce surplus, even though the mines, whose laboring population needed to be fed and clothed, served as magnets for the proliferation of markets.[3] Such was the lack of coin that barter in exchange for forced labor predominated in the surrounding agrarian hinterlands. The challenging terrain and the lack of adequate transport also inhibited the growth of markets. What markets there were received little attention from Spanish chroniclers, perhaps because they did not seem to be out of the ordinary, perhaps because they were so few in number. On the other hand, travelers who later made their way to Lima and Cuzco almost always included commentaries about the markets in their travelogs, often dwelling on the exoticism of the female vendors who predominated in them.

Not until the end of the nineteenth century did Cuzco's urban residents begin to clamor for an official market. The growth in population and the need for Peruvians to represent themselves as a modern nation (Peru gained its independence in 1821) were driving forces behind Cuzqueños' decision to build a permanent market. For Cuzqueños, their desire to be modern held even more urgency, because in the eyes of sophisticated Limeños living in the nation's capital, Cuzqueños were marginal provincial rubes. Cuzqueños admired the parks and plazas of Lima that had been inspired by "French models." Cuzqueño society was rigidly divided and segregated according to status and race. Old aristocratic families, many of whom owned large estates in the countryside, did not hesitate to express their shame over the visible presence of Indians who were dirty and of female hawkers who stepped outside of ideal Spanish gender roles. They were also sensitive to the serious problems of sickness caused by the lack of potable water and a sewage system, and they expressed their desire for "a decent market" (Garmendia 1968). The word *decente* in Spanish does not convey the sense of *adequate* but rather of *appropriate* to a society aspiring to European ideals, and a powerful correlation existed between acceptable "descent" and "decency." But "decency" went beyond the ability to trace one's blood to a proper family. It encompassed ways of dressing, speaking, and behaving. Cuzco's colonial society considered it uncivilizing and unhygienic to have an "infectious" environment in the center of the city. They thought it better to hide the uncivilized side of Cuzco from potential foreign industrialists and investors, even if the infrastructure for a modern market could not be built right away and even if there was no way to get rid of the vendors (on whom urban residents depended heavily). Urban residents urged that not only the market but also beer taverns (*chicherías*) and gambling joints be moved away from the center.

From the Market of Miracles to the Market of Modernity

Discussions began in the early 1900s to build a modern market. The southern railroad was constructed in the late 1800s, and the first locomotive reached Cuzco in 1908. Hydroelectric power finally provided electricity to Cuzco in 1914. Driven by the vision of Manuel Silvestre Frisancho, a dynamic mayor, Cuzco's first official market was completed in 1925 at no small cost. The manager and engineer responsible for its construction received gold medals and were feted by Cuzco's "respectable" residents. The municipality bought the land from the Santa Clara monastery. Initially the Santa Clara market, its name was eventually changed to the San Pedro Cascaparo market because the San Pedro train station and church were located across the street. Trains that served the tourist destination of Machu Picchu and points beyond, including the warm valleys of Quillabamba and Maldonado, stopped at San Pedro, and many lowland products—fruit, peppers, coca, and tea—could conveniently be unloaded and then bartered or sold at the central market. The stockyards previously located just off the central plaza were moved to San Sebastian, about twenty miles outside the city. In the words of one historian who witnessed these transformations:

> The dirty and fetid city of the 19th century gradually began disappearing between 1912 and 1930. The Plaza de Armas, a primitive and repugnant market with llamas and mules surrounding its fountain, a popular image of colonial Cuzco, was transformed by the prefect Juan José Núñez. With the help of "The Ornate Cuzco Society," and public fund raising, the plaza acquired its actual form as a French park. The work was inaugurated Jan. 1, 1912, and thus ended the folkloric "Market of Miracles," that ancient market where hot peppers were still used as fractions of coin. . . . Thanks to the work and vision of Frisancho, the open air markets of Mutuchaca and San Francisco disappeared. (Tamayo Herrera 1981:131)

The coming of the modern market was welcomed by many Cuzqueños who noted that "the 29th of May should be designated as a holiday, the day on which the Santa Clara market will be inaugurated, a project that will fill an immense void in the progressive evolution of the capital. . . . It is an exceedingly important work of decoration and local hygiene" (Archivo Histórico Municipal [AHM] 1925: Leg. 85). In 1930, after the market had been constructed, Cuzqueño Braulio Lesanta proudly commented in a letter on March 14 that Cuzco was on its way to becoming the "Rome of America" (AHM 1930: Leg. 91).

In the late 1990s, when I was doing my work on Cuzco's markets, Cuzco's population had grown to more than 300,000, yet its industrial infrastructure had changed little since its reconstruction in the 1950s after a major earthquake: It boasted a brewery, a Coca-Cola factory, a fertilizer operation outside the city, and several textile factories. Today, its biggest industry is tourism, which, since the end of the civil war, has brought in more than its total population per year, all of whom must eat.[4] As economic conditions have worsened and urban congestion has increased, vendors have come to flood the streets surrounding the indoor San Pedro market, and Tamayo's prediction that Cuzco's open air markets would disappear has not been borne out. Some vendors work at semipermanent stalls; others squat on the ground in a greater state of impermanence. The official market sprawls down the streets, into the plazas it once abandoned, out to the suburbs where new middle-class residential settlements have sprung up, under the railroad tracks, and up the sides of the hills, where peasants who have migrated from the countryside and many of the vendors who work in the markets live. Wholesalers with their huge Volvo lorries have replaced the llamas and mules that once stationed themselves outside the San Pedro market.

In turn, because of the urban congestion, the wholesalers have been pushed down below to Avenida Ejército, where they operate out of their lorries and storage depots. Avenida Ejército is an immense area of rickety structures four to five rows deep on both sides of the railroad tracks. The vendors in this market range from the poorest of the poor to the wealthy operators of the startling, fantastic contraband market. Cuzco's wildly expansive markets have always been the lightning rod for contentious battles raging over municipal control of sales taxes and licensing fees, the proper image Cuzco should present to itself and to outsiders, and the economic and social behavior of intermediaries who supply Cuzco's residents and its growing number of hotels with most of their food and merchandise. One of my first journal entries describes how I felt when I first went to Avenida Ejército:

> I walked down the General Buendía market from San Pedro Cascaparo. It was as if I had entered yet another world. All along Buendía were *ambulantes* (itinerant vendors), some with tents, but basically it was a makeshift scenario, a dizzying variety of goods being sold in fairly unpleasant hygienic conditions. And if it rains, as it has started to, very early in the season, the ground turns to a sea of mud. One passes *carne foránea* and *pejerrey* (foreign meat and fish), all unrefrigerated.
>
> Suddenly, I seemed to enter a different polity, with its own social relations, rules, and regulations, organization of space, politics, and mores. Avda. Ejército: city state of the low, the cheap, the dangerous, the desperate. Solid structures where people eat and sleep and drink and sell and store their goods; vendors huddled on the ground with plastic mats before them; one group of vendors comprises a union now because the police tried to oust them and they decided to take a stand and move from the ground to "tarimas," stalls built of wooden planks. Those are harder to remove. It reminds me of land invasions in the countryside. "La tierra es para quien la trabaja" (The land is for those who till it).
>
> The vendors, most of whom are women, occupy their space strategically, using every subterfuge they can think of. Dotting the bleak and extremely muddy and smelly landscape, where the dogs have no trouble finding garbage to eat, are huge lorries belonging to the wholesalers who provide goods to the retail vendors "from above."
>
> And at the far end of the railway avenue is a tangle of rusty metal objects, a space in which all manner of used metal things are thrown together and from which other objects are made anew. I suppose you could call it "the junkyard." And much of the junk is stolen. (field journal notes, August 29, 1998)

Avenida Ejército informal and black market, 1998.

There are striking similarities between my initial impression of this market in 1998 and those made by a group of nuns, businessmen, and property owners in a letter to Cuzco's mayor more than fifty years earlier, in 1935. Hygiene, theft, congestion, and garbage are commonalities in our characterizations of the market. The following is their description of this market of modernity, a description not so very different from the market of miracles that Tamayo described:

> The street adjacent to us is packed with vendors of dried goods, household products, itinerant vendors, and all kinds of hawkers who converge on the market with their products, filling the entire sidewalk and street so that it's impossible to reach the doorways to houses or stores which is where they position themselves by preference, making themselves totally immobile. Given the scarcity and total lack of culture of these people, whenever we ask if they would allow us free passage or would leave these places, we receive insolent reproaches and never achieve our objective.
>
> Given the megalomania that reigns among them, they steal whatever is at hand, even metal and bolts, anything that can't be secured; the worst is that, given the antihygienic state that exists among them, by temperament, in addition to blocking free passage to our stores or houses or along the sidewalks, they create a detestable and nauseating sight because they leave

all sorts of garbage they do not remove and neither do the police, that sticks to the bottoms of our shoes.

The only person who benefits from this state of affairs, which we conceive of as abnormal, totally contrary to the culture which we appreciate in Cuzco, is the landlord of the market who exacts charges from all the vendors who do their business, bothering and hurting us. (AHM 1935: Leg. 98)[5]

Spatial Models and Maps

Most notable about these descriptions of Cuzco's markets is the emphasis on space. Space is a critical resource and factor of organization for market vendors. The ways space is mapped through Cuzco's markets also serve as codes of communication that are meaningful to all Peruvians. There is more rhyme and reason to the superficial chaos of the market than meets the eye. To speak of "space" and "spatial relationships" might seem a bit abstract and intangible, yet for market vendors, spatial relations are vibrant, critical to their ability to sell well, to gain an edge in the marketplace, and to fight back against what they consider to be unjust repression on the part of municipal authorities. We do not usually think about space as an active dimension. Instead, we think of time—the creation of history and of movement—as active, whereas space consists of coordinates that constitute a physical locus. Social geographer Dorinne Massey (1992:70) argues that even though space and time are different kinds of concepts, they are "inextricably linked at multiple levels and space and spatial relations are also implicated . . . in the production of history—and thus, potentially in politics." In her words,

"Space" is created out of the vast intricacies, the incredible complexities, of the interlocking and the non-interlocking, and the networks of relations at every scale from local to global. What makes a particular view of these social relations specifically spatial is their simultaneity. . . . But simultaneity is absolutely not stasis. Seeing space as a moment in the intersection of configured social relations (rather than as an absolute dimension) means that it cannot be seen as static. . . . Space is not a "flat" surface in that sense because the social relations which create it are themselves dynamic by their very nature. It is a question of a manner of thinking. It is not the "slice through time" which should be dominant though but the simultaneous coexistence of social relations that cannot be conceptualized as other than dynamic. Moreover, and again as a result of the fact that it is conceptualized as created out of social relations, space is by its very nature full of power and symbolism, a complex web of relations of domination and subordina-

tion, of solidarity and cooperation. This aspect of space has been referred
to elsewhere as a kind of "power geometry." (Massey 1992:81)

The lack of a diversified productive economy, the prevalence of cheap labor that can be tapped into informally for purposes of generating revenues for
formal enterprises, and the wealth of Peru's natural resources have contributed
directly to the explosion of marketing as one way for Peruvians to try to survive. Carlos Vilas (1999:15), reporting on labor conditions in Latin America,
tells us that the Economic Commission on Latin American and the Caribbean
found that nine out of every ten new jobs created in the 1990s was in the informal sector, concentrated in low-productivity unstable activities. Yet the
ability of the developing regions to take advantage of Peru's cheap labor and
raw materials is not all that defines spatial relations in Peru's markets. To grasp
how marketing structures and dynamics are shaped by spatial relations, we
have to look from above, below, and within. It is this combination of perspectives that has often been lacking in analyses of regional markets. The ability
of Cuzco's vendors to read the codes of spatial relations in the existing markets and to manipulate or challenge them may give vendors the good fortune
of success or the bitter salt of failure and desperation. Spatial relations have
"*both* an element of order *and* an element of chaos," as Massey (1992:81) has
observed. Learning to read these codes constitutes a stage in the informal
apprenticeship of vendors, many of whom start out as little girls accompanying their mothers to market or wending their way alone in search of helpful
strangers after having been orphaned or abandoned in the countryside. Lucre's
memories of how she established herself emphasize drawing on her mother's
contacts and the generosity of strangers:

> [I arrived] by foot, from Urubamba to Cuzco . . . in half a day. I left there
> at 5 in the morning. I arrived at 3 in the afternoon. . . . Here, there were
> people who knew my mother. I went there. I spent the night with one
> lady. . . . I said to her, "please, Señora, lend me," at that time, it was silver,
> "fifty centavos." . . . I came to the market and I bought a banana. Then, that
> little banana I took to the Plaza de Armas in a small bag. There I sold it
> and I earned a little money. Once again, I returned to buy a few oranges
> because I had a little extra. And once again.
>
> Then there was a lady in a hotel in the street where the Hotel Colón is.
> One day, she said to me, "bring me a banana." "Yes, mother, I'll bring you
> one," I said. I brought her the banana, and the señora said to me, "I'll buy
> all your bananas but first help me peel these potatoes." So I helped the
> señora peel the potatoes, almost a *carga* (100 pounds). Then she gave me

food, drink, and she bought all the fruit I brought. So, I didn't have to spend on anything.

I boarded at that lady's and, little by little, I got better. She had a son and since I didn't like him, I took my own room in Nueva Alta. . . . I bought myself a little bed with what I had earned. I had my little room but I was always at that lady's. . . . "Mama Lola," they called her. Always, the lady would say to me, "sell your fruit wherever, but return this afternoon and peel the potatoes," to the point where I was running in circles. She gave me lunch, she gave me my food. That's how I came to have my job. I spent my time in that job and it never went to my head, nothing went to my head. That's how I bought my bed, the little things that I have in my room, everything that I need. That's how I have lived and I have lived.

Some of these codes are like second nature to many dwellers of highland regions. Although the discussion that follows may make it appear that the dizzying network of social relations across space in which vendors are involved operates as a closed system with daily adjustments and regulations, vendors' daily uses of space and the ways in which these spatial relations are shaped by social processes create the conditions for innovation (change) as well as upheaval and dramatic reordering of these relationships.[6]

Andean peoples have a long tradition of learning to use space to advantage rather than being constrained by it and are even able to find ways to work around the obstacles that their natural topography presents. The spatial models in which vendors work, which they also sometimes revise partially, replicate ecological and agricultural models that have long endured in the Andes. Ironically, these models have been developed by Quechua highlanders who did *not* use central markets as a primary means of creating their subsistence base. Instead, because the primary variable that determines what people can cultivate in the steep Andean highlands is altitude, dwellers of the sierra had to learn how to make the most of altitudinal differences. They did this by attempting to control strips of land that extended from the valley bottoms to the high windy slopes and plains. Within each altitudinal zone, they could grow and control different kinds of crops and livestock, ranging from low-altitude fruit trees, peppers, tea, and sometimes coca leaves, to valley maize and early potatoes, to a staggering variety of potatoes, barley (introduced by the Spaniards), broad beans, lupines, and high-protein grains, to potatoes that could be freeze-dried, to alpacas and llamas.

Another way they asserted social and economic control over their environment was indirectly, either through trade with other communities or through establishing colonies of settlers in different ecological zones, some of which could be located at great distances from their home communities. To make such a system work effectively, highlanders had to cultivate social relations intensively and possess agricultural knowledge. It is not surprising, then, that Quechua highlanders often correlated location (above and below, inside and outside), together with the products grown in that location, with social relations to which they attributed higher or lower value or status. They found ways to transfer these practices and knowledge to the very different spatial worlds of urban markets.

There are many kinds of markets in Cuzco. In addition to the fifteen street markets that range in size, kind, and permanence, Cuzco also has two kinds of supermarkets and grocery stores. El Chinito is used by middle- and upper-middle-class residents, but the small grocery stores that sell gourmet items such as specialty chocolate, cereal, trail mix, cheese, and wine are frequented by the thousands of tourists who flock to Peru for its camping, hiking, and rafting trips. The tourists also find these stores a convenient dumping ground for whatever supplies they no longer need when they are ready to move on. Most of these stores are concentrated in Cuzco's center, but eventually, a scattering of these specialized luxury tourist items makes their way to the most informal markets.

In addition, there are periodical open air and festival markets in Cuzco's suburbs, such as San Jerónimo and Qalqa. The periodical open air markets usually take place once a week and attract many more peasants from the surrounding region than the permanent markets do. More barter takes place in these markets, and an abundance of agricultural products and animals sold directly by producers can be found in them. Many central market vendors from time to time shut down their stalls and travel to one or more of these markets. The festival markets are similar but take place only once a year. Some permanent vendors shut down and travel to festival markets in the hopes of doing good business. At festival markets, vendors often offer special foods, clothing, or religious paraphernalia that are found only at that time of year: stuffed peppers, roasted guinea pig, or candles and relics for particular saints. Finally, the tourist circuits have generated market activities at particular archaeological sites, and some vendors follow the tourist tracks, especially on weekends. At the artisan tourist markets, a fantastic array of textiles, vests, ponchos, gourds, belts, ceramicware, and other goods greets the strolling tourists.

Cuzco's "permanent markets" are strategically located where there is a sufficient concentration of population and proximity to the wholesalers. The main permanent markets of Cuzco—San Pedro, San Blas, Rosaspata,

Open air rural market, 1991.

Wanchaq, and T'io—are located "inside" and "above." San Blas caters to an artistic, Bohemian, and intellectual neighborhood, Rosaspata and T'io to middle-class professionals, and Wanchaq to workers and middle-class customers. Many more people flock to the San Pedro market, partly because it is the oldest and most familiar market. It has a wide range of products, and the informal markets ringing it give customers more options. Finally, there is the Avenida Ejército megalopolis below the bridges of Cuzco. As vendors move outside and below, they are viewed in more and more negative social terms by Cuzco's urban residents, with the exception of the black marketeers. However, their views are not necessarily shared by the vendors themselves.

The circuits that vendors establish and follow and the locus of their market operations are not appropriate, in an economist's eyes, for making a profit in abstract terms. Yet the vendors are embedded in a long historical tradition of organizing themselves in space and time in ways that allow them to survive and to maintain access to goods, clients, and information they deem important. The household strategies that vendors develop involve spatial considerations. To make sense of these strategies requires us to take into account the macroeconomic and microsocial forces at work.

Household Structures and Strategies

Most vendors are women who head their own households. Rather than seeing this as some kind of aberration of the nuclear household, it might be better to consider that for centuries Andean people have moved between multiple labor sites. Although there are some exceptions, it is generally men rather than women who have migrated to mines, lowland plantations, and textile sweatshops or, more recently, to construction sites in cities, for long periods of time. Women's history of movement is somewhat different. Many have remained in the countryside, responsible for organizing agricultural activities and caring for their families. However, after the Spanish invasion, many Spaniards took indigenous women as concubines and brought them to the city. These women and their children had to seek a living in the cities once they were abandoned. They turned to two occupations, domestic servitude and marketing, often in a step pattern. In addition, even women who remained in the countryside periodically made forays to the mines or provincial cities, selling crafts or whatever agricultural surplus they had. Over the years, this pattern has changed as women have settled permanently in cities, married, and had children. But one thing has remained constant. Men often are absent for long periods of time; quite a few of them abandon their wives for mistresses; others die, leaving their wives as widows; and many women seek escape from their domestic situation because of physical abuse by their husbands. Even when their husbands do work, their jobs often are less stable. Women's marketing is more steady. They rely heavily on their mothers or other relatives for child care. Some men with unstable work also share in child care, but they become depressed, seeing this as a sign of their lack of virility.

Because most of the retail vendors are women, I direct my attention mainly to them, pointing out the kinds of patterns that men follow when appropriate. Women strategize about where to locate their marketing operations in light of what their relatives in an impressively far-flung extended family are doing to contribute to the household economy. Both the migratory movements of their households and the economic activities they cobble together constitute survival mechanisms, although perhaps not in a functional sense. These practices allow them to diversify and thereby avoid devastating risks. I say that their strategies are not necessarily functional because they might not stretch their energy and resources if not for the dysfunctional nature of the dismal national economy and the gender ideologies that often prevent women from occupying higher formal sector positions. The strictures on economic dynamism are now such that more men are joining women in informal marketing.

From Rags to Riches?

How do families cobble together an income? Salcedo describes how two brothers, Juan and Vicente, built their sidewalk vending operation in Lima:

> It was a strange impulse that caused Juan to consult with his younger brother about the decision he thought he would make. In reality, it concerned two decisions, but they were closely linked. One, to dedicate himself to selling clothes; the other, to make Carmen Olmos his wife, the same Carmen Olmos who had provided him with his first underwear and socks to sell while he was in the army barracks.
>
> But, in addition to needing the advice of his younger brother, Juan needed Vicente for the work that he was about to undertake. That night, while Vicente hung up his first pair of socks, Juan, his older brother, decided to invest his savings from his army service in the purchase of merchandise.
>
> The next morning, Juan Díaz bought socks, shorts, nylon stockings, and handkerchiefs. Afterward, carrying a small suitcase, he arrived at the fruit stand of La Parada, where he and his mother had gone the day his mother bought Vicente an enormous blue suit.
>
> Relationships get lost in the fog of ancient generations or inherited friendships that are but one step removed from the ties of kinship, [but] one fruit vendor still had a fond memory of Señora Julia.
>
> Next to the fruit stand, located at Aisle "A" of the retail market, Juan decided to set up his little suitcase. Upon seeing the suitcase on the uneven ground, the fruit vendor offered him one of those flimsy crates in which avocados and passion fruit are shipped. The crate was typical of those used by the fruit vendors of Lima: some flexible wooden slats were enough, a rough surface full of splinters, held together by tiny nails, almost slivers. The flimsy crate was the first pedestal for Juan's suitcase, as if his suitcase had acquired greater importance standing half a meter above the ground.
>
> It was the first day. After that, now and then, the little suitcase, in addition to the trousers and the "Presidente" socks, sometimes also carried soap and "Bividis" ("BVD" brand of men's underwear). And Vicente became Juan's assistant, while Pedro, the older brother, kept working in General Motors, and Elías Serafín in the Barbones silvershop. (Salcedo 1993: 68–69)

The women working in Cuzco's markets resort to strategies similar to those of Juan and Vicente, relying on existing networks to help them set up their businesses. They also carefully consider where to locate their economic activities, when to perform those activities, and how their work can take advantage of the schedules, contacts, skills, or resources that other household members control. In the cases I reviewed, rarely was a husband or male partner part of the calculations. For example, Donata, one of the vendors I got to know, sells the famous fresh baked bread of Oropesa in the central market. Her daughter Celia helps her by going to the train stations or truck stops to sell bread before she goes to school in the morning. Donata's husband has no steady work and mostly stays at home with the kids, although he does help bake the bread at night. In another case, two sisters began their business with a juice stand inside the market. They made enough money so that now one runs a roasted chicken operation while the other sells dried goods in Puquín, one of the main entry points to the city from the countryside. The sisters have turned over the juice stand to Doris Amachi, their youngest sister. In yet another case, Baudelia makes breakfast in the market. Her mother-in-law takes care of the kids. Her brother continues to live in the countryside and facilitates the transport of products for her sister to process for the breakfasts. A final example is that of Eva, Lucrecia, and their mother, Laura. Eva and Lucrecia share a house. They are all crammed together outside the main market. Laura sells vegetables, and Eva and Lucrecia sell spices. Laura lives with her youngest son and daughter-in-law. Eva's twenty-two-year-old daughter sells pork rinds down the street, and Eva turns over a little of what she makes so that her daughter can continue attending teacher's college. Her ten-year-old son also comes to help in the afternoons after school.

Household strategies also involve spatial considerations. Women rise at 3 or 4 A.M. every day and do not return home until 8 or 9 P.M. After doing housework and preparing their younger children to attend school or accompany them to the market, many of them get their merchandise from larger retailers or wholesalers, often located at a great distance. To haul those goods to their stall, they have to take a cab or hire a tricyclist or human cargo carrier (*cargador*). Both time (distance) and money (time) intervene to determine whether they use an expensive cab or a slow *cargador*. Much as they may want to work close to home, they have to consider where the wholesale depot is located, the economic activities of other household members, and the flow of traffic, which determines potential consumer demand. I met one woman who was very excited about working in the Rosaspata market because it was so close to where she lived. But she resigned herself to becoming a vendor in the San Pedro area because it was just too far to the wholesalers, and the flow of potential clients was so much greater in San Pedro.

Vendors spend a lot of time talking about flows of traffic and observing these flows as they sit at their stalls, wend their way to the wholesalers or back to their homes (usually located above the city in one of the shantytowns, or *barrios jovenes*), or travel to special festivals. They constantly calculate how to organize their vending in accordance with new possibilities of capturing more clients or windfall profits. In fact, stall control, the occupation of a space, is one of the most controversial and politicized aspects of marketing. Vendors try to operate stalls in markets or stores in their houses on the periphery of cities, where urban migrants reside and truck traffic is heavy. They do not want to work at a site where the flow of people or transport is light, one that is too far from gathering up points, or one that is under the constant surveillance of municipal agents. Consider the logic that Juan and Vicente used in Salcedo's narrative:

> The first comparison that Juan and Vicente were able to make between their suitcase and prosperity was the distance that separated them from those more experienced vendors who owned tricycle carts. The cart had two wooden wheels forged from the leftovers of automobile-like tires. At one end were two curved handles that allowed the wooden platform designed for fruit vendors, but used by other vendors, to be pushed. The distance between a crate and cart of mangos was a genuine leap of progress. . . .
>
> The municipal police demanded their "contribution." If you didn't pay, the suitcase was taken and you had to get it back from La Victoria municipality, paying a fine as well. Among all the municipal inspectors, the one who stood out was fat Caramala. The man wandered among the carts and suitcases, taking ownership of clothes or stepping all over one or another primitive display of merchandise. He announced greater reprisals if the itinerant vendors didn't pay up. Juan and Vicente rapidly understood that the cart wasn't only useful to display their clothes but also, and above all, to escape the voracious municipal inspectors. (Salcedo 1993:69, 70)

Many women strategize by having family members control stalls inside and outside the central market. Legally, the unions prohibit this, but it happens all the time. People love to hide their stall secrets. In one case, a highly respected market union leader had a large stall outside but was gradually planning to vacate it and set up a permanent store. When he did, he told no one where it was. People rapidly got wind of its location, but only after business at the new store had begun to boom. Other vendors may have informal stall operations outside one of the markets and then may set up stores inside their homes because most of their homes are near truck routes. This is so because originally many of the vendors established themselves in makeshift neighborhoods high above the city whose land they occupied when they migrated from their rural home communities to the city. One woman's husband and children ran the store in the house while she sold spices outside the central market.

Although it was hard for me not to feel sorry for the women down by the

Tricycle cart planted in front of wholesale warehouses along Avenida Ejército, 1998.

railroad tracks, several of them told me that they preferred being there because it was so much closer to the wholesalers and saved them a lot of trouble. They also paid far less, if anything, for the right to occupy their space, and they were a little further away from the arm of the municipal authorities. After a major confrontation with municipal police, who forced the informal vendors outside San Pedro to cut back the size of their *tarimas* (platforms of wooden slats on which they placed their goods), the vendors began thinking about where they could make up their losses now that they were forced to carry a much smaller inventory. They had heard about a Saturday open air market that was not too expensive to get to and that seemed to be doing very well. Some of them decided to experiment and include a trip to Huancarani in their weekly marketing schedule. In yet another case, a woman inherited her stall from her mother, and her husband assisted in the apple operation by riding a tricycle and selling their apples all over the city. Lucre, now a highly respected and well-established vendor, explained to me what her early days were like:

> *Linda:* Who usually bought from you?
> *Lucrecia:* People in the streets.
> *Linda:* Were they housewives or peasants?
> *Lucrecia:* Housewives, also people who worked in the streets, all of them

bought from me. Also, when there was the earthquake of 1950, I already had three children. Even then, I continued selling my fruit. During the time of the earthquake, everything happened. It was disastrous, but always forward, always forward, wherever you can imagine, I went to sell my fruit, here in Sacsayhuamán. Sacsayhuamán wasn't like it is now, guarded. Everyone used to play there so I took my fruit, I went with my pot, with my meat, to cook for my little children. On foot, I climbed up there weighed down by my little children. They played there, in the sun . . . while I sold and did business and I also cooked because I have never let my children go hungry, because I suffered so much in my life, from the time I was a little girl. Frankly, I've worked very hard, very well. . . .

Linda: When you changed from selling fruit to selling vegetables, how were you able to establish yourself in the market?

Lucrecia: I was able to establish myself in the market because I had a stall. This is my stall. With the money from the shoe business, I began. My husband had made a trip for his political work to Lima, had spent too much, and without my knowing it, he had sold the stall. Since I was feisty, I said to him, "Very well, you sold it, but we have lots of kids." I grabbed a place toward the outside, not like this one, one outside, and to get vegetables I had to get up at 4 in the morning, 3 in the morning, to get them from the same owner, because if I got them any other way, I wouldn't earn as much as I needed to. Because I had to cook and take care of my children all of whom were very young. I cooked here, inside the market. That's how I did it.

Linda: Where did you go to get the vegetables? What was it like?

Lucrecia: Below the bridge. Here in Avenida del Ejército. There, everyone from Urubamba, Yucay, Huayllabamba, arrived, at 4 in the morning, 3 in the morning. We were already grabbing them, without paying and, then, at 11, 12, they would come and make you pay to the very last cent.

Linda: So afterwards they charged you and they knew how to find you?

Lucrecia: Yes, they knew so I would just bring the vegetables here.

Linda: By yourself?

Lucrecia: Always with a porter. At that time, there weren't tricycles, only porters.

Linda: When did you begin selling vegetables?

Lucrecia: About twenty years ago, I began selling vegetables. Then I sold manioc. I sold a little of everything. It wasn't just one thing. That's how I earned enough to support my children. My life was sad. It wasn't like the lives of others, who have a mother, who have a father.

Linda: And when your mother sold, did you at six years old, begin learning from her?

Lucrecia: Yes, sure, I learned from my mother.
Linda: And what did she sell?
Lucrecia: My mother sold peppers.
Linda: Peppers? Here outside?
Lucrecia: My mother's stall was inside the market. Like mine now, my
    mother also had her stall.

Seeing the burden placed on informal vendors who are often in danger of
losing their space, I pondered the advantages and disadvantages of stalls and
stores. There's no question that vendors dream of clean environments with
running water, light, quiet, protection from thieves, and freedom from harassment by the authorities. But they have at least two advantages: flexibility and
greater movement. They can decide, obviously not without serious calculation and forethought, to switch to a different product or to carry more apples
and fewer grapes. Store owners remain stuck with their inventory for a much
longer time. Movement serves them in two different ways. Vendors without
permanent stalls may find that because of greater foot traffic near their businesses, there is a greater likelihood that they will make a sale. Also, they may
move to a different location if they find they are not getting enough business
where they have initially set up. Although these are not huge advantages, they
are ones that many informal vendors take carefully into account.

Even though stalls are supposedly available for rent to anyone, kin relations
weigh heavily in who controls stalls. Stall rights often pass from mother to
daughter, with multiple female relatives, ranging from sisters to cousins to
aunts, occupying adjacent stalls. The traffic in stalls involves kin ties, barter,
and reciprocity rather than a simple payment of rent.

Another significant consideration in where market women work is with
whom they work. Market women work to make a living, but they also work
to socialize and escape the dismal conditions at home. Many women explained
to me that they would rather be in the market, where they could see their
companions, and they dreaded staying at home, where they might be subjected
to domestic abuse or to suicidal depression because time weighed too heavily
as they considered their bleak economic and domestic state. Sociability also
has a pragmatic economic side. Much of the competition between market
women takes place not with their companions but rather with those selling
similar products elsewhere. There are government controls on prices in many
cases, but these controls are ignored if all the vendors of a particular product
decide to raise or lower the price. Therefore, it is important for vendors to feel
solidarity with their companions, who will help them out if they need to go
do an errand or are ill and who will share important information with them

about prices, possible incursions by the authorities, or the presence of unwanted creditors.

The ability of vendors and their families to use spatial relations to their advantage extends beyond economic returns, sociability, and risk avoidance. It also allows them to embark on some wonderful innovations that may yield economic returns. The willingness of small vendors to experiment with new spatial arrangements is widespread, even though they may not have a cushion of capital. Take the example of Hilaria Pumacahua. Hilaria approached me in the plaza, selling woven belts and carved gourds. She had some beautiful gourds, carved with exquisitely detailed scenes of daily life, accompanied by narratives that explained the scenes, also carefully carved on a surface that was about the size of a grapefruit. I asked her who had made the gourds, and she told me that her whole family had helped out. They had learned from artisans in Huancayo who had moved to Lima during the civil war. Because the same kinds of gourds were plentiful in Quillabamba, they were now making them in Cuzco. She herself was from Chincheros. She explained that her husband buys ceramics here in Cuzco, then travels with them by train or truck to Lima. There he sells the ceramics and then buys tapestries from San Pedro de Cajas and brings them back to Cuzco to sell. That's where he learned to make these *burillados,* as the gourds are called. Hilaria sells the gourds and woven belts, making a circuit from Cuzco to the tourist markets of Ollantaytambo, Pisaq, and Chincheros. Her family still has land in Chincheros, although they live in Cuzco. They use the land to grow basic subsistence crops: potatoes, tubers, broad beans, and maize.

I found that one of the most important and distinctive ways in which knowledge of spatial relations and marketing skills comes together in Andean highland markets is the awareness among vendors of how agricultural rhythms affect supply and demand and hence the prices of products. This knowledge is not limited to vendors, although they may be more acutely aware of abundant and scarce products than are urban residents in general. Prices rise and fall in accordance with the availability of products from the countryside; vendors constantly consider how they can take advantage of these rhythms in deciding from which wholesaler to buy or whether they can tap into the social ties they have maintained directly with some *campesino* producers. Realizing that these rhythms are unpredictable because of good or bad agricultural seasons, vendors may decide to invest in diverse products, evening out costs and risks. But to do well at the latter kind of marketing, they have to pay constant attention to what is happening to prices in different locations. Although the prices of some basic products, such as bread, are supposedly set annually by the municipality, these prices are rarely enforced, and vendors inside the central market reach a consensus to raise or lower prices in accordance with perceived supply and demand. They gauge the latter in part according to the price at which wholesalers offer them goods and in part according to their own knowledge of agricultural calendars. The prices of goods sold outside the central market are far more erratic, however, and vendors have more discretion (and take more risk) in determining appropriate prices.

Space and time come together in Cuzco's marketplaces, creating the dynamic knowledge on which market vendors rely to try to make a living. Their knowledge of the layout of the city—where people work and live, the gathering up points of produce on the outskirts of the city, the location of wholesalers, and the social ties vendors cultivate with wholesalers and *campesino* producers—and the rhythms of agricultural and religious calendars contribute to the creative ways in which market vendors and their household members knit together flexible economic activities. The knowledge that vendors have of spatial relations allows them to defend what they consider to be their rights to space, taking advantage of the semblance of chaos that so bothers municipal agents and upper-middle-class residents who would like to contain the vendors permanently in one rationally organized place.

Notes

Portions of this chapter are paraphrased or reprinted from my article "Market Places, Social Spaces in Cuzco, Peru," *Urban Anthropology* 29:1 (April 2000): 1–68.

1. In Ecuador, central market nodes for the barter of commodities were called *tiánguez* by the Spanish chroniclers, and long-distance elite traders of specialized products from outside the sierra were called *mindaláes*. For evidence of the presence of pre-Hispanic regional markets in the Andes, see Espinoza Soriano (1987). He describes at least four kinds of commerce that existed under the Incas: that controlled directly by the state, exchange between residents of a single ethnic group, exchange between different groups, and long-distance trade undertaken by professional merchants. The latter three were unregulated by the Inca state. See also Salomon (1978, especially 143–71), Hartman (1971), and Rostworowski (1970, 1977).

2. Few scholars have focused solely on the history of Cuzco's markets. Information on them is scattered, but Hardoy (1983), Samanez Argumendo (1992), and de Azevedo (1982) sketch some of the main aspects of the organization and transformations in commerce in Cuzco over a 500-year period. The Municipalidad del Cuzco (1993) prepared a document, "Proyecto para la Construcción del Mercado Popular de Ambulantes de Qosqo: Sustentación y Sintesis Condensada de Los Estudios," that summarizes much of the information from these sources.

3. Langer (2002) provides a perceptive analysis of the complex interaction between subsistence and export economies in conjunction with mining, textile manufacture, and mules and llamas for transport of commodities, and of how after Independence, these dynamics stimulated indigenous production for markets until the late nineteenth century.

4. According to an article in *El Comercio* on January 4, 2001, in the year 2000 Cuzco received 470,000 visitors, far more than its total population of approximately 300,000 (Silverman 2002: 891).

5. In its early days, the market was considered a municipal rental property, turned over to the landlord who bid the highest at an annual auction. The landlord paid the municipality for the right to rent market stalls to vendors, and he was responsible for collecting those rents and maintaining the infrastructure of the market.

6. The narrative structure of text ironically makes it difficult to convey this simultaneous dynamism of spatial relations, yet it is important that the reader have a starting point from which to understand the Cuzco markets. Unfortunately, this initial description of spatial relations of the market may give the impression of flatness rather than of chaos and order clashing and mixing together in sometimes unexpected ways.

7. This is based mostly on anecdotal observation, but I noticed a marked shift in the visibility of men as vendors at the lower tiers of the informal marketing system. Men have always been part of the informal economy as wholesalers or higher-tier intermediaries, but it was surprising to find more men selling clothes, hardware, or pirated compact discs and cassette tapes on the sidewalk. It seems that women still heavily predominate in the sale of fruit, produce, bread, dry goods, and meat. Lesley Gill (1997) has documented the transition men have made from being miners to participants in La Paz's informal economy and in the coca economy since a major sector of the economy, tin mining, has shut down.

2

Dried Goods, Soup, and Fried Eggs: Exchange Relations

María Inés Caballero Huachaca sits behind her counter, her hair tightly pulled back from her face, her chef's apron covering her billowing green polyester blouse. A wide, satisfied grin spreads across her face, almost from ear to ear. Her little girl sits next to her. She watches the two men and two women, seated on long benches across the counter, quietly eating their breakfast of fried eggs, rice, and coffee on her white tile table. The two women talk to each other. When they finish, they thank Inés, as she calls herself, and then leave. No money has exchanged hands and, seemingly, no products either. But Inés's case is not particularly unusual except that she herself has some unusual qualities. She is optimistic and has a sunny disposition. This was evident when I barged in on her business and she accommodated my probing queries with the same equanimity with which she treats her clients.

Inés used to run a stall in the informal market outside the San Pedro central market, where she sold cosmetics, soaps, powders, and lotions. It was not doing badly, but things changed when her husband abruptly quit his job in a fried chicken joint because he was sick of it. At almost the same time, the future for the informal vendors ringing the central market became precarious. They began receiving daily threats from the mayor of Cuzco that they would be thrown out. Inés's unemployed husband began working with her at her outside stall. But after three months, as Inés explained it, "We looked at the street and wondered where the money would come from." Her husband became desperately depressed on the days when there were few or no sales. He could not abide staying home and taking care of their two young children. Inés decided she had to find a way to "escape" the tension of the outside market.

Inés Caballero Huachaca, eating one of the fried egg breakfasts she prepares, 1998.

She worked as a cook for two months to try to accumulate enough money to rent a stall inside the central market. She succeeded in renting the stall, but she still did not have the raw goods—the eggs, rice, and coffee for breakfast and the french fries and vegetables for soup for lunch—to make a go of it.

Inés told her neighbors what she was trying to do, and they came to her assistance. Some of the market women gave her advances on the food products she needed to start her operation in the "breakfast section." In return, she prepares cooked meals—fried egg breakfasts and french fries and vegetable soup lunches—for them. Rather than directly buying their meals, the other market women exchange their goods for their breakfasts and lunches, a barter system that also allows Inés to accumulate a little surplus that she can put toward preparing additional meals that she sells to other customers for cash. Also, many market women decided to eat their lunch at her stall. No one keeps exact track of the exchanges, and Inés admits that sometimes she forgets to make some of the women pay, even though she owes them nothing.

In addition to serving breakfast and lunch at her stand, Inés also delivers lunch to a network of clients in and around the market. She does this while people are eating lunch at her stall. She has to make sure to collect the plates and the cash for her deliveries before the end of the day. This is one of the most onerous tasks because sometimes people leave without paying her, or she cannot find the time to collect the platters. Often, her husband or her older child helps with deliveries and pickup.

Inés tells me "God is great." She is a Jehovah's Witness. "With the pace of work, I haven't been able to attend meetings lately at the salon but, no matter, God has been good to me and my family." At thirty-two, Inés has four children, ages thirteen, ten, four, and two. She reflects on why she likes her fried egg operation so much: "I maintain myself well. While I sell, I cook. Everyone eats well. There is rarely anything left over from my lunches, but if there is, I can feed it to my children, something I could not do with my cosmetics."

Inés's services are useful to other market women who need sustenance quickly while they are working for long hours in the market. Most of them cannot afford to leave their stalls for long. Inés's success at starting up her new operation is due not only to economic rationality. Her ability to cultivate social relationships because of her generosity, calm, and good-heartedness appeals to other market women. Although she is keenly interested in trying to achieve a better life for herself and her children, she has not rejected her roots. Originally from Abancay, she speaks Quechua. Her mother still lives there, farming the land, but it is too far away for Inés to visit more than once a month. Many market women who have roots in the countryside prefer to identify themselves as mestizas, but Inés, who also speaks Spanish well, considers herself a *campesina*. In her words, "I have always worked in the fields and I love it. How nice to turn over the earth. The 'outfit' [*chamada*] that we *campesinas* wear is beautiful."

Unlike some women I interviewed who talk openly of the spite that often characterizes competitive relationships between vendors, Inés has had a different experience in the marketplace. She gets along very well with the other women, and they all help out in taking care of each other's children and stalls.

Now that Inés's indoor operation is going well, her husband works the cosmetic stall by himself. But he looks back on his restaurant job with some regret, thinking he should not have given it up because it was steady work, whereas the unpredictability of market vending is tremendously irritating. Now the economic situation is so bad that he wonders whether he can find another job with wages.

Within the San Pedro market a dense network of relationships exists whose threads, in turn, are interconnected to yet more strands. The vectors of this complex web extend far beyond the market. In this chapter, we take a quick tour through the markets of Cuzco to find out how the vendors who work in them establish social and economic exchanges that enable them to initiate and maintain their businesses. These exchanges, at the retail level, are not readily apparent if one is searching solely for a neoclassical economic model or Austrian model of economic rationality at work. The exchanges entail other considerations, including two qualities that are difficult to systematically define: trust and the style in which one offers and receives goods and advice.

Viviana Zelizer (in press) argues that many social scientists have mistakenly assumed that intimate and impersonal relationships are always inimical and that the interaction and interpenetration of capitalist and noncapitalist circuits and exchange relations are damaging and dangerous. Indeed, they sometimes can be, but in many cases the very existence of different kinds of circuits that structure a single economy ameliorates the most harsh and brittle aspects of either intimate (based on kinship and the betrayal of those ties) or impersonal (nonreciprocal and rationalized) exchanges. From her own research and analysis, Zelizer suggests,

> Corporate circuits, local monies, and caring connections obviously differ in their settings and contents. We should resist, however, the ever-present temptation to array them along a standard continuum from genuine, general, impersonal markets at one end to non-market intimacy, at the other. . . . In all three types of circuits we find intense interpersonal ties commingling with regularized media and transfers. In all three, for that matter, we find ties that vary greatly in their intensity, scope and durability. Differences among the three types of circuits depend not on overall extent of rationalization or solidarity but on variable configurations of media, transfers, interpersonal ties, and shared meanings attached to their intersection. (Zelizer, in press: 18)

Inés stands out because of her skill in spinning and weaving together these threads that constitute strategic social relationships, but many other vendors and their clients are engaged in exactly the same kinds of activities. These relationships may involve direct barter, indirect barter, and forms of delayed payment that are mind-boggling because they involve so many separate informal contracts. Behind material commodities stand the labor invested in them, but their value is also partially the product of the selective social ties between producers, processors, vendors, and their clients. These ties take on a multiplicity of forms, depending on the kind of relationship involved. Establishing and maintaining these relationships become ever more important factors in vendors' ability to survive in the cutthroat marketplace.

Likewise, when national economies grimly march into deep recessions, and high unemployment and hyperinflation grip middle- and lower-class families, they too resort to swapping, borrowing, and bartering. With the imposition of neoliberal economic measures and currency crises that strike unexpectedly, barter (*trueque*) clubs have sprung up, abruptly halting the relentless march toward a purely commodified economy. Instead, people bring what they have—either goods or services—to swap for what they need, receiving scrip or barter money known as *créditos* rather than currency. Although supply and demand partially determine the value of goods and services, social ties also count. These networks are defined by a disconcerting yet often comforting "combination of competition and neighborly solidarity," as Clifford Krauss (2001: 6) reports from his investigation of barter clubs in Argentina. In addition, as so many people report, reliance on barter offers hope, keeping families afloat and less apt to fall into deep depression, both economically and emotionally. In some cases, a resurgence of cultural pride has taken place as indigenous communities return to a pure barter economy, rejecting currency altogether. In both the Peruvian and Argentinian cases, barter networks and clubs have encouraged people to increase home production of a variety of goods (Krauss 2001). The government itself has recognized that these networks serve as a safety valve and, ironically, as a training ground for learning basic marketing skills, something that could come in handy if the economy improves. Finally, they are a principal means by which young people meet each other, perhaps an equivalent to our somewhat antiseptic malls.

The informal exchanges of products can be fraught with far more tension than that in Inés's operation. I wanted to interview both women and men in the markets at the retail level, but the men were few and far between. One day, I had almost given up my search for a male vendor to interview and was walking down the steps of the market to leave from one of San Pedro's side exits. Along both sides of the aisle were "stores," the Andean version of 7-Elevens or mom-and-pop operations. These stores carry all sorts of basic dried goods, most of which are not produced in the Andean countryside: sugar, rice, little packets of spices, Jello, paper, prepared chicken, cookies (both sugary and salty), canned milk (big and small), cocoa, ground coffee in bags, Quaker oatmeal, noodles, powdered milk, detergent, and soap. Usually, high in the corner on one of the shelves, is an *ekeko*, a little ceramic man, painted in colorful clothes with paper money pinned to his collar and a half-smoked cigarette in his gaping mouth. He is weighed down by all sorts of merchandise: miniature bags of rice, flour, sugar, ceramic pots, coca leaves, and a wicker shopping basket. The *ekeko* is the good-luck man of economic success, and many market women keep him hidden among their wares, tending to him by making coca leaf offerings to him and lighting his cigarette once a week.[1]

Behind the counter of one of the stores stood a man. I immediately went

Mom-and-pop store in a formal San Pedro market. Photograph by John R. Cooper.

over to see whether I could interview him. I hadn't realized it at first, but his wife was also there. He was not reticent about being interviewed, so I set up my microphone and tape recorder and began asking him about his work. His name was Juan Roa Apasa, a timid soul, soft-spoken yet willing to talk to me. However, things changed rapidly. When I started interviewing him, his wife was busily preparing little packets of rice and noodles, spices and salt, and bottles of cooking oil. We were constantly interrupted as his wife directed him to deliver the packets to different market women. The women put in their orders in the morning, and Juan and his wife, Paulina Paucar, were responsible for delivering the orders to them in the afternoon, keeping careful track of what each market woman owed on scraps of brown wrapping paper. Juan scurried back and forth, and each time he came back, I asked him another question and got a snippet of an answer. As we proceeded, it became clear to me that my timing had not been good. If I had been at all sensible I would have graciously bid farewell at that point and left Juan and Paulina to their frenetic operation. I was acutely aware that Paulina did not like me. I think she feared I was a tax agent who was going to report her for not keeping track of her receipts, and there are plenty of undercover tax agents in the markets. I dogged Paulina and Juan stubbornly. Juan was willing to share his view of how things worked with me, but Paulina, the powerhouse behind the operation, had an excellent tactical solution to my pesky presence. She smiled distantly at me and spoke in a softer and softer whisper that I could barely make out. The microphone, as good as it was, certainly could not pick it up. And she made sure that the delivery orders Juan had to attend to came faster and faster. They were both happy and relieved when I left, and as frustrated as I was, I too was glad to finally call it a day.

Juan and Paulina are from the "provinces"; she hails from Paucartambo, he from Qanqawa, a tiny herding community above Sicuani. He came to Cuzco and began attending elementary school at age nine. He originally worked in the Coca-Cola factory; she sold small piles of spices outside the San Pedro market. They still earn something from selling a part of the harvest from their remaining lands in the countryside. Little by little, they saved enough to start up the store in 1968.

In the middle of this rocky interview, Juan suddenly confided to me, "I have faith in El Señor Jesus Cristo. I am not Catholic or Evangelical. I read the Book to know. I believe that saints, legally speaking, are human beings, from what I know. They have faith in Father, the Creator. When they die, they stop being saints. They are remembered as those who serve God." Later, I think that Juan was trying to explain to himself and me why he bothered to talk to me at all because it was annoying his wife. According to the Bible, his demeanor could be characterized as saintly in the face of such harassment.

Juan and Paulina get their goods from traveling salesmen and wholesalers on a fifteen-day advance basis, but they do not bother to keep careful track of their inventory. After looking up and down the rows and rows of stores, I could not help but ask out loud how they made a profit if they were all selling exactly the same thing at exactly the same price. In fact, the store next to theirs belonged to their daughter, and they were not competing with her. When they told me that the neighboring store belonged to their daughter, a number of the surrounding storekeepers burst out laughing, as if they had managed to pull off a good trick on me. Market share obviously is important in making a profit. I asked Juan, "How does one store rather than another attract a faithful clientele?" Again, everyone laughed. Juan explained patiently to me, "Peru has almost no productive enterprises. Everyone is a *negociante* [businessman or wheeler-dealer]. Haven't you noticed that in the streets there are nothing but dried goods, shoe, and clothes stalls, one right after another? But we do create a faithful clientele, especially among the people of the market. We offer them goods on advance without making them pay interest. If the market women sell well, they pay us back right away. If not, we give them two or three days." I prodded further, "And what if they don't pay?" Paulina snapped, "They always pay." And Juan added, "We don't ask for documents or note things down. We're not like the banks. These are questions of trust."

Banks operate according to trust as well, but that trust is backed up by evidence of collateral and creditworthiness. In the informal marketplace, the circulation of products, even at the scale of this operation, is still motivated by trust. Juan and Paulina provide the dried goods to the market women they have come to know, who then use them to make traditional soups that are purchased, just like Inés's fried egg breakfasts, mainly by people working in the marketplace. If the circuit of debits and credits, or "delayed reciprocity" in the language of anthropologists, were eliminated, the entire circulatory system would come to a screeching halt. As a consequence, aside from the ongoing indebtedness of people such as Juan and Paulina, or of market women such as Inés, the delicious cheap breakfasts and lunches that sustain those who work in the marketplace would disappear.

Products circulate along channels of trust and need among market women. As we will see in the chapters that follow, the ability of market women to organize politically also relies on these same criteria. This is not the only way in which value is set in the marketplace. Between vendor and client, other contradictory factors intervene. Vendors pride themselves on having their *caseras,* literally "housewives," a term that refers to both the wholesalers who provision them and the customers who buy from them. In chapters 4 and 5, I discuss in more detail the wholesaler-retailer relationship, critical to determining the price at which vendors sell to their clients. It also bears on the ability of market women to get along with each other. In the best of all possible worlds, market women make a profit. However, their desire to make a profit is tempered by their desire to get along with their fellow vendors. Otherwise, daily life can become hideously unpleasant. Therefore, market women selling the same product work hard to set the price at which they buy from wholesalers and at which they will sell to their customers, not surprisingly taking careful account of scarcity, quantity, and quality. Sometimes, a vendor will strike out independently and take the risk of having to buy high and sell low. But she may also hit the jackpot, incurring the wrath of her sisters while making a windfall profit.

How are products exchanged between vendor and customer? *Caseras* receive preferential treatment. They always get better quality and a *llapa,* a little extra, thrown in. Sometimes, vendors are willing to sell their goods to *caseras* on an advance basis, expecting repayment at different times, depending on their own financial needs. As Rosa Quispe, a powerful butcher of lamb, pork, and beef in the central market, explained, "If it's a well-known client, we let them buy the meat 'at credit,' for a month or give them a *llapa*. We know that they'll pay us back at the end of the month when they get paid. We write down the person's name and amount of credit in a notebook. If they don't fulfill their obligations, then they will have to buy from then on outside."

Interestingly, *campesinos* who have come directly from the countryside also often receive lower prices, and vendors are sometimes willing to use barter rather than coin in the exchange. As the afternoon wanes, depending on whether the product that a vendor is selling is perishable, the price will decline so the vendors can make more rapid sales. Once it is clear that products are going to rot by the next day, they are often placed on the ground in wicker baskets and given to desperately poor people who wander through the markets early in the morning and at dusk, seeking a little food.

Many vendors try to obtain their products in ways that may give them a slight advantage over other vendors. For example, Señora Enriqueta Sana sells spices as an *ambulante* (itinerant vendor) outside San Pedro. She told me, "I get my spices from wholesalers who bring them from Puno, Juliaca, and Arequipa. I also buy them from the producers themselves who bring them from their land and then I can buy them at prices that are a little bit lower. Sometimes, I buy some spices from wholesalers who bring them to us. We organize among ourselves to buy them and we have to know, more than anything else, what season it is. Depending on demand and scarcity and if there is scarcity, we accept a little more comfortable price from the producers because we know otherwise they will sell to the wholesalers and we will have to pay more. I make money but it's a small amount because there's so much competition among us. I only know about my earnings at the end of a day if I sell a kilo or when I've sold the entire amount of each product. I don't keep an account book but I do note down what merchants give me on credit."

In addition to scarcity and the number of intermediaries in the chain from producer to vendor, transport is important in setting prices. Melchora Rayo, a worn-out woman who speaks only Quechua, has smuggled herself into the central market and made herself a fixture. She sells potatoes, broad beans, and carrots as an *ambulante,* sandwiched among other established vendors. She buys from wholesalers as well as producers, but in small amounts of twenty-five pounds at a time. The difference between her operation and those of her fellow vendors is that she buys from wholesalers located outside Cuzco in the distant suburbs of San Sebastián and San Jerónimo, and she doesn't pay for a license inside the market. This allows her to sell more cheaply and annoys the other permanent vendors. In addition, she sells in very small portions, something many market women enjoy doing because their margin of profit is greater.

She doesn't make much of a profit and doesn't know how to write, but she proudly informed me, "I keep everything in my head and don't forget anything. I've known how to work since I was very young. I had no other way to support my children so I came to the market to sell. I started with credit from a wholesaler because I had no capital. Once I sold everything from that wholesaler, I bought more from someone else with what I had earned, and then I sold that as well. That way, I could start paying back the first wholesaler."

A final variable that vendors consider in setting price is whether they might do better spreading their risk over multiple products, especially if it looks as if sales are slow. Ofelia Tingo Arias sells unrefrigerated fish in the unregulated market of General Buendía as an *ambulante*. She buys fish from wholesalers who bring it from Puno, Juliaca, and Espinar in amounts of twenty, ten, and even five kilos. In her words, "If sales don't look great, I buy more variety— pejerey, trout, and caracha."

Domérica Hermoza, lover of music and soap operas, astutely plays the market. From day to day, the array of exceedingly small piles of produce and colored yarns she sold by the railroad tracks changed. I had not seen vendors selling such a range of products in such small quantities, so I asked her how she chose what she was going to sell. She explained, "I sell both in small amounts and in quantity. I pay attention to what others are selling, how they are doing, then I do an analysis, trying to figure out what I can sell, given the capacity that I have. In one day, I make about 2 or 3 soles but sometimes if I make 10 soles I can save 5 and use 5 for my children. Part of it goes to pay what I owe and part of it goes for food. I use a little to buy a kilo of sugar, of rice. I take home what's left of the vegetables to cook in the house. There isn't much business because there isn't much work. Today I had to use loans for these little things, barely. Borrowed from the wholesalers. Oh well. They know me, I go, I take. From this, all that's left are these two little piles, really, one little pile. They don't know. If you do it this way, you're left with very little. It's a race, they say." What Domérica does is gauge the market, trying to assess what products are scarce and therefore in high demand, and how much of them she should buy so that she can repay her loans and sell them quickly. She also seems to consider whether the leftovers can be used as food for her children.

The arrangements these vendors describe rest primarily on normative economic considerations that would apply to most markets. However, they clash to a great degree with the emphasis vendors place on long-term relationships of trust, the ability to get along with their neighbors, and the enigmatic quality of interpersonal relations between vendor and *casera* that most market women describe as "*how* one sells." The language of selling is an art that combines with the shrewd calculations of merchants situated in an ideal web of personal relationships. Although the highland markets of Cuzco cannot be contained in the latter matrix alone, nor can informal buying and selling be reduced to the usual laws of supply and demand. Finally, perhaps because of the appalling saturation of the marketplace that leads most market women to shrug their shoulders in anguished recognition that, at most, they may earn a dollar or two each day, many market women perceive their world as an iron cage tinged by flecks of possibility and unpredictability. Nanci Salazar, an energetic, seemingly optimistic young vendor of dried goods (wheat, barley, corn, beans, lentils, and peanuts), told me wistfully about her future, "My future? My dream is to work in a hospital, my career, which I had. . . . In the market, everything is suffering. I have suffered enough with my children, enough, because we can't take care of our children. While we are here, we aren't taking care of our children. In the house, there's no one to take care of them. Everything is in disorder. I want to stay at home. Yesterday, I decided not to come. It was so tranquil. I staying in my house, I cleaned it, and I went out for a walk with my children. How lovely. And, again, back to hell. The market is hell because it is our house, we are here everyday, from dawn to dusk. In reality, I don't like it. Sure, I like working for myself. I don't like being exploited. To work for myself. At times, I look at my husband, other people, they get fired, they have to depend on someone else. I think I depend on myself."

Baudelia Cataldo is one of the San Pedro Cascaparo union leaders. She was elected secretary of defense.[2] Anyone in the union who has problems with union authorities can turn to her for help. In considering the state of the market, she too perceives it as a powerful symbolic and real microcosm of Peru's economy: "The market is the center of necessities, the center of our failure in economic terms."

Elizabeth Layqa, a woman selling potatoes inside San Pedro, assesses her situation: "My husband is a simple worker. When there's work, he works. If not, he doesn't. I am the only one who maintains the family. My children are screwed. I don't want to bring them here, because, as they say, 'Why does the informal market grow?' I don't want my children to walk like I am suffering. The market is hell. There are ladies in the market but they don't know how to respect each other, they fight just to fight with each other. So, I don't want my children to sell in the market."

It is striking that both Nanci and Elizabeth describe the market as "hell," an unsettled, sealed-off "house" where people spend a lot of time bickering. However, because they work in their house from "dawn to dusk" to sustain their families, their house needs to be well managed economically, and its social relations must be kept well oiled. The tension between relentless interdependence and ruthless competition requires exhaustive and constant attention on the part of the vendors. In these conditions, the circulation of fried eggs, soup, and dried goods makes this hell a little more bearable.

Notes

1. Enrique Mayer (2002: 3–4), paraphrasing Arnillas Laffert (1996: 133), describes the *ekeko* as "a popular god that ensures luck in trading," and he points out that "to be effective, however, one's *ekeko* figurine has to have been stolen or given as a gift. A bought one is useless, and the good fortune it is capable of bringing is likely to abandon a person as easily as it came." Here, as in so many other instances in the informal economy, the appropriate activation and nurturing of social relations and generosity are critical to success in buying and selling commodities.

2. The secretary of defense has two major responsibilities: protecting vendors from abuses and injustices on the part of municipal authorities or clients and mediating in conflicts that may develop between vendors.

3

Bitter Salt: Household Structures and Gender Ideologies

The lives of Cuzco's market women cover a wide spectrum of experiences and relationships. In their conversations, they nevertheless repeatedly returned to certain themes. These days, anthropologists are supposed to inure themselves somewhat to the perception of their interlocutors as victims. While I could see how market women acted to improve their own livelihoods, seek out alternative paths of upward mobility for their children, and establish domains of peace, faith, and satisfaction in their work, I also found myself commiserating with them as they told me of their suffering. Some readers may think that I was told these stories because the market women thought maybe I could help them. Occasionally that was true, but not usually. As some of their narratives show, they suddenly mentioned to me ordeals they had had to endure in their home lives in the middle of a discussion about the more mundane aspects of their marketing (where they obtained their products, how they decided the price at which they should buy and sell, whether they made a profit, and how much). They told me these things because their narratives also expressed and distilled daily burdens that they bore, withstood, and feared. Also, in so many cases, if things had been otherwise, these women believed fervently they had the intelligence, skills, and savvy to have built better lives for themselves. Why was it that things could not be otherwise and what were the patterns of household structure and gender ideologies that seemed to imprison so many of the market women?[1] Finally, were there particular conditions that allowed market women to gain upward mobility, such as education, age, household composition (including whether they were married or single or had children), and the employment trajectories of other household members?

In looking at the household structures and gender ideologies that shape the lives of market women, it is apparent that generation and education contribute to differences between them. Though not in a deterministic fashion, these differences tend to channel women into distinct sites in the hierarchy of the marketplace. Second-generation market women who have obtained some education tend to be married, they often work in the more established permanent stalls of various markets, and their husbands are employed part-time or full-time in lower levels of the government as clerks and janitors or as construction workers. Rarely, however, is the employment of their husbands stable. Market women who work more informally tend to have less education, and many of them, even if they are married, receive no support from their husbands, who often abandon them. Finally, there are a few women who work in the markets, especially at the wholesale level, whose husbands are also deeply involved in marketing as cattle dealers, long-distance truck drivers, or wholesalers gathering up goods. One of the major findings of my interviews was that even when market women remained married to men who were employed, they were often left to fend for themselves because the husbands remained absent as long-term migrants, abused them, spent their money on a mistress, or drank it away. Not surprisingly, younger, more educated women, having witnessed the lives of their parents, were initially more wary about marrying and having children, but they often felt pressured by their parents to follow the same bumpy path.

Mothers and fathers of market women offered dramatically different role models. Few of the women with whom I spoke had fond memories of their fathers. In talking about their childhood they often told how they assisted their mothers, who had to live with drunken, irresponsible husbands. Their mothers were rarely passive in the face of their tribulations. Rather, they became heads of household and managers of the economy, putting into action all the resources and skills they had at their disposal. If they had to move, they did. They even called on their in-laws to take care of young children. Yet their behavior was not without contradictions that colored the behavior of second-generation market women even more. Many a second-generation market woman pursuing a promising career, in which her mother had dearly invested her meager capital, had been sidetracked by the attention of a young man. The daughter became pregnant, abandoned her career, and married the young man. Subsequently, the latter often abandoned her entirely, established a second relationship with a mistress, turned to drinking, or simply was unable to find steady employment. These alternatives are not simply domestic "situations." Although the family histories of market women do not conform to nuclear families, the ideal, partly propped up by the conservative Roman Catholic Church and less entrenched Evangelical Protestant faiths, is that of a married couple with children. Another social ideal projected by the middle- and upper-middle-class in Peru is that a married woman is considered of higher status if she does not have to work and can remain at home. Therefore, women often reluctantly abandoned their aspirations, and men felt compelled to establish families. Yet by having a family they at once demonstrated their virility and felt trapped by it.

The state of the Peruvian economy does not provide steady jobs for the majority of the population. According to Centro de Estudios Democráticos de América Latina (CEDAL), a nongovernmental organization in Lima that maintains labor statistics, only 20 percent of Peru's working-age population had stable jobs with wages sufficient for the monthly family food basket (about $400 in late 1998; Chauvin 1998). Vilas (1999) reports that industrial employment in Peru declined precipitously in the 1990s, concomitant with the expansion of self-employment and employment in microenterprises. The decline resulted from a number of factors, including changes in industrial organization, the work process, and production techniques. However, as Vilas (1999:16) specifies, "the unbalanced opening of the economies, the overvaluation of the real rate of exchange, implicit subsidies of imports as part of an anti-inflationary balance-of-payments strategy, and the contraction of credit," all economic policies implemented since the mid-1980s, explain the decline of manufacturing, the expansion of the informal sector, and the greater number of men working in it.

Florence Babb (1998:53–56) has reviewed research on the sexual division of labor in different cultures and how this division and changes in it may affect women and men's status. Although market women experience remarkable autonomy and may participate in politics, they also experience a "secondary sexual status" because of men's employment in export or external trade. If the export or manufacturing sector declines and the only economic option for men is at the retail level of the informal economy, they may feel emasculated in the eyes of their spouse and other close family members, as well as in the eyes of society in general.[2] Babb (1998:137–43) also found that men and women valued each other's work, that women valued men's work more highly, and that men recognized that women worked harder because they had a "double day," caring for children and working outside the home. Although my own interviews confirmed her findings to a large extent, I found that men felt that they were perceived as incapable if they were forced to work in informal occupations. They blamed themselves for their failure as breadwinners even though they actively participated in political demonstrations or federations that targeted national economic policies as the cause of underemployment and un-employment. Gender ideologies have patterned the market economy in such a way that women generally occupy the lower rungs of retailing, but more and more men are being forced to join them. And the men do not have the skills or the knowledge that women have acquired across multiple generations, passed from mother to daughter, to assist them in their undertakings. Further-more, the men themselves, having internalized these gender ideologies, may be somewhat abashed about selling herbs or underwear on the sidewalk. These, then, are some of the ways in which household dynamics and gender ideolo-gies shape the lives of the women of the market who are both tough and frag-ile, desperate, stoic, enterprising, and fed up.

In this chapter I transcribe the stories of several of the women who work in the market to give readers a glimpse of how gender ideologies, household structure, age, and generation have constrained or enhanced the options avail-able to them in their employment trajectories. Some of them have established stalls and are doing well for themselves, others are powerful wholesalers, still others sell along the sidewalks with semipermanent stalls, and many are spread

Ambulantes *of vegetables and fruit on a side street, 1991.*

out along the railroad tracks of Avenida Ejército and the streets of Cuzco, with their meager wares in little piles and baskets.

▶ ▶ ▶ ▶

> My husband was the son of a wealthy man. His father had estates [*haciendas*], real estate, a soap factory, here in Cuzco. It was the brand, "León." Now he [her husband] has lands here in Concebide, a house here, one in Lima, another in Tacna. He is a rich man indeed. He fell in love and stopped studying. He finished high school . . . and also became a mechanic. He studied mechanics in the Polytechnic. And I said to him, "If you aren't going to study, well then, the two of us." And he bought his car, he began a tourist agency. He took care of nothing but tourists. And he didn't know how to drink. He was Evangelical. People who smoke, drink, evil vices, always backward. He never smokes or drinks. All this time, forty-four years of marriage, he has never drunk.

These are the words of Doris (known to all as Dori) Argondoña Martínez de Gutierrez. She has a large, extremely successful warehouse where she sells a variety of dried goods in bulk across from the San Pedro market and next to the train station. Most of the day, she sits in a big chair watching the action on the streets. Her hair is short, she is big-boned, and she wears a colorful blouse and skirt. She has a wise, canny look and a strong character, and she doesn't have to worry much about whom she trusts and whom she doesn't. She is known commonly by other market women as one of the "tomato queens," but her rise to a powerful position in the market hierarchy was not without conflicts, as I found out when I asked her how her household worked and who contributed to the household economy. Dori had already struck terror into my heart because of the description of the tomato queens that I had heard from Lucre, the successful vegetable vendor with whom I had become good friends. Nevertheless, for whatever reason, Dori took a liking to me, offered me a seat on a lovely cushioned chair with a back to it, and freely began talking. Things were closing down because it was approaching lunchtime, so it was fairly quiet. I asked her about the history of her work in the market, and this tough, no-nonsense woman of proud bearing began to weep. Her granddaughter came along and wiped the tears from her eyes. I think she was remembering her abandonment as a child. We talked until lunch. I left and returned to continue the conversation afterward:

> My mother worked in the market. She sold vegetables. I didn't finish studying. I finished elementary school and began working. I was very young when I got married at sixteen. There's my daughter, my only daughter. I

have a daughter, God bless. I've worked a lot. I've confronted life and I've taught others how to work until you drop. I've never been an egoist. Working, one can overcome all and that's what I've done. There are many people who have lived having seen the way I live and how I help others. I've dedicated myself to working all the days that God has given me. I am not familiar with vacations. But yes, now, today, I can take pleasure in all the work I've accomplished because my daughter is a great professional. . . .

I'm from Urubamba, from the Valley of the Incas. I came here at age thirteen. My mother was a widow, that's why she came to Cuzco. My mother worked in vegetables and that's how I learned. . . . She had her stall inside, six meters, a big one. My mother had to sell her fields because she was a woman, she didn't have brothers or a husband. She had to sell them. How could she work them? And with seven children, three boys, four girls. One boy died, one girl died. She is sixty years old. . . .

The household economy? Does my husband contribute more? No. Both of us contribute. I keep track of what he earns and he does the same with me and we both use the money. From the beginning, we have pooled the money, for whatever. . . . I didn't work for about two years after my baby was born. My godmother was still alive until my daughter was two years old. So, I didn't work. My godmother left [died] and my mother said, "I'm going to travel. You take charge of the stall." I was overjoyed that she wanted to give me her stall. "I'm going to make money, I'm going to work," I said. My father-in-law was appalled. He said, "No, where do you think you are going? A poor young girl going to the market? No, no, no, no, it can't be. What will people, society, say? You have to leave off this business." He [her husband] said, "Papá, you can't impose yourself. She and I, we are creating our family and if she enjoys working like this, then she can do it." That's why he left the soap factory. Because he was employed by his father. In the factory, my husband earned a salary. He said, "No, papá, I'm going to make myself independent and my wife too." He [My husband] said, here's an apartment. He provided me with a servant, a nanny, to take care of the baby. We began to work, work, work. . . .

My husband has never ceased to collaborate with me in everything. This is very unusual. There are many abandoned women here. He is special. I would say that he has another mentality, he's very respectful of people. . . . My husband, he said . . . "I'm going with her, the two of us. Into the street, wherever it may be." Since then, everyone has minded their own business. No one says, "She has money, she doesn't have money.". . . Likewise with my brothers. They didn't get along with him because he was an Evangelical, they said, "No, one who doesn't drink, that one's a savage that you can't invite to a fiesta." Then I wouldn't go either. If he doesn't go, I don't go. For me, he and I, and my daughter. . . . We've never had a bad moment.

The difference between Dori's rise through the ranks and that of many other market women is that Victor, Dori's husband, for idiosyncratic reasons perhaps, decided to break out of the gender ideologies that imprison so many couples. He disobeyed the wishes of his parents but had enough capital to establish the foundation for both him and Dori to be successful, independent entrepreneurs. Dori inherited her mother's marketing stall and knowledge of marketing. Victor and Dori had unique qualities that served them well in their quest to create their own livelihoods that went against the grain of traditional expectations. Victor was much wealthier than Dori, and his Evangelical religious faith may have contributed to his willingness to support his wife in her desire to establish an independent economic enterprise. He recognized the future potential of the tourist industry and established one of the very first tourist agencies, with two huge Chevrolet Impalas that he used to take tourists on circuits of the nearby ruins.

Chapter 5 describes how Dori became a tomato queen who controlled the gathering up of most of the tomatoes for the city of Cuzco, and how Lucre, who in character is actually very similar to Dori, was a leader in breaking up that monopsony. However others perceived Dori's position as a powerful wholesaler, she was innovative in the methods she used to establish herself. Here, though, what stands out in comparison to some of the stories of other market women's households is the ability of Dori and Victor, because of their existing capital, creativity, and religiosity, to keep at bay the expectations that Victor's much wealthier family had of their daughter-in-law. Very subtly, Dori also uses her own kind of "double vision," a term coined by W. E. B. Du Bois, the famous African American intellectual. While she rejects some of the values of her husband's family, her repeated references to how her husband has "another mentality" stands in for the social etiquette of a "decent" family that treats others (and here's the slight blur caused by the double vision), including women, with respect and gentility.

Nanci Salazar, thirty-four, does a more modest but nevertheless bustling business, also selling dried goods from a stall in the San Pedro market. She is married. She had pursued a career as a nurse and even completed her studies at an academy. She says she didn't have the proper connections to get a job in the hospital after she finished her training, despite ranking second in her class. She complained that the positions were filled by people they brought from Lima. The story of her life is not unusual. It centers on her middle-class aspirations and her rejection of patriarchal brutality. In her words,

> My father is alive. My mother, no. We've had problems since we were very little. My mother died when . . . I was eight, the others seven, six, and fifteen

months. My father wanted to split us up. My aunt, she took care of us, she is like our mother. My aunt was like "the ancient ones," very brusque, but we put up with her and because of her at least we've been able to stay together. My father did not understand us. He preferred being with his lover and was more concerned with her than with the welfare of us, his children.

My father was brusque. I suffered at school when I was an adolescent. He wouldn't help us buy clothes. He used awful words, he didn't care how we looked. Now, as my children are growing up, he still says, "Why are you buying your children toys, why toys for your children?" "No," I say, "Papá. You didn't give us any, but I *will* give them to my children." He sees this and gets bitter.

It's a terrible struggle. Sometimes I think all of this has left me very sensitive and traumatized. Sometimes, with just one little thing, I begin to cry or get nervous. People know my sisters, we are all very loving.

It's only my brother. Sometimes he is nice, sometimes ugly. . . . He probably got this from our father. We are very different in character. My father and aunt's characters are ugly. Sometimes they say, "How did all of you grow up so differently [from us]?" Sometimes, when they insult us, it doesn't matter. We've heard it all before. If it were the first time, I would be totally traumatized. I'm stronger now. And my sisters and I, we have all begun to work, by ourselves, without any help. I married without help from anyone. My father just said, "Oh, my daughter is getting married."

Nanci is doing quite well for herself and has built up a loyal customer base. Her husband, also from Cuzco, had been in the army. He now works on contract as a mechanic for the Cuzco Municipal Council, but his work is unpredictable. They have only two children, and she is adamant that she doesn't want more because of how difficult it is for them to make a living.

In contrast to the relative comfort of Nanci and Dori's situations, the lives of Eva, Domérica, Alejandrina, and Bernice are far more typical of what I encountered among informal, uneducated, second-generation vendors. Although these narratives do not constitute the kind of meticulous quantitative data that might reveal to us more clearly the possibilities for upward mobility among the children of market women, they suggest powerfully that it is limited. These narratives are highly personal in the detail they offer, but it would be a serious error to conclude that we can separate out or contrast personal life circumstances from the general economic conditions in Peru that allow few to succeed and so many to fail or stagnate, despite all the efforts their parents invest in their future. Women put their children first in spending their meager earnings, yet few of their efforts pay off. The reasons for this have to do with the interactions between Peru's economy, broader macroeconomic and political processes, and interactions between husband and wife, their children, grandparents, and aunts and uncles.

Eva Carhuarupay is originally from the rural community of Urcos. She has a wonderful display of spices outside the central market. She hasn't paid her license fee for her stall in a long time, and her future here is in grave jeopardy. Her masculine face is badly scarred. She has had some education, making it all the way through the sixth grade. She has a good sense of humor and is tough and curious. Every time I went to the market, Eva greeted me in her floppy straw hat and called me over to chat with her. She delighted in my primitive Quechua, flaunted her command of a few carefully chosen words in English that she used to attract tourists, and berated me for not spending more time with her. No matter how bad her prospects (and in the few months I was there last, they declined precipitously), she joked with me and put her companions' qualms to rest about my intentions. Eva had been selling since she was little. She began by selling lemons and cooked food. Her mother also sold cooked food. She lived in Urcos with her mother for twelve years and has been living in Cuzco for the last thirty-five years.

My father abandoned me when I was very little. I have seven children, four sons and three daughters. I began selling here in the market twenty-two years ago as an outside vendor when I had my first child. I saw itinerant vendors lining the street and thought, "Why can't I do the same, but just stay in one spot?" My husband was very abusive. He took up with a woman from Urubamba. My daughter told me that this "dog" was with my husband. I spied on the house of my in-laws and I saw my husband and this woman coming out of it together. It was like having my whole world crash down. I hadn't suspected it since he had been away for three years, at one point in Qalqa. My husband abandoned me eight years ago. He had been a contract worker for Electroperú and sometimes contributed some money to our household. But mostly he drank it away.

I had been married once before when I was fourteen. It hadn't worked out. I married my second husband, who almost immediately began beating me. He beat me when I didn't want to be with him. He beat me when I was pregnant. I went to my mother's to have my first child. Afterwards, he came looking for me and he talked so nicely to me and tried to make me go home with him. When I resisted, he bit me, just above my lip. [She still has a scar from this incident.]

My husband wouldn't let me wear new clothes. If I had any, I had to hide them. Now, I don't care about new clothes. I wear whatever I have. After my husband abandoned me, I alternated between hating him and trying to get him back. I went to Urubamba several times. He's not working but his woman is a teacher who earns good money. But they aren't married. My in-laws don't care about their grandchildren. My mother-in-law and my ex-husband are pimps [*alcahuetes*].

After my husband left, I started drinking with my companions. One day, I realized I didn't have any money for food. Now, I get up every morning at about 6:30 A.M. I work until midnight. I come home from the market at 8:30 at night and cook for my kids, grind the spices to make hot pepper sauce [*ají*], and wash my clothes. I hate dirty clothes. Washing them is a little like meditation for me. I'm used to it. It's a peaceful time. I don't have any friends, certainly not in the market.

It appears that violence and abuse run very deep in this family. Others in the market say that Eva is a violent woman and quick to use corporal punishment with her children. Eva herself used my interview with her partly as a vehicle for confessing her past problems with drinking. I am not entirely sure why this was so, but I found that it happened frequently with market women who were suffering. Perhaps they saw white outsiders as possible ecclesiastical representatives who might be able to help them, or perhaps they wanted respect for having surmounted temptations or repented past transgressions. It also could simply be their articulation of fairness.

Even more dejected than Eva is Bernice Alvarez, who runs a fruit stand by Avenida Ejército.

Abandoned mothers, we are forced to work. At times we have bad nights without anything to eat. Here, everyone wants things cheap. . . . What are we going to do? This is our work. . . . I've sold stuffed potatoes, shish kebab, breakfast, lunch. I changed to fruit because there were no sales. From fruit, enough to live, that's all. For the stomach, for the fare, nothing more.

My mother takes care of my children and I take care of my mother. They stay with my mother. My first husband left with another woman. There's no lack of problems with my second husband. It's not the same as with my first. He doesn't give me anything. They drink, they spend. For my children, I have to kill myself. I have three children from my prior husband, one from my second husband [ages fourteen, thirteen, eight, and one]. He doesn't help me maintain them. My mother doesn't work. She's a *campesina* from Apurimac. So many things happen in life. . . .

My father used to help my mother but he doesn't work anymore. So many failures. His friends took him drinking. The problem with fathers, really, with all men, is drink, spending money on beer. They invite their friends. It's a vice they have become accustomed to. Now my father is with my mother. One of my uncles died that way. They had been drinking and he went with them on the road to Quillabamba. On the way, he had a fight with his drinking companion and the man threw my uncle out of the truck. After that, my mother made my father stop working.

My father was a cattle dealer. He earned lots of money and then he would spend it all. He brought us money when we were little. But once we got older, nothing. My mother said [to him], "The worst is if you die and no one will support me. Better that you stay at my side because a family without a father has no meaning." The children land up being delinquents, vagabonds, pickpockets. Because, really, they pay no attention to their mothers.

My father, even now, how much he has beat us. Whatever mistake, he puts us in line. My father is very brusque, he's violent. He believes any little bit of gossip and takes it out on us. He has never said, "My children are saints," never. He is always beating us, always punishing us for whatever little mistake, he has never given us any leeway.

Again, one finds the odd conjunction of disparagement of drink and violence (the repeated use of the word *brusque*) associated with men and the need and desire for a father figure who symbolizes the family, however broken up that family may be.

One day I decided to go down to Avenida Ejército to speak to women who were not as well established as those working behind the semipermanent stalls just above the railroad tracks in Polvos Celestes (Blue Dust). The place Teófila was taking me to was horribly dirty and smelly. The steps down were basically a bathroom. The dust was swirling everywhere. We greeted Alejandrina Wayka, who was sitting in front of a huge pile of bags of salt and some rocks of salt. Her long, angular face was lovely. She slowly began telling me the story of how she came to sell salt there.

I had gone to Lima to work as a domestic servant. I was one of six children. Things were going well for me there. I was saving money, but I was called back here to support my brother because only one of us could be a professional and he was studying to be a teacher. When I came back, I met my husband, who was also studying to be a teacher. I started working in different ways in the market.

I was from Colcha, Paruro. The priest there is very good. I began selling vegetables, then food, then fruit. Then I got a little stand in Avenida Ejército and set it up as a little store. That's where we all slept together too at first. That was seven years ago. Now we have our house in Santa Ana. Then I got to know a man and together we began selling salt that we bought from wholesalers. The salt comes from Juliaca.

Two years ago, things changed for me. My brother and my husband were traveling from San Jerónimo to Paruro. There was a truck accident. My brother was just about to get a permanent position as a teacher and he had been working part-time already. He was permanently handicapped. My husband was also badly injured. He lost one eye. He has had four operations in Arequipa. Now I support my brother, my husband, and our three children. The priest in Colcha gave us money after the accident. No one else in the truck was hurt. Life is sometimes very sad.

The story Alejandrina Wayka tells is especially tragic. In her case, it might seem as if fate was responsible for her present situation, but her family made strategic choices, inflected by considerations of appropriate roles for men and women, that led her to become the sole breadwinner. Rather than being allowed to pursue her own future in Lima, she was called back to support her brother because he had been singled out to be the family's star, their hope for upward mobility. And her sacrifices eventually extended to supporting her husband, who was also pursuing a career as a teacher.

Women do try to fight back against abusive husbands. Inés, age thirty-two, the seller of fried egg breakfasts and lunch soups in the San Pedro central market, also tells of horrors at home. "I suffered with my first child. My husband did not treat me well. He took advantage of me. I lived with my sister.

Alejandrina Wayka, salt vendor along Avenida Ejército.

I didn't want to get married. When I got married, I was all alone, without my family. My husband beat me. Now, it's been almost two years. He hasn't beat me. One day, though, I beat him with a big spoon. His relatives also attacked me, until my blood flowed. I put up with it because of my children. He beat me because my first child is illegitimate, from a man in my community in Abancay, not of my husband. I came to Cuzco when I was fourteen."

The final story that gives us an idea of the complexity of household relationships and gender roles among women vendors is that of Domérica Hermoza, down by the railroad tracks, whom we met in chapter 2. Domérica was selling her limp vegetables spread out on a little plastic tarp in front of her—spinach, celery, lettuce, scallions, carrots—a small pile of rock salt, and her brightly colored yarns. She wore a floppy straw hat, and although her face was oddly childlike, her eyes seemed very old, her hands worn and callused. She herself was knitting away. I cannot explain what transpired in our meeting that caused Domérica to decide to talk almost non-stop about her life experiences. When I went back to visit her a week later and offered to take a photograph of her for her, she was close-lipped and frightened and wanted me to leave. She whispered to me as she pushed me away, "People will see us. People will talk." Domérica had neither mother nor father to serve as direct role models for her, and it was unclear how old she was, perhaps in her mid-twenties. She learned by the seat of her pants, from the images she saw on television, from those she fantasized about through music on the radio, and, not to underestimate its influence, from the Catholic Church.

> I'm here trying to figure out what to sell because otherwise, one stays in the house crying, desperate that a husband bring home money. My husband is a little bad, I don't want to explain. He drinks a lot, doesn't obey, gets bitter. I say to him, "I have five children who need clothes, food." He says to me, "Don't get involved in my life, pay attention to your own."
>
> My husband works but only brings home a little money. He is a journalist but the stores that had ads didn't pay up. He used to work part-time for the municipality and earned 50 soles daily if he worked. But if he didn't work, then he didn't even make a quarter, a fifth of that. So, there wasn't any money and he left off working there. Now he wants to do art. He doesn't earn anything. Even if he earns 1 or 2 soles, he drinks it away.
>
> I am from Cuzco. I don't have parents. I never knew my father. I knew my mother. When I was very little, though, my mother began to live with another man and we suffered enormously. I went to study and work in Lima. I lived in Lima and sold whatever I could there, cookies, whatever. In San Martín de Porras. That's where my husband lived. He's from

Ayacucho. We got to know each other here in Cuzco. We were neighbors in Huancaro, next to the Parish of San José Obrero (the orphanage).

I like Lima but I didn't like the rancid atmosphere. The smell was always of fish, . . . well, it's ugly . . . like being shut inside a big pot. You can't breathe. You don't have anything to breathe because, well, it's like you're a flying saucer, as they say. I couldn't stand it. It really bothered me. All alone I was, with another family that I didn't know, because I had problems with my stepfather. He beat my mother. And because I talked about these problems, I wasn't able to live that way. Better that I go. I was the last of the children. . . . I didn't have my father so I went to work. I suffered two years, weeping and weeping.

I don't remember when I went to Lima. I didn't have any documents. I wanted to go to another country. They were supposed to take me to Italy, some nuns, who made me suffer in Antabamba. I grew up in Antabamba. They brought me as a baby there, near Chumbivilcas. . . . They [the nuns] were going to take me to Italy. They didn't succeed because others didn't want me to go. They put up obstacles. So I thought, I'll go to Argentina, but the same thing. I didn't have any documents. I didn't have a birth certificate. If I had bought a passport, they would have given it to me, but I had nothing. I came to Cuzco. I had a lawyer fabricate all my documents— a birth certificate, a certificate of baptism. That's why I don't know how old I am. And because I wanted to leave and go to another country, I increased my age so they would give me documents as an adult but, nevertheless, they said, "You're going to repent having done this. We know you aren't that age. Others lower their age and you are raising yours." . . .

I didn't have a chance. Because of my husband. My husband abandoned me with my one little boy alone after we had been married four years. Afterwards, we got together again. Now we're together, but what for? Why did I get married? To live unhappily. I have studied, up through the third year of high school. I wanted to study more. My head hurt a lot. I couldn't concentrate. Even now, I can't concentrate. . . . I've tried to take care of many things. I haven't deliberately created this situation. . . .

My name is Domérica Hermoza. I chose my own name. I used to be called Carmen. Because I was born the 16th of July [Saint's Day for the Virgin of Carmen]. But I decided to call myself Domérica. I watched a soap opera and I liked that name. She was a pretty young woman, short, all beautiful. She wore pants. I liked her. "How I would like to be her!" I said to myself. She rode horses, walked in the countryside, with her hat, her whip, I don't know, and when the young men bothered her, she beat them up, and then she left. It was all so detailed. She was called Domérica. "How I would like to work in the fields, go to the countryside," I said to myself. I had a dream. And I haven't even had a chance to ride a horse. Well, maybe one day I still will. . . . But that's why I gave myself that name. I came from Lima and the lawyers said to me, "You want to change your last name, first name?" I said, "My first name, yes." I said so because fewer people use this name than Carmen. I don't like everyone using my name. I want to have a name that no one is familiar with. And just recently, I heard on the radio that a terrorist has started using my name. She isn't using Domérica but rather Doménica, they said. She gave herself that name. A terrorist.

I listen to the radio. When I have time in the morning, I get up and I put it on. I always listen to programs that come from Lima. In the evening when I get home, I listen to Radio Solár because . . . I am a musician of everything. I like everything. I can't say what I don't like. Sure, our religion tries to prohibit us. Listening to music, you aren't supposed to be too happy. But I can't, I can't control myself . . . and I have to listen to music that pleases me. Because I listen to special music—*huaynos* that I like, waltzes, boleros, I love boleros. I also like musicians from other countries, Rafael, Julio Iglesias, El Puma, Pablito Ortega, lots of them, women too, and I have special ones, I like everything, *cumbias,* but well-picked, they are beautiful and seem like a symphony to me. That's why when my husband does his program, he says to me, "You're going to listen." I say, "But if you put on ugly music, I won't. I'd rather listen to another program." I don't listen to it. My husband was working before on Santa Mónica Radio, then on Radio Lider. But now he's on Radio Mundo. But there's no income. He has to pay for the time he uses on the radio. . . . He's not an employee but a dependent. . . .

There isn't any money. Everything in life is painful. Everything is scarce, scarce. There's no money, no money. . . . He owes a lot to the radio and he can't work. I have friends in the market, one in the neighborhood, our neighbors who talk with us. But you know, there is always someone evil. Whenever you have something, there is always jealousy. . . . When you sell something, whatever, it appears as something else and sometimes you sell nothing. I used to sell very well. For how long now, I don't know, I haven't sold well.

Domérica has embarked on a path that, though still in its nascence, may lead to the kind of identity that many market women appear to have crafted for themselves out of their consciousness of existing gender and racial ideologies in Peruvian society. She is well aware of the pressures on women to be docile, suppress passion, and keep their opinions to themselves yet shoulder enormous responsibilities. She seeks escape from these cages through a variety of means, only several of which I have included here. One escape is geographic: going to another country/place, whether it is Italy or Argentina. (The first thing she asked me was whether I was from Switzerland.) Another means she uses is imagining herself and striving to reinvent herself as the soap opera woman Domérica, who takes care of herself, fights back, wears pants, and strides through the countryside on foot or on horseback. This is not just an idle fantasy. She took Domérica's name, and she has gradually built a reputation for herself as someone shrewd who does not always follow the path of other vendors. For example, instead of selling one or several products of the same kind, she views the market of potential products as a kind of stock market, reads it with great scrutiny and care, and then picks her products accordingly. She has also built a reputation as someone capable of experiencing miracles and curing others (see chapter 9). Finally, while I was sitting there with her, I witnessed her generosity to others, even when she was doing poorly.

In terms of racial ideologies, she has not rejected her roots in the countryside even while she has maintained a cosmopolitan interest in international music and other places. Not only does she see the countryside as a positive locus, but she also continues to mix together Quechua and Spanish systematically (see chapter 7) in her speech. These contradictory characteristics come together in many market women. They do not act as ideal women; they are entrepreneurs who give to those who are less fortunate; they live in the city and are street smart; they listen to boleros and watch soap operas from Mexico and Brazil yet often find comfort thinking of their relatives in the countryside (*campo*) or perhaps imagining that life in the countryside represents freedom from the horrors of city life and poverty.

Sociologist Mitchell Duneier, writing about men who informally sell books and magazines on the streets of Greenwich Village, New York City, does not romanticize the straits in which the men find themselves, but he is careful to delineate how they have struggled to create informal infrastructure on the streets in the form of social relations, sleeping spots, minimal hygienic standards, and such. To make these informal structures materialize takes a great investment of energy on the part of the men and a conviction that it might be possible to better one's life. Yet the very informality of the structures often makes them invisible to passersby. In more extreme instances, the sight of life on the streets—vendors napping, children playing inside crates, bags of old clothes, men peeing into bottles, the poverty of the merchandise being sold— appears repugnant, indicators of a down-and-out neighborhood. If these reprehensible "signs" are eliminated, many policy planners, politicians, and city residents believe, the neighborhood will not be dragged down. Fix the broken windows and hide the signs of poverty, and the neighborhood will rally and become better. Duneier's intensive field research led him to somewhat different conclusions:

On these sidewalks, the vendors, scavengers, and panhandlers have developed economic roles, complex work, and mentors who have given them encouragement to try to live "better" lives. This is the story of the largely invisible social structure of the sidewalk. For many of my readers, and certainly for myself, these redeeming aspects of the sidewalk have come as a surprise. At first glance, it strikes us that the visible practices of the street create an atmosphere for crime. . . . But it cannot correctly be assumed that certain kinds of human beings constitute "broken windows," especially without an understanding of how these people live their lives. . . . To be sure, there are some "broken windows" on these blocks. But mainly there are windows that look broken to people who are just passing by. Because Americans ruthlessly use race and class categories as they navigate through life, many citizens generalize from the actual broken windows to all the windows that look like them—and assume that a person who looks broken must be shattered, when in fact he is trying to fix himself as best he can. Only by understanding the rich social organization of the sidewalk, in all its complexity, might citizens and politicians appreciate how much is lost when we accept the idea that the presence of a few broken windows justifies tearing down the whole informal structure. (Duneier 1999:314–15)

The possibilities that Domérica has latched onto reappear in the lives and demeanor of so many market women. Their donning of identities that diverge from the norm is obviously in flux and variable, but they have a transformative dynamic power, a salve that acts as a subtle challenge to the weight of unhappy, suffocating, and sometimes terrorizing sacrifice, the bitter salt that only rarely manifests itself as tears coursing down the cheeks of tough market women such as Nanci, Dori, Eva, María Inés, Alejandrina, and Domérica. It keeps them going when they have little else to justify their huge investments in small things.

Notes

1. I do not mean to suggest that these entanglements were unique to market women. Rather, the position of women and men in the lower ethnic and class strata of Peru's social fabric creates particular household and occupational patterns and conflict-ridden relationships. Many domestic servants experienced similar tensions. For example, see Gill's (1994) excellent ethnography of domestic servants in La Paz, Bolivia.

2. Norma Fuller (1997) studied Peruvian men between ages twenty-two and fifty-five in Peru. She found patterns of fragile and unstable masculinity, in part because of the contradictory desires of her subjects to be "family men" and to demonstrate their virility socially as independent (in the streets, with the "other boys") and capable of earning a living. Those who didn't have work were simply "poor devils." Her study, though limited to middle-class men, reveals patterns that my own research suggests extends to working-class men such as the husbands of market women.

4

Straw Hats: The World of Wholesalers

The subject of this chapter is the world of wholesalers in Cuzco's informal markets. Despite the challenges I faced in interviewing and getting to know wholesalers, I was able to learn about their businesses, how they acquired their goods, the risks they faced, and their relationships with each other and with producers and retailers. Wholesalers inhabit a shadowy world. With relative ease I was able to stroll through the streets, stopping to chat with one or another vendor or buy my daily vegetables and fruit from the inside markets of San Pedro, Wanchaq, Rosaspata, or San Blas. It was another matter to approach the wholesalers, let alone figure out who they were, not least because they were almost invisible, sitting inside their trucks or warehouses down by the railroad tracks, sheltered inside their stores or hotel lodgings, or pretending to be retailers. I was always a little frightened of them because of their skill at deflecting unwanted queries with offputting and sophisticated fabrications.

The organization of market wholesalers in highland Cuzco does not resemble the well-ordered hierarchy of "buyers in bulk," corporations, or "commercial vendors" of the United States. In Cuzco, you can find out who is who only by knowing someone who knows who is who. Although wholesalers in Cuzco's informal markets engage in speculation and price fixing, it is not institutionalized, and there is no identifiable futures market. But wholesalers take high risks, organize into informal cartels, play the market, and sometimes make a killing. It is possible to see the consequences of these behaviors and to hear about them, but it is far more difficult to obtain anything resembling reliable statistics about the livelihood of these key figures or about the scale at which they operate.

With Teófila accompanying me, as much for moral support as for her acquain-
tance with some of these women and men, toward the end of my research time
I began wandering among the trucks and warehouses along the tracks where
many of the wholesalers spend all or part of the day, selling their wares, talking
to fellow wholesalers, playing cards, and drinking *chicha* during the frequent
lulls in business. The probability of being robbed skyrockets here, and I felt very
vulnerable. Most of the pickpockets are looking for wholesalers who have hit
the jackpot or have a reputation for consistently doing well, but a silly-looking
gringa in a nice rain jacket whose pockets seem full also is a good target. Lucre
told me the sad story of her son, a wholesaler in Lima who at age thirty-six was
locking up for the night after a good day. He went to a nearby bar, and when
he came out he was accosted by a group of men wielding a board with nails
sticking out of it. They threw her son down and punctured his stomach in
multiple places with the board. He died a long, painful death. Josefina Solorzano
Cárdenas, a wholesaler I got to know, said that the things she feared most were
"thieves, assaults, murders. They cut our aprons. They notice if you have money,
they grab you, three or four of them, and if you resist, they murder you. It's
worse in the city, but not so bad in the countryside. You can't walk with nice
clothes [looking closely at me]. They'll take your nice jacket, your shoes. If you're
grabbed by four or five people, they'll suffocate you, grab you by the throat."

Being even a little more successful in an economy where getting by is a
struggle brings its own unique kind of risk even as that success may provide
part-time employment for others.

I cannot say I was able to keep the hours of the wholesalers. Their most
important business is conducted at about 4 A.M. with retailers. The retailers
rush down to the tracks and load up a porter, a lucky tricyclist, or a taxi with
the goods they have bought for their stalls for the next few days or week. Some
of them have special information they are loath to share, but many of them
converse about prices and the quality of goods as they make their way to the
wholesalers from the *pueblos jovenes* where so many of them live. This hectic
rush abates by around 7 A.M. Later in the day, some of the wholesalers may
go to truck stops on the outskirts of the city and harass arriving *campesinos* to
turn over their agricultural products to them. Teófila assured me that even
though I could not manage to get down to the trucks so early, I would have
better luck on Saturdays because the wholesalers often spent the whole day
there doing business. As for those who conducted their business privately
behind closed doors, it would be a matter of chance if I managed to interview
any of them. One hotel in Cuzco caters to wealthy wholesalers who deal in
clothes, and retailers work out their deals at the hotel.

Blue Eyes at the Saturday Market

It is hard to imagine that the railroad tracks can become any more congested or frenetic than they already are on a normal weekday. But on this Saturday, we move slowly, shoulder to shoulder, scurrying to make room for the taxis and tricycles that roar by us, only inches away, honking impatiently. There is no real road down here, just one carved by rumbling vehicles that make people move out of their path. The trucks, lined up in rows, keep their motors running all the time and spew exhaust.[1] Next to them are tons of potatoes, mountains of squash and cabbage, and loads of oranges. On the other side of the road is the Saturday animal market: squawking hens, chicks, goats, puppies, rabbits, and lambs. Teófila suddenly grabs my arm and says, "Look." She directs my attention to a woman issuing orders next to a huge lorry. A number of *campesinas* and market women surround her. She is light-skinned, her straight dark hair pulled back, her face shaded by a large straw hat. She wears a brown, knee-length skirt and a magenta polyester blouse, flat shoes, and stockings. Her name is Paulina. Fully cognizant of her status and the attention it commands, she allows me to listen in on her business dealings, and she even includes me in an odd way in the conversation she is having with her admiring audience. The conversation is a little hard to follow because I have tried not to reorganize it. Instead, it reveals some of the complex principles that lie behind these exchanges.[2]

> Campesina: Is this enough?
> *Paulina:* Yes. That's enough. Look, look. That's just enough.
> Campesina: Over there are those little ones [referring to some potatoes].
> *Paulina:* Hurry, hurry, my mother [a metaphoric form of address in Quechua, usually said with endearment and often referring to a woman who is older]. And don't be stubborn in giving them to me. Just turn them over to me.
> Campesina: Okay then. I'll give you these.
> *Paulina:* Just give them to me for my child. You only gave me a kilo.
> Campesina: Isn't it sufficient for all of the children?
> *Paulina:* You need to give me just a little more. A kilo isn't enough, my little mother. Give me just a little more. Now, that's fine. I don't want them just for me.
> Campesina: They always come like this in a bag. What have you brought?
> *Paulina:* Grass. Carrots. Hurry. Hand the bag over to me. You have to give that to Señora Juana. Give me change. Hurry. Hurry. It's getting late.
> *Teófila:* Have you already finished your business?
> *Paulina:* Yes, Mamá.

Teófila: There's no one like her. Already leaving. Are you a wholesaler?

Paulina: Yes, mother. I'm a wholesaler. Hmmm.

Campesina: You owe me a sol.

Teófila: You gather [goods] from everyone?

Paulina: Yes. That's how it is. I have to help.

Linda: And why are you doing it this way?

Paulina: Clearly I'm going to help everyone. I'll buy from everyone in this row.

Paulina: How much must I give to Señora China?

Wholesaler's daughter: You have to give her 1 sol.

Market woman: She'll land up buying from everyone to the end of this row.

Linda: So all of them are your friends?

Paulina: Yes. Yes. Because if I don't buy from all of them, they'll say, "She only gets from her," "She's only bought from her."

Linda: That's great. Then, you buy from everyone. Where are you from?

Paulina: From Urubamba. [In an aside to another woman] Thank you, little mother, for that.

Linda: From Urubamba.

Paulina: Yes. And you, where are you from?

Linda: From the United States.

Paulina: Ay. How beautiful. A little *gringa* here in Cuzco. [Aside] I'm going to pay from those, from the potatoes.

Linda: May I watch? How is it that you buy from everyone?

Market woman: Look! Another one with blue eyes who is following you [referring to me, the anthropologist].

Paulina: Perhaps she will be my heir. That's good.

Market woman: You [meaning Teófila and me], too. Why don't you buy from everyone? The Señora buys from all of us in this row.

Linda: How beautiful. That's very good.

Paulina: Yes. That's how I come to have silver [money] in a huge bag.

As the first part of this conversation reveals, wholesalers such as Paulina prefer to have a steady clientele, just as retailers do. The generosity of wholesalers, in part, is an effort to ensure that producers will keep returning to them. They also want to corner as great a market share of producers and retailers as possible. Therefore, they balance their efforts to acquire goods at the lowest price possible and sell at the highest price possible with gathering up as much as possible and as quickly as possible from as many producers as possible. As becomes apparent later in this chapter, Paulina works as a wholesaler who sometimes sells the products she has brought directly from the countryside and sometimes exchanges them with producers for other agricultural products. She must constantly calculate her profit margin.

The conversation with Paulina continued as we both became more curious about each other and our respective "business" in the market. Paulina and the women she was exchanging products with called attention to her high status and mine. Her status derived from her work as a wholesaler; her ownership of land in the Yucay Valley, a very fertile and beautiful region; her husband, who may or may not be foreign born; and her "fertility," reflected in the number of children she has. In contrast, my high status came simply from being a foreigner with blue eyes.

Linda: You must be a rich and powerful woman.

Paulina: Aha. I am a rich and powerful woman. [Everyone laughs.]

Market woman: She has always been a rich and powerful woman. It's nothing new. For all these years she's been a rich and powerful woman.

Paulina: A porter is hauling my silver.

Linda: You also sell?

Paulina: Yes, I sell.

Linda: What do you sell?

Paulina: Grass.

Linda: Do you sell to everyone?

Paulina: Yes, to everyone. To them, too.

Linda: She sells grass to you?

Market woman: Yes, and buys from all of us. From all of us. When we don't have money, she gives it to us and she gives us the grass as a present. She gives us ears of corn as gifts.

Linda: Yes. That's good.

Market woman 2: Look, and what is this?

Market woman 3: They are new potatoes. And how much is an *arroba* [twenty-five pounds]? Sixteen soles.

Linda: Do you also have farmland?

Market woman 1: Yes, she has an estate.

Paulina: Keep them [the potatoes], mother. We already got some yesterday when we came.

Market woman 2: She already got some. Sixteen for an *arroba* of potatoes. They are delicious.

Market woman 1: She has an estate, mamá. One of her estates is for sale right now.

Linda: What's her estate called?

Market woman 1: In Yucay. Why don't you buy it?

Linda: Yucay is beautiful.

. . . .

Paulina: Are you familiar with it?

Linda: Yes, I am. It's pretty.

Paulina: My estate is for sale. And my husband is also for sale.

Market woman 1: No.

Paulina: One with blue eyes is for sale.

Market woman 1: How shameless. She wants to sell Señor Denis.

Paulina: My husband is a *gringo,* one with blue eyes for someone from the United States.

Market woman 1: There's the little girl but her eyes are no longer blue. Green eyes, not blue ones. When she was little, she had blue eyes. When she was a little baby.

Teófila: But she does have light colored eyes.

Paulina: But she no longer has the eyes of her father.

Here, Paulina, Teófila, and the market woman are discussing two different subjects. The market women continue to encourage Paulina to purchase new potatoes from them, but Paulina explains that she has enough already. They are also discussing one of Paulina's children, who apparently was born with blue eyes that have since changed color. Nevertheless, their lightness is considered by all of them to be a sign of high status, calling attention to how, in Peru, phenotypical characteristics continue to be correlated with social status markers.

Market woman 1: She has eighteen children.

Linda: Oh.

Paulina: I'm pregnant right now. With this one, nineteen.

Market woman 1: So she can leave the estate to all of them.

Paulina: Next year, twenty.

Market woman 1: And now. Who are you going to leave the estate to? Tell me.

Paulina [to her little girl]: Bring me the little bag.

Linda: Is that your truck?

Paulina: No, it belongs to those young men. These little potatoes that I have bought I'm going to put away.

Linda: All those?

Paulina: Thank you, little mother. This woman should give me great thanks.

Market woman 3: So, buy from us, Señorita [referring to me].

Teófila: You're going to be overloaded carrying all of that.

Paulina: Now, yes [lifting up her loaded carrying cloth].

Market woman 1 [referring to Paulina]: All that she earns just for her big belly [for her pregnancy].

Paulina: Sure. Here it is. Eh.

Market woman 1: Ay.

Market woman 2 [giving Paulina some tomatoes]: You had better add these
   because you're dropping them.
Paulina: Now we're going. Until later. Have a good trip.

The Chains of the Market: Fertile Profits, Warehouses of Debt

This not unusual yet complicated conversation between Paulina, the wholesaler,
and a number of vendors and direct producers gives us a glimpse of the place
of wholesalers in the informal markets of Cuzco. Paulina is wealthy, possibly
married to a man who owns a large amount of land in the very fertile Yucay
Valley just outside Cuzco. The way she manages her business is intriguing. As
a wholesaler, she brings carrots and grass in bulk directly from the countryside
and does two things.[3] Some of it she sells to retailers. Some she exchanges for
other agricultural products, such as tomatoes or new potatoes, that are usually offered to her by peasant producers or, in some cases, other retailers. She
then resells these products to other retailers. It also appears that in many instances she buys up these products as much to maintain good relations with a
steady clientele of retailers as to make a profit. While I was there, she seemed
willing to accept all products that the various women offered her, although they
quibbled about price and quantity a bit. Both she and the other women also
wanted to make sure that I understood her high social standing and wealth,
manifested in the blue eyes of her husband and my blue-eyed presence, her big
belly, her numerous offspring, her heavy load, and her generosity.

Paulina is only one kind of wholesaler that I found in the Cuzco markets.
Others operate with differing amounts of working capital and rely on differing strategies to obtain and market their products. Some wholesalers amass
their products directly from villages and locate themselves permanently near
producer sites in provincial capitals, large towns, or districts. They own warehouses, corrals, and even commercial stores.[4] Others do a booming business
for the very reason that they operate on the fringes in the black markets, having figured out how to cross national borders without paying tariffs.

Marina Ordoña is a black market wholesaler. She runs an enormous used
clothes store in Polvos Celestes. Her store is jammed with people sifting
through the clothes and shoes, which she buys in lots. Marina sits at a little desk,
calmly watching the action and occasionally stating the price of things that her
two employees show her. She is the final arbiter in bargaining, and here there
is plenty of bargaining. Marina is slim, well dressed, lackadaisical, soft spoken,
and sharp. Years ago, she was selling new clothes that she had acquired from

factories in Lima and Juliaca (Puno) when she met a woman who encouraged her to consider selling used clothes from Chile. She traveled to Chile and brought back a little merchandise. She found that it sold well because people were poor and the clothes were cheap. Soon she was traveling there every week. She has been very successful, and her profits exceed $500 per month.

Julia Chacón is even more able to dissemble than Marina Ordoña. She is extremely powerful but presented herself to me as a humble vendor who buys in small quantities from producers who come to her in Cuzco and who resells to merchants going to the mines. She insists she very rarely deals in potatoes, but Teófila tells me otherwise. Her straw hat gives her away, and when I ask her what kind of taxes she pays, it becomes clear that she is operating with substantial capital because she cannot use what would be equivalent to our "short form" in the United States. Julia sells potatoes in large quantities and has her own warehouse by the railroad tracks, three employees, and a telephone, something one rarely finds among wholesalers or retailers. She tells me that when she first started selling, she used to offer credit and confine her transactions to those with whom she was well acquainted. They often formalized their relationships through rituals of fictive kinship called *compadrazgo*. Now,

Potato wholesalers in front of a depot along Avenida Ejército, 1998.

she rarely offers credit and sells her goods as cheaply and quickly as possible to the first comer because the competition is so great. She tells me, "When the prices are good, we are frantic; when they are bad, we just sit here, bored."

When I lived in the countryside on and off between 1974 and 1993, I was able to get a good sense of how wholesalers dealing in agricultural products and meat operate. Many of them were children or relatives of large estate owners (*hacendados*), and they knew the *campesino* families who served as peons on their properties well. With the passage of Peru's 1969 agrarian reform, when hacendados lost most of their land, they entered into commerce and whole-saling, taking advantage of their already extensive social ties of patronage with *campesinos*. For example, I was always struck by the number of stores in the district capital of Huanoquite, Paruro, where I spent a year and part of several summers doing field research. The population of the district capital was less than one thousand, and that of the district as a whole was a little more than four thousand. Even more impressive than the number of stores was the lack of regular buying and selling that took place in them. Most were sparsely stocked with merchandise, but they were extremely popular sites. Groups of men often sat quietly drinking, sometimes starting quite early in the morning. They continued swilling, passing the bottle well into the night, with the store owner solicitously serving up rounds of beer or pure grain alcohol. Every once in a while, a little girl or boy dashed in with a handful of coins and shyly stood there until the owner took notice and allowed her to purchase a candle, some noodles, bread, or sugar. It was not until I started my work on urban markets that I understood one of the raisons d'être of these stores.[5] They were wholesale operations, open most of year with a sparse assortment of dry goods and basic necessities for sale but functioning primarily as gathering-up sites during the harvest. Nevertheless, contracts between the *hacendado* or wholesale owners of these stores and *campesinos* were established long before the harvest during the socializing and drinking that took place all year.

Other wholesalers operate on a greater scale than the local wholesalers. They are dedicated to serving as "the ships of the highways." They gather up agricultural products and livestock from the fields of *campesinos*, from highway pickup points, from weekly markets (*ferias*), and from local wholesalers. They own or sometimes rent huge lorries and usually do not live near producer sites. They converge on weekly markets and buy from producers, or they buy directly from the wholesalers who have been gathering up goods in local districts and keeping them in their stores and warehouses. They often travel from one department or city of Peru to another, specializing in particular products.[6] One kind of wholesaler subcategory concentrates on the weekly markets. They own trucks and carry nonagricultural goods that *campesinos* want. They sell or exchange their goods and gather up agricultural and livestock products at the same time.[7]

Wandering wholesalers occupy a much lower level. They accost *campesinos* at truck or bus stops or along the road, trying to make them sell their products immediately. Wholesalers who have large amounts of working capital are generally men, but these intermediaries tend to be women. They use public transport or go on foot, but as the big wholesalers do, they try to bring small gifts for producers.[8]

Several different kinds of intermediaries work on a small scale in the countryside. Although they cannot be characterized as wholesalers, they often participate directly in providing goods that eventually reach wholesalers. Some *campesinos* complement their agricultural activities with commerce, traveling to communities where they buy, sell, or exchange specialized goods, including nonagricultural items. This kind of activity has been common throughout the Andes for many years and involves a deep knowledge of social etiquette, the value of different products, and strong social ties, often through marriage.[9] As is true throughout the world, both the foot peddlers and the captains of the ships of the roads, the truck drivers, are eagerly awaited as much for news and gossip as for the merchandise and money they bring.

It is difficult for wholesalers to gain the commitment and loyalty of *campesinos* to sell a portion of their harvest to them, especially because wholesalers want to have these promises in place at the beginning, not the end, of the growing season. *Campesinos* appreciate knowing that they have a sure buyer who will be responsible for transporting and marketing their surplus, but they worry about the vagaries of the harvest. Will they have enough for themselves? How much should they set aside as surplus, and how much should they hoard to put on the market in times of scarcity, when they can get a better return? Given these concerns, wholesalers do their best to insinuate themselves into the lives of *campesinos* in a manner that will diminish the risk and uncertainty that they face. These wholesalers speak Spanish and Quechua and may have extensive knowledge of the agricultural region in which they work. Many of them operate with a large amount of working capital and deal in tons of different products. How do they do this? They are the larger-than-life godfathers and godmothers. The metaphors of family and kinship, as envisioned hierarchically (father-son, mother-daughter, grandmother-grandson) occupy center stage in the world of wholesalers.

Such wholesalers also occupy local political office as mayors, municipal councilmen, governors, and prefects. They willingly accept requests to serve as principal cargo holders in religious fiestas. They are the godparents to couples marrying and to the children born of these marriages. They are delighted to offer credit to peasants who buy bread, sugar, cookies, flour, drinks, beer, canned milk, jam, coca, and liquor from their stores, but they expect to be repaid with a portion of the peasant's harvest. They often provide the same peasants or their children with a place to stay when they come to the district or provincial capital.

When the time comes to negotiate a contract, they draw on all of these social relationships, reminding their fictive kin of their obligations in a highly ritualized series of actions. First, they arrive offering a ceremonial drink (*t'inka* [Quechua]) to the *campesino*. They approach him using terms of endearment, such as "dear heart" (*sumaq sonqo* [Quechua] or *cariño* [Spanish]). They bear gifts called *k'utuna* (Quechua), consisting of bread, small bottles of alcohol, salt, coca, and sugar, with sweets and bread for their godchildren. When the contract is consummated after the harvest, the wholesaler again brings a farewell gift to the *campesino* called a *k'acharpu* (Quechua). All of these gestures are modeled on the structure and dynamics of native agricultural and livestock rituals that involve offering food and drinks to the earth, the mountain spirits, and even the livestock so that they will reciprocate with wool, fertility (in the form of a good harvest and plenty of livestock together with its manure), and water. These elements constitute the very basic sustenance of a *campesino* household. These ritualized exchanges so closely integrated with production itself for *campesinos* take a new twist when they are activated by wholesalers and reinserted into circuits of exchange integrated with commerce and commodification.

Josefina, the wholesaler who cautioned me about the dangers of thieves, worked down by the tracks. She did not hesitate in telling me about her business. She apologized for not having a chair and offered me a sack to sit on. She was sitting inside her warehouse with her legs stretched out. She wore a big, floppy straw hat. The cool warehouse, piled high with potatoes along one side, was a welcome relief from the dust and sun beating down outside. She was accompanied by her husband's nephew and her dark-skinned, slim son. Josefina had grown up with her father because her mother died when she was three years old. I asked her why and how she had become a wholesaler. I was particularly interested in her case because there are not very many women wholesalers who go on the road. She told me, "From when I was ten years old, I always wanted to sell something. That's how I was born. I used to sell coca and coffee in the Valley [of Lares], and then I dedicated myself to this business. It has always pleased me to buy and sell. My father was a farmer in the Lares Valley. He bought cattle, butchered it, and sold the meat. My mother

also loved business. She worked with mules in Qalqa. My father was originally from Urubamba. [Qalqa and Urubamba are located in the dynamic agricultural valley of Urubamba, not far from Cuzco.] My father originally
worked with mules too, selling sugar and cheese. We would travel through
the Urubamba Valley with the mules. I can't walk like that anymore though.
I am forty-two years old."

I asked Josefina how her business worked.

We travel very far. For example, right now, there aren't any potatoes near
Cuzco. We travel far, to Andahuaylas, not to the town itself, but to the
heights of the puna. That's where we go. We make contracts, then eventually when the deal is airtight, we go there in a truck. We give the *campesinos*
money, and on the day they harvest, we put the potatoes in sacks, we weigh
them, we pay them, and we bring the potatoes here from Huancarani,
Acobamba, Huaynapata. We know the peasants who work. We buy directly
from them. It doesn't make sense for us to buy from the others who gather
up products because they gather them by the *arroba* [twenty-five pounds],
and they are all different colors. Other merchants want only one color, one
variety, and they won't accept them if we sell them all mixed up. *Perichosa,
sica, mariva*, these are the varieties they sell.

We go along, asking for people who grow potatoes. They tell us, "that
guy there, that guy," and we go to their houses carrying with us little breads,
soft drinks. Without a gift, we don't go, for their children too. That's what
they want, because if we don't bring things, they just turn their faces away—
"What have you brought, why have you come?" We don't bring food. We
bring jam, oil, bread, to give away. We make the contract when they are
harvesting.

We also give them advances before the harvest. When someone in their
family has a problem, if someone's sick, if they have an emergency and we
know them, then they come to us and we give them an advance for a certain date. No matter what, that's what we do. When they come, we put
them up, we feed them, we protect them from the robbers, that too. That's
the way they too have trust in us.

The *campesinos* engaging in these negotiations, like the market women
dealing with Paulina, understand fully that these wholesalers will make a profit.
Olivia Harris is an anthropologist who has spent many years working in
Aymara villages of Bolivia. In one article, Harris (1995:307) traces how villagers regard money and its uses and finds that "money seems to have a largely
neutral value." Harris assumed that villagers would resent the exploitive practices of intermediary traders, such as wholesalers, and regard their relationships with them as antagonistic but necessary, but she found otherwise. In her

conversations with *campesinos,* they seemed to accept the exorbitant profits made at their expense by these intermediaries. As Harris (1995:308) puts it, "It transpired that they were fully aware of the inequality of particular trans- actions, but justified them by the convenience of the traders coming out to the countryside, thus saving them an arduous journey. One woman trader described as 'bad' by most people did indeed wrest a living from the peasants by charging high prices or selling for credit to be repaid in kind at harvest time. However, it was not these activities that people were alluding to when they called her bad; rather, they meant that she was mean in not offering food and hospitality. Other traders who combined profit making with generosity were described as good."

Canadian anthropologist Inge Bolin (1998) has written a book based on long residence with Quechua herders who live high in the Andes at about 13,000 feet above sea level. She argues that the moral principle of respect predominates in everything the Chillihuani herders do, from the organization of their every- day work activities to their cycle of ceremonial rituals to their relationship with natural forces. One way this respect manifests itself is in the vigilance Chillihuani exercise to ensure that competition does not prevail, even when winning and losing clearly take place. For an outsider, the "rituals of respect" that character- ize the dealings between wholesalers and *campesino* producers at first glance seem paternalistic and unnecessarily obsequious. Yet it is probably the case that the traditional emphasis the Quechua have placed on suppressing competition is even more vigorously enforced in this highly exploitive and competitive eco- nomic relationship, which certainly does not favor the *campesino* producer. Ironically, then, a principle that encourages harmony and control of hierarchy and differentiation in one social and economic setting contributes to and per- petuates exactly those inequalities in another.[10]

Josefina makes it clear that, from her perspective, wholesale transactions are high-risk and difficult operations and that no matter what kinds of terms she could offer producers, they would turn their faces away if she didn't approach them with the expected gifts.

> We always travel. . . . Once, twice, three times a week, if there are sales. We don't have a truck. We contract an express truck. There is a lot of competi- tion. There are *campesinos* who offer the price here in Cuzco just to screw us, just to make us lose face. The number of merchants and the lack of work creates this competition. Everything is competition. You can't buy anymore with tranquility. You buy at 800, others at 850, another at 900. And you have to pay the cost of transport. A woman can't carry the sacks. I have to have a man who can carry the sacks and I have to pay him as well. The potato

business requires great strength. One has to fill huge sacks, weigh them, put them on the scale. One needs strength. We sell all day until about 6 P.M. We will sell to anyone. We sometimes give products to the retailers as advances. If they don't pay, well, we fail. We can't do anything about it. If we complain, we'll also lose money because complaining requires time. One needs money to take that path. If we don't know the market woman, even though it hurts our heart, we won't give her credit.

Profits are equated with fertility. Even when they are joking, market women in general and Paulina, as a wholesaler, equate both pregnancy and profits from their wholesale operations with fertility. Profit is the reward that wholesalers reap for taking risks and making arduous journeys to the countryside. Harris (1995:309) also finds this, noting, "Indians consider that people who travel deserve to compensate their expenditure and effort by making a profit. . . . People who make money to give birth in this way are thought to perform a valuable social service. Money when it returns in the form of profit is fertile, not through the process of planting and maturation, but through exchange."

This mutual understanding functions more like mutual mistrust as wholesalers and *campesinos* get down to the dirty business of besting each other. Before the contract is sealed, *campesinos* play wholesalers against each other to drive up the price that wholesalers will offer them. After the contract is sealed and wholesalers arrive months later for their goods, the exchange of gifts notwithstanding, wholesalers rig scales while *campesinos* mix the quality and variety of potatoes or wool, for example, always being sure to put the best, biggest, and finest at the top of the sack. They may mix the potatoes with a few rocks or make sure some of the wool is wet. Sealed contracts do not prevent wheedling, whispering, and angry shouting as *campesinos* feign scarcity and wholesalers discover hidden expenses that *campesinos* owe them.

Wholesalers are well aware that most *campesino* producers act as individuals. This gives them an important edge. They gather information and take advantage of the lack of organization among producers, forming a kind of cartel among themselves to keep the prices they pay to producers low. In addition to manipulating *campesinos* through friendships and godparenthood, then they are also able to manipulate supply and demand to a degree.

Wholesalers and producers depend heavily on creditor-debtor relationships for the smooth functioning of circulation. They offer producers credit without interest as advances. This may be the most important attraction for *campesinos,* who, like most farmers the world over, always have a cash flow problem. The creditor-debtor relationship appeals to *campesinos* for more than simply the availability of cash. *Campesinos* draw on a metaphor of production and reproduction in conceptualizing their debts to wholesalers. The Laymi *campesinos* of Potosí, Bolivia use the same word for manure and debt: *wanu*.[11] Manure, of course, is used as fertilizer and eventually should result in a better harvest. Likewise with debts. "The Laymi believe that it is good to have both credit and debt relationships. In the metaphorical association of debt and credit with manure," says Harris (1995:309), "we can detect a vision of circulation itself—or rather delayed circulation—as a fertilizing force."[12] Thus, money itself can serve as a fertilizing force, even when the underlying terms of exchange are unequal.

Notes

1. They used their trucks' power source to keep their radios blasting, but sometimes it also seemed that they were making a symbolic statement about their availability of capital, which allowed them to keep their engines running for most of the day.

2. I have translated the conversation between Paulina, me, Teófila, several market women, and one *campesina* into English, but it took place in both Spanish and Quechua, with the speakers switching from one language to the other. The use of Spanish or Quechua (see chapters 7 and 8) depends in part on whether the person to whom they are speaking is of higher or lower status and whether they are monolingual Quechua or Spanish speakers or bilingual. This particular conversation is complicated by my intervention in Quechua. Higher-status people, such as wholesalers, use Quechua instrumentally, to obtain the best deal from *campesinos*, for example. My use of Quechua was also instrumental (an attempt to be included in the conversation), but it had the added effect of drawing attention to me and creating laughter because it was paradoxical that a blue-eyed, high-status foreigner would want to speak the language of the Incas, which has been associated with low status and denigrated for so long.

3. Grass is in demand because many families living in Cuzco still raise guinea pigs (*cuyes*) in their households and feed them the grass. Guinea pigs have always been an important source of protein for Quechua people. They are also used for curing and divination, and some families have succeeded in setting up small businesses, raising the animals for sale. Grass is also used as fodder for llamas, whose home traditionally has been at high altitudes in the puna. Until the introduction of mules and horses by the Spanish, the llama was the principal beast of burden in the highlands, organized into large trading caravans that traversed the Andes and, during the colonial period, frequented the central plaza, carrying goods to the market. They were also valuable for their fiber and meat. Today, they serve an additional function. Tourists love having their photos taken with Quechua women and children, dressed in their finest traditional outfits, together with a llama or two, and the plaza once again is occupied by llamas, which must be fed.

4. In Spanish, these local or village wholesalers are known as *acopiadores mayoristas locales* or *rescatistas del pueblo*.

5. Catherine Allen (1988) spent many years working with the people of Sonqo in southern highland Peru, trying to understand their worldview or cosmology. In the

course of her study, she inquired into the effects of the money economy on the Sonqueños. She reports, "As Sonqo becomes increasingly incorporated into the money economy—and as Sonqueños raise more cash crops and state that life without money is impossible—conversation turns less to the *saqra llaqta* (demonic town) and more to the *saqra tinda* (demonic store). Nocturnal travelers, they say, hear voices and singing as the hillside opens beside their path to reveal a rich Mestizo store full of manufactured goods, bright lights, laughter, and music. The urge to enter is nearly unmasterable, but the fool who does so finds that the store soon vanishes, leaving him back on the path and deathly ill" (1988:111). Many *campesinos* feel less negative about the monetary economy than Sonqueños, but they are all aware that within the money economy, usury and unequal exchange are characteristic, especially in dealing with wholesalers.

6. In Spanish, these wholesale transporters are known as *transportistas mayoristas*.

7. In Spanish, those belonging to this subcategory of *transportista* are known as *rescatistas de feria*.

8. In Spanish, these women are called *rescatistas minoristas ambulantes* or *alcanzadores independientes*.

9. In Spanish, these intermediaries are called *comerciantes campesinos* and *rescatistas de comunidades*. Giorgio Alberti and Enrique Mayer (1974) edited an excellent volume titled *Reciprocidad e Intercambio en los Andes Peruanos* in which the contributors wrote in detail about Andean highland rules of reciprocity and calculuses of exchange. They argued that market dynamics destroy the principles of reciprocity that are integral to Quechua culture, but since then, research has shown the remarkable adaptability of *campesinos* that has permitted them to move between the world of the market and the world of the gift, defending themselves, at times successfully, from terms of trade that they consider too exploitive, resisting the inroads of a totally commodified society. However, I am not saying that *campesinos* are not exploited if one objectively calculates costs of production and the profitability of serving as an intermediary in the chain of circulation. I only observe that *campesinos* themselves have found ways to take advantage of and manipulate this structure. Sometimes they embrace it or are able to stave off or channel in an unexpected direction what they find offensive about it.

10. Bolin takes to an extreme the idea that respect, activated by the Quechua as a moral principle, encourages harmony and equality. In fact, even in many isolated highland villages, paternalistic relationships exist that rely on such "rituals of respect." The dynamics between *campesino* producers and wholesalers is not particularly novel, but the way in which the market economy, with its emphasis on competition and individualism, interacts with these rituals of respect that are not part of a market economy is quite interesting.

11. Harris (1995:309) states that *wanu* and *manu* (the Quechua and Aymara word for "loan") are used interchangeably. This is not surprising because Quechua speakers often use word play to make a point.

12. See also Allen (1988, especially 93–94 and 169–70).

5

Harpies and the Empty, Dirty, Overpriced Bread Basket: Regulating the Market Chain

In this chapter, I focus on the hostility aimed at intermediaries in general and at wholesalers in particular. I examine the ways in which government regulations and transgressions affect exchange and incite hostility among intermediaries and the views that retailers and consumers have of the behavior of intermediaries. The chain of market intermediaries linking consumer to producer often is more elaborate than meets the eye, and its very complexity makes it difficult to consider how it might be simplified or eliminated (see Babb 1998:86–89). As we learned in chapter 4, wholesalers such as Paulina exchange products with both producers and retailers, and some wholesalers, such as those who live in the countryside, may also operate as producers. To further complicate matters, alliances and competition characterize relationships between wholesalers. Finally, the chain of intermediaries within the informal market economy is closely intertwined with the production and sales processes of formal economy businesses, and the chain itself facilitates the circulation of products in an inefficient economy with poor transport systems and great geographic obstacles.

The relationships between retailers and wholesalers and those between wholesalers and *campesino* producers are generally personal, often long term and face to face. This is not true of the relationships between wholesalers and consumers or between consumers and producers, who are separated from each other by a chain of sometimes seventeen or eighteen links of intermediaries. These relationships are impersonal and anonymous, just as they are in the United States. But the U.S. government is directly engaged in making decisions about interest rates, and market information is transparent. Because this is not the case when markets are informal and information circulates by word of mouth or painstaking statistical assessment that is already out of date by the time it hits the newsstands, consumer hostility is directed at wholesalers.[1] Retailers also protect themselves against the accusations of consumers by blaming wholesalers. Historically, state officials located in municipalities have taken primary responsibility for trying to deal with this situation. Yet as I found out when I began poring over documents from Cuzco's municipal archive, state agents have repeatedly colluded with wholesalers in creating false scarcity and fixing prices. On September 10, 1924, the mayor of Cuzco singled out the actions of wholesalers as the main cause of the high price of basic commodities and the economic crisis it created for "the proletariat." The complaining tone of his missive reverberates through the decades up to the present day:

> The public conscience is aware that monopolists are gathering up basic commodities, not only at entry points to the city, like Ayahuaico, Puquín, Huancaro, Socorro and Uma Calo of Santa Ana, but also at the Muttuchaca market itself and at the Flea Market of San Francisco where on Saturdays a certain number of women wholesalers dedicate themselves to hoarding whatever goods they can without allowing others to provision themselves in the same quantity or at the same relatively cheap price. These unscrupulous saleswomen,[2] in their desire to exploit, resell the same commodities almost immediately with a mark-up of 100 percent. There is a need for control and police intervention.
>
> We find a plague of wholesalers posted at certain distances from the City, like Poroy, Cachimayo and other intermediary points who, with impunity buy corn, wheat, flour, barley, potatoes, etc., which in turn they sell to the monopolists of this City. This illicit commerce is the reason for the excessive rise in prices of basic commodities. . . . It is worth mentioning certain master bread bakers, like Angelino Carrasco, Manuel Coronado and his brother, who are well aware of who the wholesalers are and where they engage in their illicit commerce. (AHM 1924: Leg. 84)

The Tomato Queens

Are there ways in which retailers or consumers can transform the balance of power between producers and wholesalers, or are they simply caught in between or powerless because of their locus at the end of a commodity chain? I asked this of Lucre, my good friend and a well-respected political leader and vendor. In response, she told me of her battle to break up the monopoly that a few wholesalers had established over the tomato market, cowing *campesino* producers and leading retailers to raise the prices at which they could sell.

Lucre: I've been Secretary of Organization. I've also been Secretary of Defense. After that, I was Secretary of Marketing. . . . I've fought with the big guys, with the big cats. I've fought, cloak and dagger, I've fought with Paulina Velasco, with Lady Dori de Argondoña. I've fought with the tomato ladies, the tomato queens. . . . They treated me as if I were stupid. They treated me like I was swine, but they landed up knowing me for what I was. They didn't grind me down. I have always stood up to them.

Linda: What did you fight over?

Lucre: They were exploiters. In other words, they had a scam going with the peasants from Limatambo and with the vendors in the market. The two of them bought up all the tomatoes that came in by truck. All the tomatoes for two people. And when they had enough, they gave them to all my companions, slowly, they said, and they didn't leave any for the peasants or the market. Only they ate. They sold everything to these two ladies. And only the ladies sold the tomatoes, inside only.

Linda: How were you successful? What did you negotiate?

Lucre: The struggle was over marketing. We formed an alliance with the "engineers" [municipal agents and legal advisors]. And frankly, we convinced the engineers, giving them all the data, of what they [the tomato queens] were doing to us, how they were treating us, was wrong. . . . We did the same with the peasants. I went to Limatambo as the Secretary, as the representative of the retailers. There, we talked with the peasants and the peasants decided to support us. And up until now, they've [the tomato queens] remained crushed.

Linda: And why did the peasants support you instead of them?

Lucre: Because they were being exploited. "Bring us tomatoes," they would command and then they would pay them whatever price they felt like. And they couldn't sell to anyone else but those two ladies. They did it because they gave them money, they gave them all sorts of things. They gave them credit. . . . At times, money commands. So, we spent two years fighting them. We had to be very careful in what we did. There was a Doctor Gloria. That Doctor Gloria betrayed us. But the other doctor [legal advisor] didn't. She still talks to me, the other doctor, she's tricky, but not with me.

Linda: In what way did the peasants support you?

Lucre: When the Limatambo peasants came, we divided all the tomatoes among the vendors. When each truck arrived, I grabbed my companions, and we had to divide up everything. And that's how I did them [the tomato queens] in up until now.

Linda: When was that?

Lucre: Oh, fifteen years, ten years have passed. But I fought to break them up. Now the peasants say, "Thank you.". . . I struggled to break up that mafia. Now, everyone has access to the tomatoes. And the peasants, everyone brings tomatoes too. Those who know me, they say to me, "Mama Lucrecia, how are you? I'm bringing you some peas for your dinner."

Regulations and Transgressions

The vagaries of harvests sometimes create alarming scarcity for urban consumers, but this in turn is exacerbated by the machinations of wholesalers, whom consumers and municipal officials then hold responsible for the "exploitation of the consumer." Over a twenty-five-year period, consumers have made repeated requests and recommendations that the municipality control retail sales of basic commodities. The view that different sectors of Peruvian society hold of state and law enforcement agents and their intervention in marketing is not monolithic. It is very much shaped by macroeconomic and political forces at work at particular moments and by local dynamics of supply and demand that naturally create scarcity or a surfeit of agricultural goods. In the mid-1920s, when Cuzco's first indoor market was established, market women at the retail level did not want municipal agents to be involved in running their markets. Afterwards, these same women experienced abuse at the hands of people who rented the market on a contractual basis from the municipality, overcharging the vendors for space and basic services. When these services failed to materialize, a clamor arose from among retail vendors for the municipality to take over management of the markets.

Consumers also eventually begged for the intervention of the municipality in controlling prices at the retail level to prevent cartels and price gouging. A number of references appeared in the municipal record in October 1924 in which consumers demanded that police be deployed to prevent "monopolists" from blocking the free passage of producers attempting to enter Cuzco with their goods (AHM 1924: Leg. 84). Nevertheless, while consumers want law enforcement to prevent wholesalers from creating false scarcity and operating in a Mafia-like fashion, they are well aware of the temptation for municipal agents to be corrupted by wholesale operations and of their generally ineffective prosecution of the wholesalers' "machine" politics, especially at key entry points from the provinces into the city.

Before the 1969 agrarian reform, consumers also asked that the municipality establish marketing boards to negotiate directly with large estates. The Municipality of Cuzco continues to this day to wrestle with similar complaints from consumers. On September 25, 1950, consumers and producers felt compelled to organize and sent a letter to the mayor of Cuzco, stating that they were planning to establish an open air market where producers and livestock raisers could sell their products directly to Cuzco's consumers, "eliminating intermediaries who always hike up the prices." They also pleaded with the municipality to enforce laws preventing retailers from selling in bulk. This caused a backlash from wholesalers, which the Federation of Workers protested, arguing that there has been "a surge of activity on the part of wholesalers in acquiring food products from the provinces. Despite efforts to combat this system energetically, it has reestablished itself with a vengeance to the point where the public cannot buy directly from producers for the simple reason that these wholesalers and retailers stake out sites at truck stops, like Pampa de Ruinas, Limac Pampa Chico, Limac Pampa Grande, across from the Central Market at the San Pedro train station, and at the Peruvian train station where, when local trains arrive, there is a veritable assault on all the products that come from the provinces, provoking the concentration of these products in the hands of retailers who then take advantage of the situation by exploiting the public consumers in an exaggerated manner" (AHM 1950: Leg. 144).

In addition to the frustration consumers express with how wholesalers control the marketing chain in the Department of Cuzco, they are even more alarmed by wholesalers' ability to bypass retailers altogether when they move huge loads of goods between departments, making a good profit, exacerbating local scarcity, and causing prices to skyrocket. On different occasions, both local and central government officials have reacted to the situation with protectionist measures, prohibiting the "export" of primary goods. The consequence is that basic goods become unavailable to the retail sector in other provinces, leaving the consumer without access to them and creating monetary scarcity. In 1924, the government imposed protectionist measures. Several people wrote the mayor on February 21, telling him, "This prohibition has led to scarcity and a lack of buyers. It has made life very difficult for those in Puno who obtain their grains and other products from Cuzco. . . . The lack of movement of agricultural products to consumer plazas has caused the halt of monetary circulation, producing a terrible economic state for producers and the halt of trade for other products, like cattle, cheese, bacon, and other goods that this city consumes" (AHM 1924: Leg. 84).

And on March 26, 1945, the fruit sellers of Cuzco wrote a letter to the mayor complaining, "We are no longer able to obtain fruit in sufficient quantity because the wholesalers send their fruit directly to Puno and Arequipa, leaving us the worst. And, many wholesalers are doing their business at the doors of the market, creating competition with us" (AHM 1945: Leg. 124).

The Pros and Cons of the "Free" Market

Obvious difficulties face municipal police and marketing inspectors trying to enforce the measures that consumers are demanding. Informal wholesale operations and the dynamic transnational black market successfully elude state control and raise prices for consumers because of the multiple intermediaries needed, yet they also create the smooth flow of products from the thousands of producers whose geographic locations are not easy to reach to the few urban centers of Peru. In a 1993 study, Fernando Romero asked itinerant vendors where their products came from. His data tell us something about the breadth of territory that wholesalers cover. Although most goods came from within the Department of Cuzco, 13 percent came from Bolivia, Brazil, and Chile, and surely the amount is increasing.[3]

The protectionist measures municipal governments take backfire because wholesalers and their black market partners need to keep money and products circulating, a complex function that does not necessarily harmonize with the availability of agricultural products. In addition, wholesalers may benefit enough from scarcity to make windfall profits that put consumers at a terrible disadvantage. Continuous debates take place among policymakers in Peru over the advantages and disadvantages of a "free market" under these conditions. On October 17, 1998, the Lima-based newspaper *La República* (1998:10) reported acts of violence on the part of "black market mafias" who were "mounting a campaign of intimidation against custom officials in Puno to prevent them from seizing merchandise that was illegally entering the country. The intimidation consists of defamation, beatings, and death threats, issued by various persons who use trucks to transport the illegal merchandise."

In addition to this obstacle to enforcement, others become apparent through a close reading of the municipal archives of Cuzco (AHM 1860–69: Leg. 2). Many municipal agents and police, charged with controlling the aggressive activities of "profit-seeking wholesaler harpies," instead collude with them. Instead of putting a stop to these monopolistic practices, they become a part of them. The alarmist tone of the *La República* report ignores just how seductive it is to custom officials, who earn little, to receive a cut in the form of bribes or to become part-time wholesalers themselves, not unlike Mafia operators in the United States have done.

As early as 1858, one man complained that the police were abusing indigenous people by trying to gather up from them the goods they were bringing to the city to sell. He added that "these agents are obviously being paid by wholesalers to do this and have even resorted to seizing their beasts of burden and water, and making them sweep the streets without paying them" (AHM 1860–69: Leg. 2, September 17 and November 12, 1858). Tadeo Salas stressed in 1859 that "the Muncipality should put an end to these kinds of abuses in order to avoid a universal scream of protest," and "the armed forces should be used if necessary" (AHM 1860–69: Leg. 2, June 18, 1858).

Especially since the 1969 agrarian reform, *campesino* producers have become more eager to market their products directly. Government and nongovernmental organization efforts to create producer-run marketing boards have met with mixed success, and *campesinos* are unable to bypass the control of wholesalers if they act as individuals in marketing their goods.

The Cuzco municipality eventually took over the management of the markets, giving up the direct and lucrative rent they received from market landlords, who until then had been responsible for their daily operations. Annual reports show that market rental income was the most important source of revenue for the municipality. The antagonism between retailers and the municipality has grown since then. The municipality must ensure that it continues to receive these important revenues and has the wherewithal to enforce the law, tracking down vendors who have not paid for their licenses and fining those who commit infractions, such as failing to keep their health licenses up to date or forgetting to wear their aprons. In addition, the agents seek to prevent the many itinerant vendors circulating outside the permanent markets from doing their business. Some of them also have licenses, but many of them take their chances, working irregularly or totally informally. I heard many a story of municipal agents who seized vendors' products, sexually harassed them, or physically abused them because of the infractions they had committed.

Liberata Condori, who sells *chicha* (see chapter 7), told me of some of the horrors she and other women experienced with the municipal agents:

Linda: Did you have problems with selling?

Liberata: Yes. We fought . . . they would try to throw me out and I would try to defend myself. There was something with a Señor Benavente.

Teófila [my research assistant]: He was terrible. My mother also clashed with him. [Teófila's mother is unusually mild-mannered.]

Liberata: He was atrocious. The municipal agents would say, "Let's insult them." They would say, "Make what you've given birth to stand up, old ladies."

Linda: How did you defend yourself?

Liberata: "No, 'my father,'" we would protest. But he wouldn't listen. He
would hold us down. Squeeze us. I would just leave my little baby and
flee.
Linda: Didn't he do something to the baby?
Liberata: No, he didn't do anything to the baby.

We can only imagine what it must have been like for Liberata to feel so much
fear and anxiety about her own survival that she would leave her baby and flee
for cover. In chapters 7, 8, and 10 I discuss how ideologies of race, gender relations, and class standing loom large in explaining why such violence accompanies efforts of law enforcement and municipal agents to control informal
marketing. Excerpts from the archival record and these interviews give some
flavor of these ideologies while they clearly reveal the legal transgressions these
women commit.

Permeable Borders

Just as territorial borders are permeable, so are those between formal and informal enterprises. Factories and established businesses, once the most powerful forces in keeping itinerant vendors off the street to prevent them from
competing with them, have turned to a new strategy, often working with these
same vendors. The many men and women selling BVD underwear on the sidewalk, unbeknownst to consumers, are the salespeople for the factories. Some
of them also perform certain production stages such as finishing or processing goods that they sell for factories or private businesses. Certainly, the huge
artisan market in Cuzco functions in this way. And in other parts of Peru, where
more industries exist, there are stories of men and women who receive part
of their factory wages in the form of products. They then sell these products
in the streets or distribute them to others to sell. Salcedo (1993:50–51) recounts
how Juan, the small-scale informal vendor, began to sell clothing for a clothing factory, and I saw many a young man or woman selling exactly the same
kinds of goods on the streets of Cuzco:

Juan began to get to know a worker from the Nova clothing factory.
Carmen Olmos showed him a small briefcase one day filled with underwear.
Now and then, the Nova workers received merchandise as part of their
payment. Juan took a pair of black underwear. The underwear were attached
to each other with a red label on which "Presidente" was written in white
letters. When he got back, Juan showed that first pair of underwear to a
friend in the barracks. Without realizing it, the friend repeated to him the

same phrase Juan had heard when he undertook his first frustrated experience as a vendor of chickens: "How much are they?" And that afternoon, in the División Blindada, he made his first sale.

Carmen Olmos continued to supply him. To the "Presidente" underwear, she added "Coqueta" stockings for women and young ladies, plastic pants for babies, white undershirts, brand BVD, for the men . . . [and] blue and pink panties of various sizes for the ladies.

The same mayor who had thwarted his first vending effort . . . became one of his regular customers.

There is no question that the distinctions between formal and informal businesses, between wholesalers and retailers, and between nations are made murky by the ceaseless flow of people and commodities. Municipal and other law enforcement agents always will be hard-pressed to implement a coherent policy rather than one shot through with contradictions and paradoxes.

Necessary Evils?

According to statistics that Fernando Romero Neyra (1993) has painstakingly gathered from formal interviews with wholesalers and informal retailers (not including the established vendors in Cuzco's permanent indoor markets), approximately 9.5 percent of retailers get their goods directly from producers, 67.1 percent buy from wholesalers, and 6.3 percent get their merchandise from both wholesalers and producers. The rest make their own products or get them from other retailers. In my own interviews with retailers, most of them tried to establish long-term relationships with wholesalers, not least so that they could have access to decent terms of credit. Economic anthropologists (see Plattner 1989) have argued that the ugly picture consumers paint of intermediaries in general as usurers does not consider the risks of the intermediary or the advantages of the terms of trade between producers and wholesalers or between wholesalers and retailers. From the perspective of Dori Argondoña, one of the tomato queens whom Lucre disparaged so vehemently, this was indeed the case. She tells the story of her relationship with *campesino* producers very differently from the way Lucre spoke of it. What she emphasizes is that wholesalers often serve as the catalyst for innovation in the marketplace. They are adept at imagining what the public might want to consume, and they have the resources and authority to persuade producers and retailers to try something new. Dori is proud of the new agricultural products she helped to introduce to the Cuzco markets:

I've worked for thirty-five years in the market. I began working in vegetables, specializing in tomatoes, squash, string beans, all fine vegetables,
peppers, cucumbers, artichokes. I brought all the best from Lima, Arequipa,
Tacna, to supply the Cuzco market, until finally they labelled me the tomato queen because I sold such high-quality goods and earned a pit-
tance. . . . I was the intermediary for the producer . . . for everyone from
Limatambo. To all of them, I gave advances, that is, money, so they could
produce and at the harvest, they turned their goods over to me at market
price. In a word, I collaborated with them more than the bank. . . . This
went very well. We got along perfectly until I retired. . . .

Before, the *campesino* had nothing. He might have land, but he had
nothing else. He didn't have money, he didn't have ideas. I brought seeds.
I washed the seeds, I selected tomato seeds, each squash seed. The agrono-
mists knew that and when the *campesinos* asked for seeds, they told them,
"Go to Señora Dori, she'll give them to you." Because I continued select-
ing seeds even though no one had taught me. It was my own idea. . . .
[Digression about the lack of knowledge among *campesinos* and how they
will not work unless they are forced to.]

Before, Limatambo did not produce squash. In 1961, I brought squash
from Lima, some huge squash. One of my squash fell and split open in the
street. I was carrying a load of them. I saw the seed. And inside the squash,
leaves were already forming. With great affection, I gathered up the whole
mass of seeds, I carried them to my place and put them in my basket. The
one who took the first squash, Infantes Pacheco, an estate owner, at that
time they still hadn't taken away his land, then Angel Nieto, another
Pacheco, Sauceda was his estate. Almost five months later, they brought me
some beautiful squash. From that time on, they began to believe in me.
Señor Angel told me that he would bring me all his squash. "You know how
to sell them."

We distributed seeds to various sites, Qalqa. And not only squash seeds.
Tomato seeds, peppers. I improved all the seeds. I even selected maracuya
seeds from Lima. But that didn't really catch on with the public here. There
were too many little snakes among the maracuya. They're even growing
granadillas now in Limatambo. They have learned to plant *kishkawaranqas,*
a rich fruit . . . garlic, celery. Only two hours away. It's a pretty zone. Everyday the producers bring them. (field notes, 1998)

Stuart Plattner (1989:220) notes that wholesalers take risks in that they
operate with less than full information about goods, the transactions themselves, and the people engaged in the transactions. "The poorer the information, the higher the 'experience' quality of the goods; the higher the transaction costs, the riskier the exchange, and the more valuable an investment in

personalized relationships." By "experience" quality, Plattner means that the quality of the goods is not immediately apparent to the wholesaler and only becomes apparent afterwards as the goods are broken up from bulk and re-sold. Long-term relationships, frequency of transactions, and past experience reduce risk.

Wholesalers can never be entirely sure about the quality of the goods they are receiving, they always have to include the costs of transport and warehous-ing, and they cannot be fully confident that the contracts they established with particular producers will be fulfilled. Few producers want to take on such costs by marketing their own goods, being forced to standardize what they grow, and not having a sure buyer for their harvests. Some retailers would like to eventually be wholesalers, of course.

The Peruvian Tea Party

When Peru's president, Alberto Fujimori, came to office in 1990, one of his first priorities, in addition to putting an end to the civil war and clamping down on the Shining Path guerrilla movement, was to jumpstart the economy. The economy was in shambles.[4] Money was almost worthless because of hyperinflation, leading temporarily to a reinvigorated barter economy. Fujimori heeded the International Monetary Fund and embarked on a now-familiar series of policies: the implementation of neoliberal economic mea-sures, privatization of state-run businesses, and restructuring. He also zeroed in on the need to tax Peruvian businesses. He declared that an 18 percent sales tax should be imposed on all businesses without regard to their scale. A whole-saler whose lorry was filled with potatoes and an itinerant vendor selling her pile of oranges on the sidewalk would be equally taxed, an atrociously regres-sive policy. The result was huge demonstrations throughout the country, un-usual in that they united all the different levels of vendors. Fujimori was forced to back off. He devised a new tax law and established the Superintendencia Nacional de Administración Tributaria (SUNAT), a bureaucratic institution designed to collect taxes and arrest or fine those who evaded them. Many whose jobs in other state-run businesses had ended because of privatization became white-collar tax workers.

The views that Peruvians hold of SUNAT are mixed, and market women share many of these sentiments. The new tax law has a cutoff point, and those below it do not pay taxes. The rest must pay either a "simple" tax (20 soles per month) or a percentage of monthly sales. Most itinerant vendors still do not pay taxes. But established vendors and those who operate at the lower end

Vendors demonstrating against taxes and the SUNAT, 1998.

of wholesaling operations consider the system destructive, unfair, and corrupt. The established retailers feel that their margin of profit is so slight and their earnings so erratic that they should not have to pay taxes. By forcing them to pay taxes, they argue, the government is actually contributing to the stagnation of the economy. Donata, a woman selling bread in the San Pedro market, explained, "SUNAT is everywhere. When we pay taxes, we cannot spend on basic goods. If we cannot spend, then others cannot work. The middle class is disappearing. We are being taxed to death."

The SUNAT resembles the U.S. Internal Revenue Service in that most citizens are terrified of it. Many of the agents moonlight as taxi drivers. In addition, they rove the markets, dressed in plain clothes, trying to ferret out people who have evaded their taxes, who are not properly preparing sales receipts, or who have more than one store or stall. If they have more than one stall or store, they are no longer able to pay the simple tax. They ask vendors about their sales and purchases in an informal manner and then compare their responses with available tax records. People therefore have to watch what they say. Because of the fear among vendors, I am using pseudonyms rather than giving the names of people I interviewed who were willing to talk about the SUNAT.

Elizabeth has a store where she sells eggs in quantity. She pays the "special" tax to SUNAT and is responsible for preparing receipts of her transactions. She commented to me, "The government is excessive. We didn't used to pay taxes. In other countries, they pay taxes and that's fine. But SUNAT abuses us. Sometimes they don't let us work. We pay and on top of that, they fine us because one of the agents has the wrong address or entered a wrong digit. They don't know Cuzco and the streets, they make mistakes, and then we get put out of business." Shortly after, I watched as Elizabeth sold five dozen eggs to a man who was obviously a regular customer. Although money changed hands, Elizabeth did not prepare a receipt. When I asked her about this, she protested that there was no way she could charge him because he was her cousin's husband, and he always bought eggs from her. All over Cuzco businesses have been closed down for different lengths of time depending on the severity of the infraction they have committed, their doors slapped with the now familiar SUNAT signs and big red *X*'s telling the public that the owners failed to pay their taxes.

What is most disturbing about the enforcement of the current tax law is that the targets are small entrepreneurs rather than the large and profitable wholesalers. If small shops do not keep their books properly, they are closed down. Large companies and wholesalers, unlike retailers or smaller-scale intermediaries, have already figured out elaborate strategies to avoid paying higher taxes or keep their multiple warehouses well hidden from the authorities by cooking the books, claiming to sell in smaller quantities than they really do, and then surreptitiously coming down to the railroad tracks to sell more. They have learned how to falsify their receipts systematically. It is easier for tax officials (who are paid very well) to target permanent retailers and semipermanent vendors who do not move from place to place. The very flexibility of operations of most vendors means that they keep changing their inventory, depending on people's tastes and supply and demand. Consequently, it is difficult to figure out exactly who belongs in a particular tax bracket.

The real question on the tip of everyone's tongue is, "Where is the tax money going?" More than one person reiterated Margarita's query, "Why doesn't the government have any money? What does it do with the tax revenues? If it used the revenues, then wouldn't there be work, projects, money? It is because of SUNAT that there is no work."

Some vendors do not see taxes as all bad. They understand the logic of paying taxes as a means of getting returns from the government in the form of improved infrastructure and services. This is certainly the view of one small storekeeper, Luís, who pays "simple" taxes to SUNAT: "It's a way of improving the country." Josefina Solorzano exclaimed when I asked her about taxes, "Taxes? Yes, we pay them, but the state doesn't pay any attention to us. It's the truth. How much we would like the government to permit us to pay a moderate tax. We're in agreement with that. Señora, I've worked for twenty years. If my profits were so great, I'd have my nice house, my trucks. I live in a rented house, in Progreso. It's not as much as the government thinks, our profits. I'm the sole support of my family. If I don't work, how will my children eat? What will they wear? How will I pay the lease of the stall, the SUNAT?"[5]

State Nightmares: Neuralgia

Why does the relationship between tax evasion and the hierarchy of informal intermediaries matter? One of the government's efforts over the last two years has been to formalize the itinerant vendors, enclose them in a building, separate the retailers from the wholesalers, and get the riff-raff off the streets. If government officials had these tax revenues, they claim, they would use them to build a market for informal vendors and regulate the wholesalers. And municipal governments have done exactly this in at least three different places in Peru: Arequipa, Cañete, and Lima itself.[6] Although some vendors have not been pleased with this policy, others have accepted it. In Lima on August 24, 1998, the newspaper *El Comercio* described the resettlement of thousands of vendors who have been a fixture for years along one of the city's main arteries:

> "Some 800 vendors will abandon Avenida Grau."—More good news for Lima. . . . The vendors will move to a commercial center in block six of Jirón Abtao. They have occupied the space for 17 years but decided to formalize their situation after conversations with municipal authorities of Lima. "For many years, we have lived free and we haven't known what it is to pay for licenses, pay taxes, or other concepts. The change will be hard and it will be a challenge to convince the people, but we have decided to do it because we also believe that it will signify an improvement in our lives," said Élmer Ojeda Salas, president of the association of *ambulantes*. The vendors looked at a lot of different places but decided on Abtao because it is close to where they are now and they will be able to maintain their habitual clientele. They have contracted 15 private police and 30 national police will provide security. They will also have free artistic spectacles every month. There are 1,200 stalls of 3 or 4 square meters whose prices vary between 3,600 and 4,800 dollars. They can finance them over a four year period.

In this arrangement the loci of wholesalers and retailers are permanently established, leading to less competition between these two categories and making it easier for consumers. But this has not happened in Cuzco. In 1993, Cuzco's municipality prepared a detailed project report to construct such a market. They designated exactly where the market would be constructed, and its design was finalized and a budget developed. In the proposal to construct "A Chain of Markets for the Supply of the City," the municipality provided a brief history of markets in the Cuzco region, observing that in 1925 Cuzco had a population of 25,000, whereas today "it has converted itself into a neuralgic center of commercial exchange which has concentrated enormous quantities of persons and vehicles, provoking disorder and congestion. The demands of those who use the central market have incited the uncontrolled occupation of the entire surrounding area, where in precarious and unhygienic conditions, basic products are retailed" (Municipalidad del Cuzco 1993:2).[7]

The *ambulante* market would be part of a greater "Chain of Markets." The "Chain of Markets," in turn, would be the antidote to the commercial neuralgia[8] besetting Cuzco. The municipality identified where population growth was occurring in order to site a number of new markets, including a wholesale market, an itinerant vendors' market, and a producers' market. It also planned to expand two existing markets. The project met a sad end when the mayor sold the land to private investors. He was unable to obtain the international financing he sought for the $26-million project, and toward the end of his term he was accused of embezzling funds for all sorts of inappropriate expenditures.[9]

The municipality argues that such a market chain is urgently needed to broaden the availability of agricultural products to consumers, improve the quality of life and income of itinerant vendors, and relieve congestion. Perhaps most important to the municipality, however, moving the vendors out makes sense because "their presence" and "the indiscriminate use of the streets of the center for informal commerce . . . are inconvenient for the conservation of the Historic Center . . . [and] are incompatible with the historical monumentalism which is the city and they ought to be displaced" (Municipalidad del Cuzco 1993:1–2). Although the municipality places great emphasis on the incompatibility of the disordered markets with the attraction and growth of tourism, Cuzco's primary industry, the reality is that the tourist circuit for the most part operates nowhere near the sprawl of the central market, and tourists find the markets fascinating, if dangerous.

From a different vantage point, however, this grand design makes eminent sense. Many of the vendors welcomed it, even though they knew they would be heavily charged for the services they would receive. They would be able to work in greater peace, with more security for themselves and their children, and eventually they might be able to amass a bigger inventory. A producers' market would mollify both consumers and producers. And wholesalers would experience more barriers to competition with retailers and producers. The project now appears to be dead in the water. I do not find it surprising that yet another huge demonstration uniting all the wholesalers and retailers took place on July 24, 1998, protesting the government's tax policies. The chain from wholesaler to retailer changes in form, adds additional links, and creates the possibility of ever more entangled business dealings, but the straw-hatted wholesalers remain the linchpins in the market economy, and the market women who buy from them have become angry at the municipality, which now attempts to throw them off the streets without providing them an alternative.

Notes

1. A major research center of agrarian studies in Cuzco, the Centro de Estudios Regionales Andinos "Bartolomé de Las Casas," regularly publishes a list of the prices of goods that make up a basic bread basket. Retailers and wholesalers alike often turn to this list in setting their own prices and trying to calculate supply and demand forces. But the list is published monthly and ultimately is of little help in trying to assess day-to-day market forces.

2. The person writing this uses the Spanish word *gatera*, which means "saleswoman" but also plays on the word *gata* (cat), implying that the saleswomen are "she-cats."

3. Among itinerant vendors, in addition to the percentage of their goods coming from outside Peru, 35 percent of their merchandise came from Cuzco, with a similar percentage from Arequipa and Puno, 13 percent came from Lima, and 4 percent came from Arequipa. Furthermore, 10.9 percent of their agricultural products came from Anta, 28.6 percent from La Convención, 12.6 percent from Arequipa, and 14.3 percent from Cuzco itself. A high percentage of woolen goods, textiles, and wool came from Lima (64.4 percent) and from San Román, Juliaca (19.2 percent). Only 13.6 percent of the merchandise comes from the same place as the vendor herself. These data are taken from the comprehensive surveys that Fernando Romero Neyra (1993:13) did for the Federación de Trabajadores Ambulantes del Cuzco (FEDETAC).

4. Interestingly, "a shamble" also is a stall used for marketing.

5. In Fernando Romero Neyra's (1993) study of itinerant vendors, he found that in March 1984, 50 percent of them had sales ranging from 1,316 to 5,258 soles. In June 1993, only 13.8 percent had sales in that range. Also in 1993, 50 percent of them had sales less than 526 soles, whereas in 1985 only 4.5 percent of the itinerant vendors had sales less than 526 soles. There has been a clear trend toward lower sale levels, but there is also a reluctance to reveal actual sales because of the possibility of having to pay taxes. Even if these annual sales figures are low, Romero calculates that the total value of annual sales of itinerant vendors in 1985 was around 160,712,856 soles, which in 1993 soles would

be about 17 soles per hour of work. In 1993, the total value of annual sales was 37,256,688 soles, or about 4 soles per hour of work. This sales level would have permitted FEDETAC to generate approximately 3.8 percent of the total as indirect taxes to SUNAT.

6. The Lima newspaper *El Comercio* reported the following on November 16, 1998: "'Itinerant vendors abandon the central streets of Cañete'—More than one thousand informal vendors were relocated to the new 'Model Market,' which was constructed by the Municipality with the support of one sector of the itinerant vendors. The vendors began their relocation at 3 A.M. leaving the principal arteries of the city open to the circulation of pedestrians and vehicles. The 'beauty of this district' and the circulation of pedestrians and vehicles has 'improved.' The new center in Ramos Larrea urbanization was constructed with the support of the municipal district and with quotas that were levied on all of the vendors. After relocating the vendors, about 50 police maintained strict control in the streets to prevent the return of vendors who were not included in the plan given that they had not paid their monthly quotas or their enrollment fees."

7. This report is part of a larger proposal, "Plan de gobierno municipal Qosqo, 1993–1995: Programa de acondicionamiento teritorial desarrollo urbano."

8. "Neuralgia: Sharp, severe paroxysmal pain extending along a nerve or group of nerves" (*American Heritage Dictionary of the English Language,* 1992 ed.).

9. Lima's leftist *La República* newspaper reported on October 17, 1998, "One of the municipal councilors in Cusco, José Béjar Quispe, declared that Salizar [the mayor] had used more than 3 million soles from the municipality for his electoral campaign, invested in public works in different sites and pueblos jóvenes, without considering how much he spent. He also said that most of the money was to be reimbursed after the elections with a loan of 6 million soles, solicited from important commercial businesses in order to construct a model market for *ambulantes.* Having failed to obtain the funds, the Cusco municipality basically finds itself bankrupt, with a debt of more than 3 million soles and not having paid municipal salaries this month. Councilors of the opposition will present a formal denunciation before the National Comptroller so that he is sanctioned for using the municipal apparatus for his own reelection in order to govern for four years more."

6

Sharks: Loan and Credit Arrangements

Street Theater and Martial Order

The first Sunday I was in Cuzco in 1998, I ambled down to the central plaza, thinking I would have coffee before heading to the market. A huge commotion was under way, and the plaza was blocked off. From the balcony of Plus Café, I watched as a martial parade made its way around the plaza, led by an impressive triumvirate: the local commander-in-chief of the army, the mayor, and the archbishop. Behind them, a banner held high announced, "With the force of reason and law, we will defend national unity." Soldiers and police goosestepped in perfect unison, accompanied by cheerful, loud brass bands. Clusters of civil servants, schoolchildren, and officials followed them, all in uniform. (The groups are selected to participate in the parade as an honor when their institution celebrates an anniversary of one sort or another.) *Campesinos,* dressed flamboyantly in their best traditional outfits, brought up the rear; they had been trucked in from different parts of the department, and special preference was given to those who had served in the army. I was told that these parades had been going on for a long time. It made sense. It was a great way to inculcate a sense of collective pride, and I, like so many others, watched the festivities, partly because with the traffic blocked, there were few places I could go until noon. The marchers in their disciplined formations made a fine sight that many a child watching would like to emulate. They created an almost surreal order that seemed to be missing from the daily lives of most Cuzqueños, who normally scurried about, trying to make ends meet and avoid being asphyxiated by exhaust fumes or run over by vehicles while keeping an eye out for gangs of roving thieves, who make their way through the rows and rows of peddlers. It was an interlude of order, albeit a frightening one: These rituals of military populism seemed to be spreading across the country. I had seen an earlier example after only one day in Lima. But Cuzco's manifestation of militarized order was a little different.

The usual vendors, including many young children, were there peddling their wares—gum drops and mints, cotton candy, cookies, sodas, cigarettes, and little cake slices—and the shoeshine boys were pocketing a few more pennies than usual, but what caught my eye was a chaotic circle of people who had gathered in front of the cathedral. I paid my bill at Plus and made a beeline over there. I found myself part of the audience watching "The *Prestamista*" ("The Loan Shark"), performed by a group of street actors whom I would soon come to know quite well. They were defying municipal orders prohibiting them from performing in the central plaza. Eventually, they would no longer be able to evade government regulations: Several months later, their street theater was marginalized, and I could only find them performing in much smaller plazas and in front of high schools, far from Cuzco's center, where the money wasn't as good but the interest in what they were expressing was still high. That day, however, the growing crowd intently watched the performance as the plot unfolded.

A poor *cargador*, a porter, was dressed in rags and *ojotas* (rubber tire sandals). These porters, who haul products in bulk for anyone who needs their services, are a common sight in the markets. This *cargador*'s demeanor was one of constant fear, desperation, and subordination. A friend of the *cargador*, the *prestamista* (money lender), wore boots, a wide-brimmed hat, a long-sleeved shirt, and jodhpurs and carried a whip. A well-dressed *campesino* sported homespun wool pants and vest, poncho, and *chullu*, a colorful knitted cap with ear tassels, topped by a felt hat, and *el nuevo amigo,* "the new friend" in the *cargador*'s neighborhood, played the part of a city slicker, dressed in a white beret, cotton pants, and a T-shirt.

Before the play began, the street actors engaged the audience in a discussion of who deserved the most applause. Intent on creating irony and satire, the actors challenged the audience to agree that the loan shark merited the most applause because he was powerful, whereas the porter was just a worthless *cholo* (half breed).[1] Then they suggested that perhaps *gringos* (foreigners or whites) deserved more applause than the *prestamista*. After this introduction, teasing out both the audience's assumptions and their doubts about their assumptions, the melodrama unfolded.

The *cargador* owes money and knows that the money lender is after him. At his wit's end about how he can pay back even a small part of what he owes, he is ever more desperately trying to figure out what to do when his friend, a powerful-looking, proud, well-dressed *campesino,* comes to visit him. The *cargador* haltingly spills out his problems to him. The situation grows ever bleaker as the *campesino* begins to realize how deeply in debt the *cargador* actually is. He owes the money lender $1,000 and has already mortgaged everything he has. In addition, he weeps as he confides to his *campesino* friend that he has cancer. The *campesino* explodes, urging him to go to the doctor and get treated because cancer kills, and if he dies, his wife and child will be abandoned. This makes the *cargador* even more distressed. The *campesino* tries to reassure the *cargador,* telling him, "For every problem, there has to be a solution. We just have to think of what it is."

Suddenly, someone knocks on the door. The *cargador* panics, knowing it must be the money lender. The *campesino* hides his friend under a woven cloth in the middle of the room and waits. The money lender knocks down the door and barges in shouting, to find only the *campesino.* The *campesino,* who had been wearing his hat proudly over his *chullu,* takes it off in the presence of the money lender and suddenly transforms himself into a quivering mass of jelly. The *campesino* and the money lender talk. The *campesino* explains that the *cholo* has gone on a trip and that his wife and child have gone with him. The money lender asks him how long they will be gone. The *campesino* replies, "Hasta fines" ("until the end"). The money lender thinks he means the end of the month, but when the *campesino* tells him, "No, the end of the year," the money lender leaves in great anger. The *campesino* uncovers his friend, who is very grateful to him. But the wily money lender sneaks back in and discovers the *cargador,* and a huge fight takes place. The money lender threatens to kill the *cargador* but then realizes he will never get his money that way. He threatens to cripple him. Finally he forces the *cargador* to realize that he doesn't owe him $1,000 but rather $2,000 because he had agreed to a 50 percent interest rate and has owed money for two months. At one point, the *campesino* suggests that the *cargador* mortgage his grandfather's house. However, the house already has a mortgage on it, held, of course, by the money lender. The money lender then says that he will agree to give the *cargador* "twenty-four." The *campesino* and *cargador* rejoice, thinking that he means twenty-four months, but he means twenty-four hours. The money lender kicks both the *cargador* and *campesino,* leaving them on the ground.

When he finally leaves, there is another knock at the door. The *cargador,* beside himself, opens the door, shouts at the stranger, and shuts the door in his face. The stranger turns out to be the new neighbor. When he learns what the problem is, he begins calmly to ask the *cargador* and *campesino* questions:

Did the *cargador* and *prestamista* go to a notary public to have the loan arrangement notarized? Were there any witnesses when the arrangement was made? Was there any paper "that talked?" The play ends as the *cargador* and *campesino* realize with relief that maybe the law will help them in extricating themselves from their plight.

The Circulatory System

The audience is deeply involved in this morality play, identifying with the plight of the *cargador*. Despite their own limited resources, when the hat goes around, everyone puts in a coin or two. The lesson "The *Prestamista*" seeks to convey to the audience is not realized in the wide range of informal loan, credit, and saving systems that operate in the markets, where most of the women have little trouble recognizing themselves in the *cargador*. They are subjected to anxiety, threats, and, ultimately, the possibility of having their source of supplies cut off if they cannot pay back their debts.

In this chapter, I take a closer look at the debit and credit arrangements in which retail market women are involved. Chapters 4 and 5 addressed the ways in which wholesalers use credit arrangements to obtain their products, which they then distribute to retailers. The credit arrangements of retail market women include informal, individually arranged loan arrangements, credit they receive from wholesalers, their participation in rotating credit associations, startup capital from nongovernmental organizations (NGOs), and bank loans. The government's policies and the behavior of private enterprises and NGOs affect the flow of capital in the marketplace and the degree of dependence of market women on loans and credit. The use of loans and credit is absolutely necessary to the functioning of the informal markets. In addition to serving as a vital safety net for retail market women at lower levels, it keeps the whole marketing circulatory system operating. Yet the more I learned about how the system worked, the harder it was for me not to wonder whether it would collapse before long. Since my last trip in 1993, the fragility of the system seemed to have increased remarkably. Increasing numbers of vendors seemed to be flooding the markets on a daily basis while the purchasing power of *caseras* (regular clients) was plummeting. It appeared that although debits and credits kept the system going, they also made retailers increasingly vulnerable to heightened anxiety, threats, and economic failure because of their credit unworthiness. Dori Argondoña offered me her description of what was happening, and it concurred with the fears articulated by vendors at all different levels of the system:

There's been a huge glut of people who want to work in the market. Today there are more vendors than buyers. How many *ambulantes* are there?
Before, the market was just this part above. Then Odria built the new
market here. Then, the area surrounding the new market also became a
market, because before it was totally quiet here. At two in the afternoon,
all the vendors went home to take care of their children, their families. Now,
come here at nine, ten at night, the people keep on working. More vendors than buyers. That's because of unemployment. There's no work, no
factories, no business that could attract the number of unemployed people
now. And now there's crime. You have to be a very intelligent mother if you
hope to give your child an education. In those times, there were people who
sent their children to the university and they graduated as doctors, engineers, lawyers, these were people who had been really extremely poor, extremely poor. Now, so many people have gone under or are living on the
edge. This is very bad.

Wholesale Credit

Market women rely on several kinds of credit arrangements to keep their businesses going, some of which are less risky than others. They buy their goods
on credit from wholesalers with arrangements to pay back the wholesalers
within a certain period of time. Almost always a prior social relationship exists between wholesaler and retailer, perhaps one that begins with one woman
recommending her friend to the wholesaler. Eventually, if the market woman
proves herself trustworthy, paying back her advances regularly, then the wholesaler provides goods on credit at a lower price to her or gives her more time
to pay back the wholesaler. The time a market woman has to pay back a wholesaler varies greatly and depends on whether the wholesaler needs capital or
cash, how perishable the product is, whether the product is part of people's
daily bread basket (i.e., an item that regularly sells faster than others), the
quantity that the retailer wants advanced, and the existing relationship between
wholesaler and retailer. A market woman with a small-scale business usually
must pay back the wholesaler in five to eight days. A larger-scale retailer must
pay back what she owes in fifteen days to a month.[2] Whether she pays in credit
or cash and how long she has to repay the wholesaler are critical variables that
affect the slight margin of profit one market woman obtains in comparison
to another. If a market woman purchases her goods *al contado*, paying on the
spot, then she always gets a lower price, but she may not be able to buy in the
same quantity as her companion who is buying on credit.

These differing arrangements are obvious in the explanations that market
women themselves offer and the calculations they make. For example, Victoria

Quispe sells meat, a highly perishable product: "We don't have capital here. The cattle dealer brings it to us, weighs it, maybe four, five, six lambs in the morning, and in the afternoon, we pay him back. We earn about 15 soles ($5.00) per day. You have to get rid of the intestines, the fat, so the meat loses weight when we sell it. We earn about fifty centavos a kilo, but sometimes only twenty." Another butcher of beef, lamb, and pork, Rosa Quispe, explains her system: "I go to particular wholesalers. They travel and bring back the goods. I look at the quality, trying to decide what it's worth. Every time I go to buy, we bargain. It partly depends on supply. Sometimes, I get the meat on credit and I have to pay more. I have eight days to pay them back. If I can't pay them back, they'll never give me meat again. They'll cut me off. The competition is intense. When I sell the meat, if it is someone I know well, then I let them buy the meat *al crédito* with a month to pay me back or sometimes I give them a *llapa*, a little extra. I know they will pay me back when they get their salary at the end of the month. I write down the person's name and the amount I've given them on credit. If they don't pay me back, well then, they'll have to buy from the *ambulantes* outside."[3]

In contrast, Aidé Tito Romero sells homespun wool fiesta clothes as a

Aidé Tito Romero, well-established vendor of fiesta clothing in San Pedro Central Market, 1998.

wholesaler to four retailers, but she also sells to "*ambulantes*," as she calls them: "They (the retailers) pay me in cash if they are *ambulantes*, but if I have long-time clients, I'll wait twenty-four days. I buy everything in cash. I raise the price to the *ambulantes*."

One woman selling potatoes explains her arrangement with wholesalers: "It depends on whether or not they know us. If they trust us and we've worked with them for years, they give us three, four sacks of potatoes. If not, they give us one or two sacks. They bring us different kinds of potatoes—*ch'aska, blanca, chita*, in succession. We have to pay them back within a flexible period. We have to beg if we haven't had sales. We usually have about three or four days to pay them back."

If a retailer fails to pay back her advance from the wholesaler, in addition to not being able to purchase more goods and having her reputation put at risk, she may even suffer physical attacks from wholesalers. "The monkey has to dance for coins," said Eutrofia, explaining succinctly why she avoids advances from wholesalers as much as possible. "One day when I got to the market, I went over to visit the fruit ladies whom I know quite well. When I got to their area, a commotion greeted me and I saw that the fruit ladies were visibly upset. One of them was weeping. She owed a wholesaler 20 soles and the wholesaler had lost her patience, begun beating her, and finally scratched her face in front of everyone. Humiliation takes many forms."

Some market vendors operating on a large scale combine different kinds of credit arrangements, buying directly from producers who may walk through the market and making advance purchases from large factories in Lima or along the coast. They also often accept agricultural produce in lieu of cash from people walking through the market. Only retailers operating at a larger scale tend to keep accounts. Just after Lucho Galdos, who runs a clothing operation in the Tupac Amaru market, explained this system to me, a woman came up with a batch of heavy jackets, and he bought them directly from her. In other cases, very small-scale vendors buy a little from one store, a little from another, and maybe even some goods from another *ambulante*, often purchasing these goods on advance at slightly different prices and payback times.

A number of retailers, in addition to making regular purchases from wholesalers, also buy from producers at weekly markets. The retailers sometimes earn windfall profits when they sell these goods in Cuzco, even accounting for their transportation costs, for two reasons. They have been able to obtain the goods for a great deal less than it would cost them from wholesalers, and they can sell the goods to Cuzco consumers, who purchase them for far more than buyers at the weekly markets.

Loan Sharks

Having wholesalers advance goods to retailers is not an unusual business practice around the world. However, this is only one way in which market women
run the risk of becoming indebted. What often happens is that market vendors cannot repay what they owe to wholesalers in the time they have agreed
on, or they face unexpected expenses. They then turn to a second form of brutal
indebtedness, dramatized in "The *Prestamista*."

At the end of a long day, coming back from Avenida Ejército, I was walking along the stalls outside the San Pedro market when I heard raised voices.
A *prestamista,* a young mestiza woman in tight-fitting pants, a polyester
sweater, neatly curled short hair, makeup, and leather shoes, was trying to get
her money back from a woman selling tomatoes. The *prestamista* began calmly,
reminding the tomato lady, "You have owed me money for three years." The
tomato lady looked down and mumbled that she simply didn't have the money.
The *prestamista* got angrier and angrier, and before long she was shouting,
"Slut. Your children were obviously never breast-fed, what a liar you are." She
could put fear into anyone who heard her expounding in such a fashion, and
because she was shouting at the top of her lungs, she terrified the tomato lady.
She also succeeded in demeaning her. By suggesting that the tomato lady was
a slut and that her children had never been breast-fed, she used powerful
gendered ideologies that contrasted wasteful antisocial expenditure (being a
slut) with responsible productivity (nurturing children and making them grow
or, even more concretely, making enough money to pay back her debts).

All of the *prestamistas* in the Cuzco market system are young women. They
dress like the young mestiza just described, and it is easy to spot them as they
make their rounds. They make loans at 20 percent interest to multiple clients.
The *prestamistas* stake out certain sectors of market vendors, lending them
funds in the morning and collecting them in the afternoon with interest. They
turn over large amounts of money and seem to do quite well for themselves.
They tend to lend in small amounts, around 100 soles at a time ($33 in 1998).
The person has a month in which to repay the loan and usually makes a daily
payment of 4 soles so that at the end of the month, the interest reaches 20 soles,
or 20 percent. I had a number of questions once I realized how fundamental
this system was to the market: Why are they all women? How do they enforce
their credit arrangements? From where do they get their capital?

It may be that they are all women because most of the vendors are also
women. In Peru, as in many other parts of the world, women tend to keep
track of household accounts, so they may have a predisposition to go into this

Cheese vendor and a loan shark counting her money outside San Pedro market, 1998.

business. However, other factors that are less obvious account for the fact that they are all women. Many of the *prestamistas* are part of an elaborate transnational cash flow. The interest rate for loans at Peruvian banks is high, but the barriers to qualifying for a loan in the first place usually are insurmountable for market women. They simply do not have the collateral, credit rating, or basic documents they need to obtain a loan from the bank. Julia Chacón, who sells potatoes and broad beans, explained it this way: "A good government would give us loans at a low interest rate so we could work a little more. They ask for all kinds of documentation for a loan. Without capital we can't work. The *prestamistas* are making loans, one says at 10 percent, the other at 20. They have to be paid a little of the interest every day. We earn enough to cover the interest. With such high unemployment, everyone's becoming a *comerciante*, everyone with incentive has become a *comerciante*, because there's no other way to make a living."

The market vendors feel they may be better off establishing informal loan arrangements instead of formal ones with a bank because if they default, they may have greater leeway in appeasing the *prestamista* than they would in appeasing the bank. This is ironic because the very informality of these arrangements constitutes a two-edged sword. Neither *prestamista* nor vendor can turn to legal means to defend their rights.

The proliferation of money lenders who seem to have a substantial amount of money to lend is partly explained by a growing transnational practice that encourages cooperation between formal and informal economies. In Bolivia, powerful merchants and drug lords obtain 5 percent loans easily from the Banco de Sol, a government-subsidized bank, somewhat similar to the former Agrarian Bank that used to exist in Peru. The men at the top of the loan system then distribute the loans to lower-level *prestamistas* (almost all of whom are women) at a higher interest rate, who in turn distribute their funds as loans to the vendors at 20 percent. This is one of the principal ways in which the *prestamistas* obtain sufficient capital to grease the entire system. It is also a very convenient arrangement that allows drug money to be laundered. Many of the *prestamistas* are involved as couriers and drug launderers at the lowest level of the system. Thus, just as women constitute the majority of informal vendors because men fill the ranks of the formal labor sector, they also proliferate as loan sharks because men occupy the more powerful and lucrative positions in the lending structure.

The loan rates cited by women who were able to borrow from banks ranged from 3 to 10 percent, compared with 10 to 20 percent from *prestamistas,* but most market women cannot qualify. Baudelia Cataldo, secretary of defense, describes the existing *prestamista* system as horrible but necessary, given the lack of alternatives available to her companions:

> Usurers? There are hundreds throughout the market. The 20 percent interest rate is an exploitation. People take out these loans out of necessity. First the rate was 10 percent but in the past four or five months, it has risen to 20 percent. But it is not a great arrangement. A Market Bank would be best. But what can we do if some of the women fail on their loans? What can we do so that they pay back? And with the crisis, it's worse. We need to encourage the *compañeras* to be more responsible. I can attest to the problem. An organization called SODECO [Social Development Consultants], a credit organization, came to us in the market. And they made loans to many *compañeras.* Many of us met our terms, but others did not. We formed a group of four, but three failed. I was the only one in the group to pay back. They are my *compañeras* but I can't lie. The usurers make problems. The law states that there is no prison for *prestamistas.* They become extremely harsh, demanding, demanding, until the person is exhausted. When the usurer sees that they can't pay back, then they won't lend again.

I myself was asked on more than one occasion to serve as a money lender. My friend Mari, who sold clothes, and my research assistant, whose mother sold fruit, both asked me for loans in the amount of $50. I felt vulnerable, wondering about the impact such a loan would have on our relationship if either of them defaulted. In the end, I was naive (or wise) enough not to ask for interest in either case, but with my research assistant, I told her that if she did not pay me back, it would come out of the money I was paying her to work with me. I felt awful, as if this economic transaction was violating our friendship and, in the case of Teófila, our professional relationship as well. I was incredibly relieved when Mari and Teófila both paid me back, a little later than they had said they would. The experience made me realize what a violent and nasty atmosphere this system of indebtedness has created in the markets because there are many cases, as Baudelia points out, in which the women default.

Eva Carhuarupay confirmed the problem. She uses loans and, in fact, could not survive without them. But her credit rating is declining rapidly. She says she often is unable to pay back the loans. The *prestamistas* then threaten to take away her goods. In that case, she has to borrow more from someone else. Once she has this kind of problem, she usually cannot get loans from the same people again, even if she pays them back eventually.

State Subsidies and Nongovernmental Support

Both the advances of wholesalers and the loans of *prestamistas* that retailers receive generally are relationships between two individuals, although the *prestamistas* and the wholesalers talk among themselves. This is why some retailers are blackballed and their businesses fail. However, another loan agency has come on the scene that operates in a different fashion. These are the NGOs, such as SODECO, the Swedish NGO mentioned earlier. Although there are fewer of them in Cuzco's marketplaces than in the countryside, they are beginning to make an impact on the market vendors. As Baudelia told me, the vendors would love to see a market bank develop that offers loans at low interest rates, and they don't much care whether it is a state or an NGO that establishes and runs it. Although these arrangements may work well for the vendors, as several women pointed out to me, the NGOs can make a good profit by organizing groups of debtors and asking for more interest than they would receive if they were simply working with individuals. Of course, their risk is higher as well.

Government agencies linked to Vaso de Leche ("A Glass of Milk"), a mother's group that Fujimori assiduously cultivated in the countryside, have also influenced the way the market's circulatory system works. Vaso de Leche provides women in Clubes de Madres (Mothers' Clubs) with basic food products and milk; Programa Nacional de Apoyo Alimentario (PRONAA), or the National Program of Nutritional Support, provides breakfasts to children. Because of the scale at which they operate, they are able to buy goods such as beans, corn, wheat, and barley directly from peasants, offering them far higher prices than most vendors can afford to pay. As Nanci Salazar complained, "In the last two months, PRONAA has been buying up beans at 2,500 soles from the *campesinos.* We can't possibly match that price. The *campesinos* sell everything to them. We can't buy at that price. We would like to file a complaint, but it is the government. They should not do this. Before it was 15 soles for twenty-five pounds of corn; now it is 18 to 20. We simply cannot do that and now the public doesn't believe that we can't match it. PRONAA gathers the products and distributes them to the *campesinos.* I think that what the government is doing is bad. Broad beans too. Before broad beans were 1 or 1.20. Now they are 1.50. They've risen so much. It's because that's the price at which PRONAA is buying."

Another well-off vendor, Julia Chacón, explained her view of government intervention of this nature in the market: "The present government is killing us with hunger. I am not in agreement with this government, with all the abuses it is committing against us, the middle class. We have never never received any support from this government. Sure, the *pueblos jovenes* [squatter settlements] and the *campesinos* [peasants] are getting help with their Vaso de Leche and even loans but we, the middle class, we have never gotten any help. Every government that enters office forgets about the middle class."

These remarks highlight the complex way in which intermediaries are part of a chain of exchange and how the government and NGOs influence the links. Because of the partial monopoly that the government has exerted over the dried goods and milk market (partly in the interest of amassing populist support from the *campesinos*), *campesinos* are no longer willing to sell to other wholesalers and retailers. Consequently, government intervention has created an engineered scarcity of these products that the public finds hard to believe. The government criticizes intermediaries who hike up the price of goods, but they themselves are hiking up the price of goods, not at the end of the chain but at the very beginning of it. This engineering has exacerbated the clash between the interests of *campesino* producers and the urban poor on one hand and of vendors (many of whom are also lower-class) and middle-class consumers on the other.

Oddly enough, organizations such as the Catholic Agency for Overseas Aid and Development (CARITAS) also enter the picture. I was having a conversation with a group of women in Avenida Ejército about their loan arrangements. They buy dried beans and potatoes from other wholesalers in fairly large quantities as well as from producers. They have established a relationship with other merchants from Puerto Maldonado who come to Cuzco to buy their goods and then sell them to the miners there. Suddenly, all of them began chiming in when one of the women started to talk about one of Peru's largest and most important factories, Gamarra. As they explained, "There's a huge factory called Gamarra Nacional. They make all kinds of clothes. But the government is bringing in used clothes from the United States. The clothes, we call them 'Americana,' are distributed throughout Peru and at very low prices, much lower than the prices of Gamarra. A pair of pants from Gamarra costs 30 soles, one from Americana, 8 soles. So there's no longer any demand. And a huge number of people work in Gamarra in various factories. Now they are firing all the workers and there will be more unemployment, more competition. Why is the government letting this happen? What about custom duties? These used clothes arrive as charitable contributions [from CARITAS]. The government shouldn't be doing this kind of thing. What will those people in Lima do when the needs become even more dire? All of this the government is doing. It should say no to these kinds of things. Why should those people be fired?" This is a case of globalization and of national government policy. The sharp increase in wealth in the United States in the 1990s led to a surplus of used clothing being exported around the world. In turn, this generated increased unpredictable competition for Peru's national textile industry. At the same time, the Fujimori government, so intent on free market policies, deliberately intervened in the market by permitting it to be flooded with charitable donations (no custom duties or tariffs) in the form of used clothing, helping to drive out its own clothing industry.

Playing the Lottery and Banking on Trust

In addition to getting advances for their goods and taking out loans, many market women participate in what they call *jugando pandero* (playing the lottery). This is a risky game, offset only by the strength of the social bonds between the players. At its worst, it functions as a pyramid scheme; at its best, it works as a rotating credit association, a common voluntary association found the world over. The number of people who participate varies, and usually they know each other. Sometimes, however, acquaintances who aren't so well known to each other are involved in order to get a sufficient number of participants. Anywhere from six to ten women agree to play. One woman is designated by the rest to collect a certain amount of money a day from the other women. Each of the women picks a number. The pot grows until it reaches an agreed-upon amount. Each time it reaches that amount, it is distributed to the women in the order of their number. In a few cases, women play *pandero* with goods such as oil and sugar rather than with money. "It's just a little bit of help," explained Nanci Salazar, but Flora Pompiya, a black marketeer, refuses to play *pandero*. "It's too much responsibility. It scares me."

Julia Chacón told me she had just started playing *pandero* with other potato vendors by the railroad tracks. "We realized we had no capital. We got together with a friend and we organized ten people, our work companions. Each day we put in 10 soles, 60 soles a week for each of us, 600 soles [$200 in 1998] in all. And we're about to finish the first game. It's really helped us. We've been able to pay our bills. We play because the state doesn't help us at all."

The butcher Victoria Quispe never takes out loans because she would be too worried about paying them back. But she does play *pandero*. "Whatever I lack in the house, rice or sugar, I buy. Or if I don't have any money, I can use it. If things rise in price, then I can use it to buy things."

The women I spoke with felt the game had at least four advantages. It constituted an informal savings account, they did not have to go to the trouble of setting it up at a bank, it was a way of achieving forced savings that their husbands could not easily get their hands on, and it was easier to save just a little each day. The risks are great, however. Women who can't contribute to the pot have to retire from the game, and I heard of cases in which the woman gathering the money fled with the daily pot, or women who had received their share vanished from sight.

Is this great circulatory system a house of cards waiting to collapse? It is hard to say. The system keeps people alive from day to day, allowing them to feed their children. Both *pandero* and the purchase of goods *al crédito* create fragile social camaraderie in the form of an economic safety net. When that net ruptures, though, given that only 20 percent of Peru's population is actually earning a living wage, I wonder what the vendors will do. And will the Peruvian government begin to reflect on the wisdom of its purist neoliberal economic measures and populist politics?

Notes

1. The concept of *cholo* is complex. As I discuss in more detail in chapters 7 and 8, some Peruvians, usually those who do not consider themselves indigenous, use the word *cholo* in a derogatory fashion for boys and men in Andean society who look indigenous, but they draw a contrast between the hard-working agriculturalists (*campesinos*) who stay in the countryside and the emasculated *cholos* who, in their racial ideology, are subordinate, lazy, often drunk, and uneducated. *Chola*, the feminine counterpart, is more closely correlated by these same people with a particular social category because of their deliberate choice of dress, their occupation, and the ties that form among them. They may be labeled as *chola* or *cholita*, but the term may be used

either positively as a diminutive or negatively. Furthermore, within a national setting, the image of the *chola* increasingly has served as a medium for creating a sense of folkloric national identity. See Marisol de la Cadena's (2000) and Robert Albro's (1997) work on images of *cholas* in Bolivia. In part, these are sliding labels that differ according to the locus of the person in question and the interaction and perceptions of the people involved.

2. For people involved in the market system, whether they are *campesinos*, retailers, or wholesalers, the "week" consists of eight days; two weeks consists of fifteen days. This may be because Sunday is only occasionally a work day for vendors, who go to regional fairs, and rather than cut back the time for vendors to pay back what they've received on credit, it is extended to Monday.

3. Implicit in her reference to a vendor being forced to buy from an *ambulante* is the awareness among all vendors that *ambulantes* usually sell the worst-quality produce in the smallest amounts.

7

Talking Brew, Butchering Patience: Conversations in the Marketplace

Race rears its head most obviously where Peru's weak economy meets its age-old biases, and blame is misplaced, as it has been for many centuries, on Indians and Peruvians who do not easily fit into a single racial category. In their more tepid but no less corrosive form, racial and gender ideologies underpin everyday conflicts that occur in the simple encounters of buying and selling in the marketplace. Language practices and market women's exchange relations with a whole range of people from the city and countryside who are partially distinguished from one another by class, gender, and ethnicity create vectors along which cultural knowledge travels. The daily economic transactions and language exchanges of the urban marketplace constitute one site where ideas about nationalism and feelings of what exactly it means to be Peruvian are debated, evaluated, and contested. In the marketplace, where they spend most of their day together, market women, with a subdued but dramatic flair, sometimes question or ridicule efforts of others to freeze racial categories or use them pejoratively. This chapter examines what we can learn about the racial and gender ideologies at work through the kinds of conversations that accompany purchases, sales, and trading in the marketplace.

How street vendors sell is as important as what they sell. In the countryside, the exchange of products takes place in a notably different manner than in the cities. In many highland villages, the principal markets take place during fiestas and are carefully scheduled in accordance with agricultural and ritual calendars. On those occasions, scarce yet highly valued goods limited to distinct ecological zones are exchanged. Often, rather than monetary transactions, true barter or trade predominates.[1] For example, purveyors of ceramics from

Puno often travel great distances to small villages to obtain maize, freeze-dried potatoes, salt, medicinal herbs, or wool for their pots. Villagers select particular pots they desire and fill them with the product the ceramic vendor wants. Most importantly, these exchanges entail almost no conversation and may even take place silently. Regional open air markets also differ from the urban marketplace. Although these intercommunity events may involve vendors and clients who know each other, many of them may be strangers, and they may find the space of the periodic marketplace alien and a little frightening.

Brooke Larson and Rosario León (1995:247) have been studying the behavior and organization of these markets in Bolivia, and they describe them well: "The cultural logic of the marketplace is also encoded in the staging and choreography of trading interactions over the course of a day. Peasant women of surrounding highland communities dominate the interior space of the marketplace. . . . Most intercommunity exchanges are conducted by peasant women, who spend long days waiting, watching, conversing, and quietly haggling over the balance and importance of the interchange. . . . To the outsider's eye, their market etiquette is extremely subtle, almost invisible." Interestingly, Larson and León (1995:247) also have observed differences in the behavior of men and women vendors, differences that are also evident in the urban markets of Cuzco: "Aymara- and Quechua-speaking women conduct their negotiations primarily in Quechua through patterned exchanges of whispers, silences, and gestures meant to coax, pressure, or appease their trading partners. The itinerant male peddlers stand in vivid contrast to the market women. Greatly outnumbered by the market women selling all manner of foodcrops and products, the men are purveyors of luxury, manufactured goods who stand 'offstage'—at the margins of the feria's interior 'feminine space' of quiet, intense negotiation over the staples of life. The most conspicuous male trader is the *ranquero,* the dazzling ambulatory peddlar who shouts out the exotic wares he has to offer."

In contrast to the subdued ambience of rural marketplaces, the urban marketplace is characterized by camaraderie hedged by controlled competition, displays of humor, sexual innuendo, and the learned skill, as one vendor put it, of how "to tease out" customers "with jokes, with love." Nanci Salazar elaborated,

> I'm very endearing. The majority of my clients, we want a person who attends to us this way, happily saying "look at this little kilo. I cooked it myself last night." But when a client asks another vendor and the vendor answers abruptly, "1.20," then the client comes back to me and asks for a little extra and I give it to them. The extra makes it 2 soles when I weigh it but I sell it to her for 1.90. It's a question of the public, how we wait on the public. At

times, there are clients you have to wait on who have sour faces and make you bitter. But you have to ignore them. Perhaps they have problems at home or even here. Everything is in a gaze. Let's say I'm selling well. My companions look at me with a sour face. These kinds of things always occur. They become jealous or if many clients are loyal to me and only buy from me, they start gossiping. Despite everything that happens, you just keep on selling and the clients keep coming back to you. I'm very endearing and my clients say, "Flajita [skinny one, intended as an endearing diminutive], you must take care of yourself."

In documenting language exchanges in the markets, I gained a sense of some of the skills market women deploy in structuring their own sense of identity. Much of the time the language exchanges of the market are pro forma and lighthearted. Many market women pride themselves on their ability to wield language skillfully. Market vendors who are first-generation migrants to the city and whose Quechua is still fresh in their minds love to engage in word play. In the countryside, in a manner similar to playing the dozens among African Americans, word play among the Quechua shines in riddles, courtship songs, and insults and often involves not a one-on-one repartee but rather the entire community as active audience, occasionally participating with their own ingenious puns and double entendres. These skills are easily transferred to the marketplace and become ever richer as bilingual participants incorporate plays on Quechua and Spanish meanings.[2] Their repartee often is also trenchantly grounded in sexual allusions and sometimes remarkably revealing of market women's views of sexuality and male and female comportment. In addition, their rich bantering sometimes hides suffering. As is true for many human beings, humor is a bittersweet salve for the injuries that some of these women have endured.

The women who sell bread or meat, in particular, pride themselves on their humor. Although it is hardly deliberate, they are the ones who most often find themselves enmeshed in angry verbal conflicts with their clients, a subject to which I return later in this chapter. It is worth noting here that exchanges, ranging from those that are wholly innocuous to ones that are brittle, may map onto occupational differentiation and stratification in the market itself. Normative and uneventful conversations between buyer and seller generally focus on the quality and usefulness of the products; the conversations have a particular structure consisting of an opening, a short negotiation, an agreement on price, a payment, and a farewell. The uneventfulness of the conversation depends on an apparent mutual trust between buyer and seller, an agreement on the price, and an expectation on the part of both client and vendor that if the transaction is going smoothly, the vendor will be "endearing" ("cariñosa," as Nanci Salazar put it) and give the buyer a "little extra."[3]

In these exchanges, context is critical to understanding why a conversation rolls along smoothly or why it escalates into name-calling and ethnic slurs. As more and more linguistic anthropologists have discerned, context is complex, broad, and culture-specific. Bruce Mannheim has worked for many years with Quechua oral narratives. He and Krista van Vleet (1998:326) have laid out the problems involved when these narratives are transcribed and then are viewed simply as "neatly bounded" prose. Transcriptions without context fail to take account of how language exchanges are shaped by an understanding by participants of the roles they are expected to play and the history of the roles they and perhaps others have played, by references to other narratives occurring simultaneously, and by a specific linguistic mechanism in Quechua that distinguishes between direct quotation and hearsay.[4]

The language exchanges of vendors and their clients may also be contextualized by omissions, that is, incidents that occurred in the past that were unpleasant or conflict-ridden and that both client and vendor recall but that remain as unspoken memory. This kind of context is hardly verifiable unless the anthropologist has acquired contextual knowledge through other modes of field research. Context also includes the relationships between the participants; references to people, places, and other vendors who represent competition; and possible acknowledgement of past deeds of reciprocity in the form of *compadrazgo,* or fiesta sponsorship. Context may include important information on market conditions. Finally, context is embedded in appropriate interactional etiquette: how rapidly the bargaining takes place, whether the client admires the quality of the produce or instead ignores or criticizes its condition as a reflection of who the vendor is, and whether the client signals that she will return again after this purchase as a loyal customer; or, in another instance, that she is seriously shopping around and not just wasting the vendor's time or that she is a one-time, ignorant buyer whom the vendor can charge as high a price as possible. Likewise, context may signal whether the vendor is willing to provide that "little extra." Many vendors ultimately lose their patience when clients do not treat them with *decencia,* decency. As we have noted in past chapters, this concept refers to a notion of behaving in a civilized manner and has often been used judgmentally against vendors. It is important to understand that vendors themselves expect to be treated with respect, as would any person when interacting with or addressing others in a social context. This is especially the case given that vendors know that they provide needed and valuable economic goods and services.

Ceramic vendor arguing with a client in Polvos Azules market, 1991.

Markets are not ideal places to use a tape recorder. I therefore directly wrote down the exchanges in Quechua and Spanish, with one of my two research assistants by my side to correct my notations and refresh my memory. In a later trip, I did use my tape recorder, and I was surprised to find that many of the women responded to my interest in their use of language by hamming it up a bit with the tape recorder, as would a deejay, or formally reflecting on what they wanted to say, as if they were presenting a speech to a general assembly of their union. The latter was more common in the formal interviews I did. Some of the pieces I taped obviously reveal their funning with a ready audience: me and their companions. However, many other nonrecorded conversations that I witnessed or participated in bore a close resemblance to those that I recorded. Both Teófila and Edgar, another research assistant with whom I worked, were children of market women, fluent in Quechua and Spanish, and familiar with the creative metaphors and their meanings that both market women and their clients deployed in their exchanges.

Race, Labels, and Language

Language exchanges in the markets take account of immediate and distant context. They also involve assumptions that the parties engaged in conversations are making, subconsciously and consciously, about race. Weismantel and Eisenman (1998:137) note, "People live in communities, and depend upon them for their survival. To recognize that the marks of a collective social life carried on for many generations are sometimes visible in the bodies even of the newly born, is only to acknowledge the fact that we enter the world neither alone nor without history, but already placed in a world not of our making."

Market women themselves may choose to contribute actively to the images others have of them, making larger than life some aspect of their identities through both language and dramatic flair. Thus, the dynamic perception of ethnic status and the use of labels emerge out of daily interactions, such as conversations, and a self-conscious construction of identity in which labels attached to people may undergo redefinition and resituation. At the same time, theatricality and the ability to assert individual agency to project a particular public image are constrained by the historical legacy of attempts by different sectors of Peruvian society, including government officials, to rigidify and idealize these labels to create static categories, using ideas about race, which also contribute to the structuring of daily interactions and ethnic identity. Ethnohistorian Thomas Abercrombie (1991:97–98) refers to the paradox apparent when anthropologists use these categories. Their use "accedes to the colonial situation itself, which continues to posit itself in the form of a relationship between two opposed cultural poles, 'Indian' and 'European.'. . . But to suggest the existence of *a* rural/indigenous culture in the Andes . . . is usually to fall victim to 'non-Indians'" essentializing stereotype of 'the Indian.'. . . We must avoid, too, essentializing *a* Hispanic urban culture. . . . In the Andes, an 'urban,' 'Hispanic' or 'European' culture exists, like an 'Indian' one only when we are studying stereotypes. I do not therefore dismiss such stereotypes as 'mere' images, since, as they are produced in, and produce, systems of inequality, they are often invested with terrible power."

Many venues exist in Peruvian society for relationships between people of differing ethnic backgrounds to unfold, sometimes smoothly and sometimes contentiously. One reason why these interactions in the marketplace captured my interest was that they expressed far more vividly and explicitly the kinds of underlying ideas Peruvians hold about race, gender, and class that create institutional discrimination in the national legal, political, and educational systems. My efforts through formal interviews to obtain a better sense of how market women and their clients perceived their respective ethnic, class, and sexual identities had not been entirely successful, although they were revealing. It was only when I decided to spend a good part of my time informally chatting with market women and wandering about the market that I learned about some of the more subtle dynamics of interethnic relationships. The formal interview responses I had gathered began to make more sense juxtaposed with the informal conversations between market women and their clients because the former were an important indicator of how market women *believed* ideal social interactions should occur, whereas the latter reflected the tensions of actual behavioral interactions, often characterized by assessments of personal character on the basis of stereotypical images of race.

Talking Brew

The close relationship between how language is used in market exchanges and racial and gender ideologies became apparent to me when I stopped by Liberata's stall for a glass of *chicha*. *Chicha* operations, where corn beer is served and tongues are loosened, turn out to be a good starting point from which to enter into the tangled world and history of racial relations in Peruvian society. Whether they are as informal as the one I describe here or as formal as Eulalia's, a well-established and famous Cuzco *chicha* tavern, I found them to be the site of significant codes of communication, a locus where sentiments that often remain unvoiced about racial discrimination in Peru are both expressed and contested.

Liberata Condori is sixty-five years old. Stray wisps of graying hair fall over her face. She has few teeth left. Despite her age and the hard knocks she has suffered, as I was soon to discover, she bustles energetically, guffaws, and generally serves as a magnet to which many passersby are attracted. Liberata sits on a small stool inside the San Pedro Market in front of the permanent stalls. To her side is a wide, white enamel bowl of chopped lima beans, carrots, and potatoes that she salts liberally and a bucket of water in which she keeps her large jam jar *chicha* glasses. In front of her are two huge plastic containers of *chicha* (maize beer), one of which has been mixed with strawberries and is called *frutillada*. One thing that has always struck me about the market is the clash of scales: huge containers of *chicha* and tiny bags of spices side by side. Liberata wears a long, blue apron that occasionally serves as a drying cloth. A number of little wooden stools surround her. One person after another, many of whom seem to have known her for a long time, come and buy their thirty centavos of *chicha* or fifty centavos of *frutillada*. Many of them also work in the market. Liberata offers them a stool, and they sit and stay a while. They greet each other quietly. Initially, little conversation transpires among them, but eventually the exchanges become quite raucous, especially because of my presence. They admire my blue eyes and jokingly suggest that I should distribute money to the vendors or that I should bring one of the vendors to the

United States, hidden in my suitcase. The conversation alternates between Spanish and Quechua and sometimes is a mix of both. One client demands "Dos chicharrones." *Chicharron* literally refers to fried pork, a dish served on festive occasions, but in this instance it is a play on words, combining the Spanish *chicha* (maize beer) with *ron* (rum). The client wants good, strong *chicha,* and he explains further to me, "Chicharrón líquido" (liquid fried pork). We all laugh.

The conversation moves from liquid fried pork to genuine fried pork and whether it is worthwhile for the vendors to prepare roasted guinea pig, roasted pork, or fried pork to sell for the upcoming fiesta days, especially Todos Santos (All Saints' Day), which is two weeks away. Liberata and two of her clients try to calculate whether it is going to fall on a Sunday; if so, they all agree it is not a good idea to invest in cooking pork or guinea pig because Cuzqueños leave the city on Sundays to go to regional fairs or the cemeteries in the countryside or outskirts of the city, and they won't be able to make enough sales. The Catholic All Saints' Day coincides with the Day of the Dead, a Quechua ritual in which people "feed" those close to them who have died over the past three years, piling their tombstones high with special bread dolls, potatoes, coca, *chicha,* and alcohol, all the while consuming the same food and imbibing liberally. They believe that only if the dead are fed excessively will they return the favor in the form of soil fertility or good sales. Liberata comments, "Boy, pork is really expensive these days." One of her customers agrees, specifying how much it costs and adding, "It's going to be even worse this year because none of us have any money."

Liberata continues to serve more customers. Soon, there are no stools left. I exclaim, "So many people come to you!" Teófila responds, "It's because of the sun. And look, most of her customers are women from the market." One of the customers says, "No, it's not the sun. In Cuzco we all drink our *chicha.* All of us." I note, "But you all seem to be coming to Liberata's stall." The customer again disagrees, "No. Only sometimes. There are so many *chicha* places [*chicherías*]. For example, just a little further down, there's another. Everywhere there are *chicha* bars." "But look at all the people here," I persist. She concludes, "That's because the *chicha* here is more natural. Yes, it's softer."

This congenial ambience is suddenly disrupted by the arrival of a new customer. She is dressed well, in short skirt, silk blouse, and stockings. She wears makeup and carries a leather purse, almost challenging the pickpockets to make her a target. She approaches Liberata in a completely different way than her other customers. Without greeting her, she abruptly and nervously demands, "One *frutillada,*" adding in a lower voice, "I haven't had any in twenty years."

After trying it, she immediately comments, "It's not very good, not very sweet." This is definitely not a *casera* (a loyal customer). She is from Tacna. A heated discussion ensues among the gathered group about whether it is better to live in Tacna or Cuzco. One customer comments, "In Tacna people like us are on the margins. We are not considered part of society." The stranger does not deny this, but she remarks, "Many people from Puno are in Tacna because many of the goods that make their way to Puno and Cuzco come from Tacna" (Tacna borders Chile). It dawns on me slowly that she's probably a black marketer.

Just when things seem to be settling back into the daily routine of information sharing and sociability, yet another customer arrives, a man. He too wants his glass of *chicha*, but as Liberata begins to prepare it for him, he exclaims, "You've got to clean that glass, it's filthy. Please wash it." Everyone protests, "The glass is not for drinking but only for pouring." Some of the very first customers to arrive are still sitting. Many of them have had more than one glass, and Liberata gives all her *caseras una llapa* (a little extra).[5] She has already given me and Teófila two glasses of *frutillada*. Liberata serves the new customer, ignoring his criticisms, and he drinks up. Soon after, Liberata's food and her *chicha* are all gone. It is close to the end of a successful day for her.

Liberata Condori and a market woman client, 1998.

Chicha ladies (*chicheras*), with their formal or informal *chicha* bars, provide invaluable services. They offer a respite to weary travelers from the country-side, who are able to feel a little more at ease in a strange place, let down their guard, and drink their *chicha*, quietly sitting and maybe exchanging a sentence or two. *Chicha* businesses are the equivalent of local taverns and cafés the world over. People come to take it easy, laugh a bit, and temporarily forget their troubles, but they also exchange important information and gossip about future prices, political turmoil, the hardships facing some of their companions, and new ideas. Their conversations, as is apparent from the brief summary here, range widely and offer a forum for intellectual debate. It was only after the unfamiliar strangers left that conversation became more relaxed again and the drinkers who had lingered reminisced about the history of Cuzco's markets, the old flea market in the Plaza of San Francisco, and the delicious food market of Santa Teresa, where the tax office of the Superintendencia Nacional de Administración Tributaria (SUNAT) has been built.

In this particular instance, lines are clearly drawn in Gofmannesque fashion between insiders and outsiders. There are patterns of meeting, greeting, appreciating and drinking the *chicha* itself, and sharing information that the woman from Tacna and the man perturbed about the cleanliness of his glass did not understand or chose to challenge. At the same time, though, this line between insiders and outsiders is not impermeable, and the presence of outsiders is also an opportunity for learning new things and evaluating existing practices and information. In fact, travelers always need to quench their thirst at some point, and their stops at the equivalent of wayside bars allow significant networking.

Charles Walker (1999:40–41), a historian who has written about the turbulent years at the end of the eighteenth century before Peru's independence in 1824, notes in his book *Smoldering Ashes* that *chicha* operations were very important in circulating information and organizing resistance movements. They were also considered hotbeds of revolutionary activity, whether or not they were, and many of the *chicheras* were persecuted by the military and police: "The rebels counted on travelers, above all muleteers and swift soldiers for their coordination and espionage. *Chicherías,* taverns featuring corn beer, were important sites for conspiracies, rumors, shared frustrations, and . . . strategy sessions. Located along the different trade routes and within the city of Cuzco, these taverns not only put Indians and non-Indians into contact but also linked different regions through talkative travelers."

Labels and Liabilities

Many of the women who run these taverns and work in the markets are called *cholas*. They do not fit into racial categories established by the Spaniards when they invaded Peru. Initially, the Spaniards had two categories: Indian and non-Indian. Furthermore, although much debate took place about whether Indians had souls and could be saved, few Spaniards entertained the possibility that education could change one's membership to a category. Thus, Peru's social structure resembled that of a caste system, and the operation of the caste system was closely linked to colonial economic welfare and fiscal policies. Interestingly, only those who were non-Indian fell within the caste system initially. Indians fell outside, and one could consider them similar to India's untouchables. Those who were considered Indian had to pay tribute or, later, a head tax. Therefore, it was very much in the interest of the Spanish to maintain these categories, as much for social as for economic reasons. Nevertheless, a number of different processes complicated their best efforts to maintain this ideal structure.

Intermarriage, concubinage, and prostitution between Spaniards and Indians produced children who could not be identified phenotypically as Indians. They were called *cholos* and *cholas*. The Spaniards developed many terms that complicated the caste system. The very proliferation of these terms represented the hopeless and concerted efforts of the Spanish colonial bureaucracy to keep Spaniards separate from non-Spaniards. The "in-between" beings of Peru have had both the misfortune and remarkable capacity to straddle worlds. Many of them who work in the market have obtained their goods from their relatives in the countryside; they often take care of their relatives when they come to the city, they help them with bureaucratic problems, and they have sometimes strategically assisted in land invasions in the countryside or urban demonstrations. At the same time, they provide food to urban residents to which they would not easily have access otherwise. They rarely call themselves *cholas* but rather mestizas, a confusing state of affairs because many who consider themselves non-Indian and part of the world of Spanish mores also call themselves mestizas. Nevertheless, others call these vendors *cholas* in a denigrating fashion. Their male counterparts also may be referred to in a negative way as *cholos*, but they rarely stand out. This is so for two reasons. Many *cholas*, especially those who work in *chicha* bars and marketplaces, have evolved a highly distinctive dress compared with that of other groups, whereas *cholo* dress resembles a poorer version of the mestizo's (Nash 1979:312). Even in a sea of people, some market women distinguish themselves in their tall, white

stovepipe hat with a wide black or colored band, their multiple cotton or vel-
veteen *pollera* skirts and brightly colored polyester sweaters, their dangling
earrings sparkling with rhinestones, and their money purses, bulging beneath
their skirts. The distinctiveness of their dress is visible primarily in the marketplace and on the travel routes they take for their business. It is associated
with the occupation they perform. Strangers may no longer label them as *cholas*
once they change into indigenous or mestizo dress and engage in activities not
associated with street vending.[6]

The very fluidity of the identities of market women means that it is difficult
to place them in a racial category, as many Peruvians would like to do. The
following examples of informal conversations involving market women took
place in various Cuzco markets. They give us an excellent sense of the ways in
which racial ideologies, like gender ideologies, undergird everyday activities
in the markets. Although most of these exchanges begin uneventfully, some
become virulent, characterized by violent and abusive language and sometimes
physical assault. It is precisely when these exchanges escalate or take an unexpected turn that these ideologies become more apparent. As Chartier wryly
observed (1979: 277), "It is often in discovering its margins or opposites and
in trying to subdue, by acts of language, that which worries it, that an established society best reveals its malaises, fissures, and phantasms." Also, the ostensibly private exchanges between client and vendor are not as closed as they
might appear. In the market, vendors work side by side; they keep their eyes
and ears open to potential clients, roving thieves, and municipal agents; gossip circulates; and vendors and clients alike turn private exchanges into public performances to gain the sympathy, support, and derision, at times, of the
general public.

The Language of Exchange

The first conversation is most typical. Elizabeth Anchaya is not an established
vendor and does not have a permanent stall. She sits on the sidewalk, her small
piles of potatoes organized on a cloth she has spread out below them. An
upper-class "white" mestiza, Faustina Mendoza, gets out of her car and approaches her. Faustina begins the conversation in Spanish, and Elizabeth responds in Quechua:

> *Faustina:* How much are your potatoes?
> *Elizabeth:* Only five hundred, little mother. Go ahead and buy some.
> They're delicious. Very floury.
> *Faustina:* Do you really think I'd buy this little pile at such an exorbitant
> price? You who come from the countryside ought to sell more cheaply.

Elizabeth: Go ahead and buy them, little mother. I also need a little money. That is why I am selling them. I have eight children. I need to buy in order to cook for them and care for them.

Faustina: So, smelly *chola*. Who do you think I am so that you can come telling me these stories? Do you think that money rains from the sky for me?

Elizabeth: But, little mother. I'm just selling potatoes. I'm not asking you for money. What did you say that to me for? If you like, go somewhere else. Go ahead. Why did you ask me? If you think you are so rich, then go ahead and buy from the wholesalers and buy a lot of what you want.

Faustina: But, what do you think, vulgar *chola,* to demand that I demean myself this way? I may even make you close down after how you've offended me. You don't know who I am.

Elizabeth: But, Señora, what have I done to you? Perhaps you'll send someone. That's what you have threatened me with. Go ahead and bring whatever shit you want. What will he do to me? Because I'm poor, you hurl whatever abuses you want. Perhaps you wanted me to give you the potatoes for nothing. I work with my labor. I'm not selling potatoes I robbed.

Faustina: Now you'll see, you insolent Indian. You've made me furious. I'll be back.

Although the nuances of shifts in language are obfuscated by their translation into English, in the original text, as tensions rise between Faustina and Elizabeth, the exchange makes explicit Faustina's underlying fears and prejudices as well as Elizabeth's adamant rejection of Faustina's efforts to use manipulative and denigrating labels. Through their choice of words, both attempt to define and control the social distance between them. Faustina, who speaks Spanish throughout the exchange, begins by addressing Elizabeth informally as "you." By the end of the exchange, Faustina has resorted to ethnic slurs, calling Elizabeth "stinking *chola*," "vulgar *chola*," and, finally, "insolent Indian." Elizabeth begins addressing Faustina with a Quechua term of endearment, "little mother." By the end, she has shifted to using formal Spanish, calling Faustina "Señora." Each also makes assumptions about the other's economic position. Faustina accuses Elizabeth of taking advantage of her because Elizabeth has direct access to agricultural products whereas Faustina does not. Elizabeth, still attempting to placate Faustina, protests that, despite her poverty, she works, investing her agricultural labor in what she is selling. Faustina becomes defensive, decrying Elizabeth's awareness that she does not work and lacks the information, the social contacts, and the scale of money necessary to buy from wholesalers. Their conflict is not only about the labor and skills needed for buying and selling. It is also about a very common strategy on which vendors rely. That is, they prefer not to sell all their goods to one customer for fear that their other loyal customers may desert them.[7] Elizabeth also calls attention to the differences in their ways of living by suggesting that Faustina, in contrast to herself, is intending to purchase goods with money that she has not earned with her own labor (that she has robbed). In frustration, Faustina issues a weak threat that she will call the authorities, and Elizabeth dares her to act on her threat. Elizabeth probably has lost a sale, but it is also likely that Faustina will not be able to obtain a better deal from anyone else because she cannot purchase from wholesalers.

Because the position of market women is both a constructed identity and an economic function created by the weak articulation of productive agricultural regions and urban centers, market women and *campesinos* in the countryside harbor intensely mixed feelings about each other. On one hand, market women have proved to be adept at courageously confronting the dangers of urban living: the immediacy of repressive authority and of the state levying taxes and license fees and the rules and regulations affecting their physical and social space. They have greater knowledge than peasants about the political workings of formal bureaucracies, political parties, and unions. Moreover, their ability to speak Spanish and Quechua provides them with an important weapon that they can use in their own defense and in the defense of their rural kin to resolve land litigations, for example, and to lobby for infrastructural services. They can also provide needed credit to peasants. On the other hand, market women themselves harbor ambivalence about their desires for upward social mobility, which may involve deliberate separation of their identity from that of their rural kin. To *campesinos,* who may proudly defend their autonomy as indigenous peasants, market women are also alienating, given that they have carved out a space for themselves in which they can make a living from the products and money of *campesinos* and mestizos. These sentiments, it seems to me, are unavoidable in a society in which racial and gender identities and categories are deeply felt and reacted to but hardly stable.

Sometimes the aspirations of market women for upward mobility are shattered by the obstacles put in their way by attempts of the state and the dominant mestizo classes to impose their own model of ideal ethnic relations. The daily experiences of market women of these contradictory dynamics do not necessarily lead them to oppose the state (in the form of municipal agents and the like) and dominant classes, although many of them do. The worlds of rural peasants and urban market women intersect; in fact, one could argue that they occupy the same world but experience it and are situated in it somewhat differently. Therefore, conflicts and tensions mark the meeting points between them.

In another conversation between Cleófila Huamani, a market woman selling rice, a food product not readily available in the countryside, and Victoria Rado, a *campesina* who has come to Cuzco to make a few purchases, the ambivalent relations between *campesinos* and market women become clearer. The entire exchange takes place in Quechua. Victoria, the *campesina,* begins the exchange:

> *Victoria:* Little mother, how much is your kilo of rice?
>
> *Cleófila:* This rice is 400 million soles.
>
> *Victoria:* How can it be that it costs so much, little mother? Just the other day, I bought some at 340 million. It can't have gone up that much.
>
> *Cleófila:* What do you want? Don't blame me for the price. This government takes advantage of all of us, cheating us. Everything is like this now.
>
> *Victoria:* But, little mother. I didn't vote for him. I'm not even registered to vote. I don't know how to read or write. It wasn't me who voted. You, yes, you [plural] voted for him and you are to blame.
>
> *Cleófila:* Shut up, big-mouthed woman. If you don't want to buy from me, then don't buy. If you prefer, go search all over Cuzco for a lower price.
>
> *Victoria:* What kind of a person are you [formal] to speak to me like this? Aren't you a woman? Or are you a man? Perhaps you were raised as a man?
>
> *Cleófila:* Smelly llama woman. Watch out or I'll slap you one.
>
> *Victoria:* And you? Who are you to have to slap me? Don't I already have a husband who slaps me? Perhaps you [formal] don't have one who would slap me.
>
> *Cleófila:* Get out of here. Don't talk back to me, mule woman.
>
> *Victoria:* You are also a mule woman but you don't even know it.

A number of underlying conflicts inform this exchange. We see the intervention of issues of gender in which Victoria derides Cleófila for her threat of using physical violence against the *campesina,* taunting her that she is a man rather than a woman or was raised to be a man. Victoria assumes that men, not women, have the right to use physical punishment. Also implicit is Victoria's assumption that having a husband is of social value, despite the fact that she may be physically abused by him. And, indeed, many market women have suffered from not having a husband even as they have gained greater autonomy and economic independence. Victoria also points out, correctly, that the majority of market women put their faith in a president who has proved to be a traitor to them, and she thus questions the value of electoral politics and literacy itself because they have led to deleterious consequences for both market women and peasants. Almost simultaneously, however, Cleófila forces Victoria to realize that the market women continue to occupy a more powerful economic position in that Victoria probably will not be able to find a lower price for rice anywhere in the market. Whether the increase in the price of rice is really the consequence of government economic policies or the consensus of market women to sell at that price, Victoria remains at a disadvantage. Finally, Victoria responds to the scathing insult Cleófila levels against her by calling her a "llama [long-necked] woman," thus drawing attention to her bestial, rural roots as an Indian. Retorting, Victoria calls Cleófila a "mule woman." The latter is a hybrid animal, and Victoria makes a claim that she and Cleófila are the product of colonial miscegenation, despite their public construction of identity as market woman and peasant, respectively.

Market women prefer transactions that do not entail defending their status and character. Furthermore, it is interesting that, just as a failed transaction may become highly personalized in a negative sense, a successful transaction may also become highly personalized in a positive sense. In successful transactions where market women offer "a little extra" to the client, efforts may be made to create a more permanent buyer-seller relationship for the future.

Man inspecting olives in vats in an informal market outside San Pedro, 1998.

Although it is impossible to predict precisely when a transaction will degenerate and therefore not be completed, it generally occurs at the moment when the criticisms a client makes of a market woman's produce and character become both personal and racist. A certain degree of bantering and questioning of prices and quality alleviate boredom, provide entertainment, and, from the client's perspective, may succeed in lowering the price. If the buyer's insults about the quality of produce command the attention of the surrounding audience of market women, they do not usually encourage competition from other market women. That is, neighboring vendors do not go to extreme lengths to persuade a client that their produce is of better quality than their neighbor's because these vendors, in turn, would run the risk of losing sales in a similar manner in the future.

Language exchanges like those just described take place from time to time in the marketplace. Despite the dominant class and ethnic categories to which mestizos still subscribe, the indeterminacy of social relations provides a space for contentious reassessment of identity and the validity of the categories that are used. Market women may be able to reject or deliberately call attention to them and thereby appropriate and acknowledge the construction of different relational categories in opposition to those used by the dominant classes. Because market women participate in similar functions, are located together in the marketplace, and often come from similar backgrounds, their conversations are not only the product of individualized apprehension of daily practices or of the imposition and insinuations of hegemonic ideas. They also speak to a more subterranean collective apprehension of experience, channeled into the efforts of market women to articulate alternative structures of social order.

Market women control access to economic goods for urban mestizos, thereby making the latter vulnerable. The pejorative racial terms aimed at market women only heighten the latter's awareness of the kinds of goods and services that, by rights of citizenship, would be made available to them were they not labeled as vulgar *cholas* and insolent Indians. The intention of those who use such labels may be to denigrate market women, but this kind of language exchange can backfire, becoming yet another political weapon of resistance to assimilation and integration. That is, if market women, by all accounts, behave respectably, speak Spanish, and are educated yet are still perceived as marginalized from mainstream Peruvian society, they may then develop a political consciousness and solidarity that they can use to mobilize against such institutionalized racism. Xavier Albo (1991:44), a Jesuit priest and ethnologist who has spent many years working on interethnic relations in the Andes, remarks that, particularly in Bolivia, a new awareness of Indian identity and of what he calls "plurinationalism" has indirectly been fostered by "urban Indians who no longer live from working the land. . . . Seeing themselves rejected in their urban upward mobility, they make this denigration their cause, and out of their culture, now more idealized than lived, they make their ideology in the city, under the slogan, 'As Indians we were exploited; as Indians we will liberate ourselves.'. . . With this global vision, concepts such as 'class' and 'syndicate,' formerly used in an exclusive manner, are no longer considered sufficient. Other concepts such as 'community'. . . and, increasingly, 'nationality' and 'nation' are privileged instead to emphasize that [their] identity is not simply synonymous for belonging to a state."

Butchering Patience

Women who sell in the meat market are among the most powerful and well established. The most tense exchanges take place between them and their clients. These exchanges often degenerate into insults. Why is this? In the municipal archives, on April 27, 1950, Guillermo Masembach went to the stall of Rocenda Caceres to buy some meat and concluded that "meat vendors seem to be among the most aggressive in the market." He complained that her "rudeness" became so extreme that "she yanked the meat out of my hands" (AHM 1950: Leg. 144, April 1, 1950). Butchers earn more money than most other vendors at the retail level. Furthermore, they are often the wives or mistresses of cattlemen who, in turn, may occupy important political positions in district capitals of the countryside. In one instance, the union of cattle dealers, involved in auctioning cattle, were accused by an upper-middle-class woman representing her husband as "tariff killers," and she hurled "insulting words, threatening us because we are cattle dealers . . . who only want to offer the public the basic staple of meat, which today is scarce in the plaza because of the uncontrolled export of meat to Lima" (AHM 1950: Leg. 144, November 13, 1950). Cattle dealers and their companions, who are often butchers, are powerful in grassroots politics and in providing a basic commodity that middle- and upper-class residents desire.

Despite their power, butchers occupy a different gendered and ethnic position than the middle- or upper-middle-class women who usually come to buy from them. Cattle dealers and their wives are deeply rooted in the rural countryside because they must maintain close relations with the peasants who take primary responsibility for raising the livestock that the dealers and butchers sell. Although peasants receive something for the labor they invest in raising cattle, calculations by a group of students from the agronomy department of the University of Cuzco showed that the value of the labor they invested was far greater than the remuneration they received. In place of receiving adequate recompense, the peasants are permitted to use the cattle they are raising to plow their fields until they are sent to slaughter. The cattle dealers establish *compadrazgo* relationships with the peasants, becoming godfather to hundreds of peasant families scattered through the countryside, and thereby insinuate themselves further into multiple local political networks. Many of them also own tracts of land in different parts of the highlands.

At the same time, the product that butchers sell at the retail level is unlike perishable goods, such as fruit, vegetables, or eggs. You cannot tell what you have. You can smell it, but you cannot be sure. It is supposed to be inspected, but you still cannot be sure. It could be bad meat and still be very expensive, especially with the decrease in the buying power of the middle class. Over and over again, in the archives, there are efforts on the part of the municipality to distinguish between cuts of meat and establish different prices and taxes. In 1935, ten different standards for beef, lamb, and pork were set (AHM 1935: Leg. 98). There are also numerous complaints that butchers "are selling rotten meat at exorbitant prices" and that they are "both a threat to public health and speculators" (AHM 1945: Leg. 124).

The middle class considers it a matter of status to consume meat. By consuming meat, they make themselves more like the elite. Sidney Mintz (1996:78, 81) has written a book on the history of the consumption of sugar, in which he observes about consumption patterns under capitalism, "In the new scheme of things, what one consumed became a changing measure of what (and of who) one was. Status did not so much define what one could consume; what one consumed helped to define one's status. . . . As an older social system (one that is not capitalist and prior to modern consumerism) becomes dilapidated, one's individual identity is called into question more. The use of consumption as a means to define oneself becomes commoner; the market emerges as a mirror of what one is, and what one can become."

Cattle dealers and butchers are regarded ambivalently and sometimes even hatefully by peasants and urban consumers. Therefore, their clients tend to be somewhat rude and untrusting, and the butchers tend to be insulted but still in control. In the paraphrased words of more than one butcher, "This is not a job for everyone. You have to have tremendous patience to put up with the way people treat us. It's up to the buyer to know the quality of the meat."

This tension between the abruptness of buyers and the patience of butchers resembles the "race-denying discourse" that Harrison (1998:619) describes as "subtle" but that "nevertheless has racializing effects that work 'between the

Butcher in a San Pedro market with a campesina *client, 1998.*

lines' and 'beneath the texts.'" She adds, "In social contexts in which overt racism is no longer acceptable, more subtly raced language appears to be more socially appropriate and morally defensible. This apparent legitimacy makes this form of racialized discourse all the more powerful."

In the complicated exchange that follows, Elena Vega, a mestiza client, accompanied by her *campesina* servant, Betti Huanca, comes to buy meat in the butcher section. She approaches Susanna Mora, one of the butchers.

> *Elena:* Señora, how much is your kilo of beef?
> *Susanna:* Very cheap, mother. Buy some. The meat is fresh.
> *Elena:* Then why is it so dirty? It's covered with dirt.
> *Susanna:* But, little mother, all you have to do is wash it.
> *Elena:* But, Señora, don't you understand that the meat is already contaminated. Why do you [plural] sell in these conditions? The municipal agents should control this. How can you sell in this manner?
> *Susanna:* But you, who do you think you are to reject the meat I'm selling in that way? If you are such a clean lady, then go buy somewhere else. You shouldn't buy in the market.
> *Elena:* But who do you think you are, refined *chola*, that you can tell me where I should buy? I can buy wherever I want.

Susanna: And you, who are you? Who do you think you are, stinking dame? You don't remember where you are from, who your grandparents are? Maybe they were worse *cholas* than I. And you, now you come calling us *cholas* without knowing who you are. Now you dress in pretty clothes, elegant clothes, you use makeup. With that, you think you are superior to us.

Elena: But you, what an insolent Indian you are. You don't even know how to treat your clients properly. I'm sure you never set foot in a school. You aren't educated or cultured.

Susanna: So, maybe you've gone to school or maybe you haven't. Maybe you're refined. Go away, lady of high heels. You're making me furious. Be careful or I'll throw this piece of meat at you.

Elena: Go ahead and throw it, greedy Indian queen bee [metaphor referring to those who opportunistically accumulate wealth for themselves]. You don't know what I'll do to you.

Susanna, speaking loudly so her fellow vendors will hear: Lady, you are rich. Perhaps you're a millionaire who made your money as a prostitute. Go to your house. Don't fuck me over here.

Elena turns to Betti, her domestic servant: What did she say?

Betti, smiling, responds: I don't know. What could she have said?

Elena, speaking again to Betti: But you know Quechua. What did this woman say to me? I won't leave things this way. I'll denounce her to the authorities.

Susanna: Right. Go ahead, bring your husbands and your lovers [referring metaphorically to authorities]. What are they going to do to me? Go ahead and bring them. If you like, I'll go with you. You're a lady like a pig with lice eggs between her thighs.

Elena: You'll see, foul-mouthed *chola.* Perhaps you don't realize the kind of power I have to do something about this. I'll come back tomorrow.

Susanna: Go ahead, stinking dame. I'm not scared of you. Bring whomever you like. How ridiculous! Surely you wanted me to give away the meat to you. You say you have money and you still look for the best. If you want the best, you should buy imported meat and not come here to try my patience.

The most fascinating aspect of this exchange is that the norm among wealthier urban residents is to send their servants to the market to make household purchases. For whatever reason, Elena came to the market with her servant and assumed that she could assert her authority without opposition. In doing so, she not only made herself vulnerable, unexpectedly perhaps, but also permitted Susanna to confront directly the kinds of racist attitudes that prevail in Peruvian society. In this encounter, again, linguistic shifts take place, moving from formal terms of address to ethnic slurs. Both vendor and client begin their conversation in Spanish, using formal terms of address. Whereas Elena begins by addressing Susanna as "Señora," and Susanna addresses Elena as "mother," by the end Elena is calling Susanna "foul-mouthed *chola*" and "Indian," and Susanna is calling Elena "stinking dame" and "prostitute." Elena begins to incite the anger of Susanna when she makes a sweeping statement about the "dirty" conditions in which market women sell their meat, using the plural "you." Furthermore, she juxtaposes her view that the market women have deliberately created the unhygienic conditions of the marketplace with her threat that the municipal agents should be called in to rectify the situation. Her statement, in turn, serves as a trigger mechanism for the market women to support Susanna in defending both her character and the quality of their produce. Also intriguing is Susanna's strategic shift from Spanish to Quechua when Elena accuses her of being uneducated and uncivilized and threatens to call the authorities. Susanna is able to turn the usual assumptions about nonmestizos being uncivilized and without education into a farce because Elena is the only one who does not understand what Susanna is saying. Even Elena's domestic servant allies herself with the vendors, and Elena is unable to control the behavior of her servant. Susanna also highlights the fact that fancy clothes, makeup, and even a supposed education are not the only skills needed to buy meat from her. Precisely at this juncture, Susanna challenges Elena's status by suggesting that they probably come from similar back-grounds, and she insinuates that to obtain money Susanna works whereas Elena resorts to prostitution, the final alternative for urban migrants who cannot find another source of livelihood. She thus draws attention to the morality of her labor in contrast to that of Elena, who probably does not work. Susanna's reference to Elena's "high heels" simultaneously is a comment upon Elena's putting on airs and her not working. Finally, Susanna displays her unique gendered identity and makes a political statement by saying that she will not be intimidated if Elena returns with "all her husbands and lovers," a metaphor for the authorities.

Mules and Bananas

Very early in my work, I strode out to the central market, hoping that some of the market women would speak to me. My hopes were not unwarranted. I found myself in one of my favorite sections, the bread section. Felicitas was eager to speak to me, and we conducted our conversation in Quechua, which she preferred, rather than Spanish. It began in a fairly boring way. I asked

Felicitas about her business: where she got her bread, where she baked it, and how much she had to pay to use the ovens of Oropesa, which is where all of the women selling bread baked their bread. But this routine dialog rapidly evolved into a far more entertaining exchange in which Felicitas's companions also participated with great gusto. It went something like this:

> *Linda:* So, how much do you pay to use the ovens?
> *Felicitas:* We pay 18 soles for each round of dough. We make bread all night. We don't sleep at night. Do you sleep at night? Why don't you come to Oropesa and bake bread with us? You won't sleep all night either. [Everyone laughs at this thinly veiled reference to not sleeping and making love, with "baking bread" equivalent to "making babies."]
> [Further routine conversation about the price of bread, earnings, credit, and the process of selling the bread.]
> *Linda:* Does your husband work?
> *Felicitas:* No, he stays at home with the kids. I have eight children. Why don't you take one of my children? I would like to give you one of my children.

Felicitas makes a sale to one of her *caseras,* giving her a good deal. A municipal agent approaches her and asks her, "Is this your stall?"

> *Felicitas:* Yes sir, this is my stall. [He turns to another woman, and Felicitas whispers to me in Quechua, "He's ugly."]

The guard asks another woman where her apron is. The woman first tells the guard that it got scorched, which is why she is not wearing it. The guard leaves, but when he comes back she has it on. The guard notes that she has lied and fines her.

The conversation again becomes routine as the bread ladies tell me how the government is bankrupt and the taxes they have to pay are exorbitant. Then Felicitas offers me some bread.:

> *Felicitas:* Try some of this bread.
> *Bread woman 2:* It's snot.
> *Felicitas:* And so are you.
> *Bread woman 2:* I have beautiful eyes like the *kapulí* [a cherry fruit tree].
> *Felicitas:* So do I.
> *Bread woman 2:* No, you're an old snot.
> *Felicitas:* You're a dirty old man.
> *Bread woman 2:* You are dumb.
> *Felicitas:* You are foolish.
> *Bread woman 2:* You're deaf. You don't listen.

Felicitas: You have a black ass.

Bread woman 2: You are a tight ass.

Felicitas (to me): You need to eat more. Why don't you take this girl?

Bread woman 2: A fly almost flew into your mouth [You talk too much].

Felicitas (to me): What did you drink that has prevented you from having children? There are baby orphans that you can take. If you have a husband, then why don't you have children? You'll have them, in time. Where is your husband? Whoa! You are here alone. We should have guards around you. Bring us some *chicha.*

Bread woman 2: Linda Violeta. Bring us some *chicha.* Bring me some *chicha.* Let's drink together. Let's drink some *chicha* for Mamacha Asunta. Right?

Felicitas: What's your name?

Linda: Linda.

Felicitas: Linda. What? Linda. Linda.

Linda: Like *sumaqcha* [the word for "pretty" in Quechua; *Linda* means "pretty" in Spanish]. What's your name?

Felicitas: My name is Felicitas. And your last name?

Linda: Linda Seligmann.

This joking around pervades the marketplace. However, I think my own status and the misfortune or fortune of having the name *Linda* encouraged the ribald nature of exchanges I often had with market women. *Linda* does not only mean "pretty" in Spanish. It also refers to a beloved and stunning baroque saint image of the Virgin of the Immaculate Conception, called *La Linda,* which has stood in one of the chapels of Cuzco's principal cathedral since the colonial period. *La Linda* was chosen as the patroness of the province and bishopric of Cuzco in the mid-1600s, and she is considered the hostess who welcomes and bids farewell to other visiting saint images that participate in Cuzco's elaborate fiesta complex, including Corpus Christi and Inti Raymi. Market women often brought up *La Linda* in conversations with me. She is considered one of the most opulent and beautiful of images, and she stands on a pedestal of silver. It is said that in the Corpus Christi procession of all the saint images of the Central Cathedral of Cuzco, she smiled upon a sacristan and gave him all her jewels to distribute to the poor (Barrionuevo 1980:61).[8]

Here I was, a well-educated foreigner, strolling through the market by myself without my husband, striking up conversations in Quechua with street women and living alone in Cuzco. In a sense, I was rupturing social codes, and the women found this quite amusing. It was also reassuring and somewhat surprising to them that sometimes I did not understand the social conventions I was challenging, given that their own aloneness and independence often prompt violent and vituperative remarks. Examples of this condemnation of street vendors' sexuality abound, especially among political figures, such as Cuzco's mayor, who did not hesitate to refer to the market women as "pimps" and "prostitutes." As I make clear in chapter 10, the women of the market are quite adept at returning the insults that government officials and municipal agents hurl at them with salacious and barbed ones of their own that also serve as commentaries on the men's humanity and ability to be responsible family members. Unfortunately, women, once again, serve as the vehicle for slamming these insults home. For example, in several cases the women suggested that the men's barbarity indicated that their mothers had not breast-fed them.

Products themselves determine to some extent the pattern of language exchanges (see also Sikkink 2001). Eva, the lively yet uneducated itinerant vendor of spices, was always quick to take advantage of business opportunities and had learned to wheedle foreigners walking through the streets by offering them coca leaves in English. She took a liking to me and, together with her sister and other companions, was always bantering with me about my sexual identity. One day, after I hadn't been there for a while, I showed up with two small bananas in my hand, and she and her companions ribbed me endlessly about how the bananas must be a substitute for my husband. Then she remarked, "You haven't come for a while because, obviously, you've been sleeping with your husband. I bet you'll sleep with your husband's brother once he leaves. We'd better guard you carefully. Worse, maybe one of us will sleep with your husband."

Hilda Villafuerte Toledo, an itinerant vendor with twinkling eyes, also kidded me: "Little *gringa*. Can you believe it? Do you eat wheat soup? Corn soup? Wheat soup is much better than freeze-dried potato soup? How long have you studied in the university? You are old because you studied too long in the university. Why don't you become my daughter-in-law? We could live in Santa Ana." I responded, "No, I already have a husband." Later on, I asked whether I could take her photograph. She agreed but added, "If you take a photo, you have to become my daughter-in-law." I retorted, "Can I be your daughter-in-law along with my existing husband?"

Hilda's conversation was particularly unusual because it kept harking back to her own life in the countryside: the foods she liked to eat (the different kinds of soup and their status in terms of a code of race, going from freeze-dried potato to wheat to corn soup) and the ritualized nature of Quechua courtship. Yet the content was not limited to the odd encounter between *gringa* from afar and precariously grounded market women. I visited Domérica several times when she was selling her vegetables and brightly colored yarn by the railroad tracks and taped the following exchange one day. The woman with whom she had the conversation turned out to be the midwife who had assisted Domérica when she had a near-death experience giving birth. Domérica spoke in both Spanish and Quechua, but her Spanish was rich with Quechua syntax. The midwife spoke only Quechua. Their conversation was punctuated by bursts of laughter.

Domérica: Take this for your grandchildren.
Midwife: Don't you have the yarn that I knitted for my older daughter?
Domérica: Aha. You should have brought me a piece.
Midwife: It was another kind.
Domérica: Why didn't you bring me a little piece?
Midwife: I don't have any more. I'll buy this other one from you, perhaps tomorrow.
Domérica: Great. . . .
Midwife: You're already finishing your business?
Domérica: Take this from me, take this.
Midwife: Where? What? Which thing? [She acts as if she does not understand.]
Domérica: Take this celery so that your belly doesn't swell up. For gastritis.
Midwife (giggling loudly; the reference is to pregnancy, really): How much?
Domérica: It's cheap. Not very much. The celery and turnip I'll let you take for only 500.
Midwife: Together with you?
Domérica: With me as part of the package too. [Midwife and Domérica laugh.]
Domérica: Do you still have your son [indirectly offering to be her daughter-in-law]?
Midwife: Yes, I have my son. Shit. He still isn't married.
Domérica: You mean he isn't engaged?
Midwife (laughs): That's right.
Domérica (to me): She says she has a son who is single.
Midwife: My son the soldier is single.
Domérica: I'd like to see him then. [They laugh.] How great. Let's see if she really wants me to be with her son. How great.
Midwife: Is this awning yours?
Domérica: No, it's rented.
Midwife: Tomorrow I'll bring the piece of yarn to try to match it.
Domérica: Thank you. [To me]: The lady makes jokes.

The plays on masculinity and femininity found in this and many other exchanges refer to some market women's self-conscious choice of clothing and their demeanor, which, in turn, mark a particular terrain of sexuality and ethnicity. Many market women exhibit behavior as hybrid females whose aggressive character traits usually are associated with men; they often refuse to tolerate racist slurs or insults and wield economic power ideally belong to mestizo men. Sarah Radcliffe has studied processes of hybridity among Ecuadorans who are considered "indigenous" because of the clothing they wear. She argues that the concept of "hybridity" should be used to refer more broadly "to the nature of cultural mixing, the bringing together in innovative ways of tradition/modernity, indigenous/*mestizo*, national/non-national. Beyond the new label—hybrid—is the way in which it makes us think of *process,* and specific histories and geographies that lie behind new cultural formations . . . while adding a sensitivity to gender relations" (Radcliffe 1997:10). In developing her thesis, Radcliffe (1997:18–19) goes on to stress that hybridity is infused by power relations such that "it is contextualized by the hegemony of a move from indigenous to Western/mestizo in which the presentation of subjects' affiliation to place has occurred through the layering of clothing on a racialized, colonized body." Finally, she notes that in these changing dress styles, women tend to retain traditional costume to a far greater extent than men.

What is particularly unusual among market women is that, as we can see in the preceding language exchanges, at the same time they are mixing both sexual identities and racial identities. In addition, the specific occupational function they perform in the market bears on how they are perceived by others. Butchers and bakers are in a more powerful position in the market than vendors of fruit and vegetables. Market women have the capacity to step out of stereotypical categories. If they so choose, they may wear the distinctive dress of a "typical" *chola* with white stovepipe hat. But they may also choose, as most of them do, to wear nonindigenous clothing. Except for the vendors who occasionally make forays from the countryside to sell their products on a sporadic basis, few of them dress as native "Indian" women. Although their personalities are diverse, many of them, while they are selling, are bold and outspoken, engage in ribald sexual humor, and are shrewd hawkers of commodities.[9] To mestizos, they often appear as particularly threatening Indians who are acting in urban ways and contaminating the public sphere with an alternative construction of gender, class, and ethnic identity. They do not fit the abstract model that mestizos have incorporated, either of ideal femininity or of ideal Indian identity. Furthermore, they are hardly comfortable or docile objects on which men can exercise their sexual prowess. Their very ability to leap out of these categories makes them more tantalizing and infuriating to those who want to use them for their own purposes.[10]

Notes

Portions of this chapter are paraphrased or reprinted from my article "Between Worlds of Exchange: Ethnicity among Peruvian Market Women," *Cultural Anthropology* 8:2 (1993): 187–213. Copyrighted by the American Anthropological Association.

1. I distinguish between barter and trade insofar as trading transactions involve an indirect calculation of the monetary value of each product, which then determines the equivalence of the quantities of products exchanged, whereas barter is a direct exchange.

2. See Seligmann (in press) for a more detailed discussion of the linguistic characteristics of verbal exchanges in Quechua and Spanish in the marketplace.

3. Leandro Medina (1991) studied language exchanges between vendors and buyers in Puno, Peru as "communicative events." In his unpublished article, "Interacción verbal en un centro de abstos de Puno," he offers several examples of these events in order to ascertain the norms of buying and selling.

4. Bruce Mannheim and Krista van Vleet (1998:326) elaborate on the different dimensions that constitute context in language exchanges:

> In its skin, Southern Quechua narrative is dialogical at several interpenetrating levels: first, a formal level in which the narrative is produced between interlocutors; . . . second, by embedding discourse within discourse by means of quotations or indirect discourse; . . . third, intertextually, in which implicit or hidden dialogue between texts is brought out through the intertextual references to other coexisting narratives; . . . and fourth, in a complex pattern of participation through which dialogue takes place not only between actual speaking individuals (as in the first sense of dialogue) but between distinct participant roles that are produced as pragmatic shadows of the face-to-face event of speaking, evoking multiple interactional frameworks. These different dialogical levels inform each other even in the dynamic process of the narrative event.

5. One learns a great deal about how Quechua and non-Quechua economic models intersect from the language that is used in the marketplace. For example, *llapa* is a Quechua word, not a Spanish word, and its usage in this context once again calls attention to the rules of reciprocity and to social and economic relationships at work.

6. Informal surveys and observations show that the term *chola* is rarely used as a form of self-identification except in joking exchanges, where it is a term of endearment (combined with condescension), or in exchanges of insults. In fact, no single encompassing term of self-identification for this diverse and intermediate category exists as far as I know.

7. I am grateful to James Scott for pointing this out to me.

8. For more details on *La Linda*, see Alfonsina Barrionuevo (1980:61) and Victor Angles Vargas (1983:134–38).

9. The explicit concern of market women with dress styles parallels Paul Willis's observations of the ways in which working-class students in Hammertown, England strive to open up avenues of alternative social identity in order to differentiate themselves from the stances and status of "ear'oles," the school conformists:

> It is no accident that much of the conflict between staff and students at the moment should take place over dress. . . . Concerned staff and involved kids . . . know that it is one of their elected grounds for the struggle over authority. It is one of the current forms of a fight between cultures. . . .
>
> Closely related with the dress style of "the lads" is, of course, the whole question of their personal attractiveness. Wearing smart and modern clothes gives them the chance . . . at "putting their finger up" at the school and differentiating themselves from the "ear'oles.". . . Counter-school culture is the zone of the informal. It is where the incursive demands of the formal are denied—even if the price is the expression of opposition in style, micro-interactions and non-public discourses. (Willis 1977:18, 22)

10. Weismantel (2001) offers a probing analysis of the sexuality of *cholas* in the context of race relations in her book.

8

Race Recipes: Alliances and Animosity

How market women perceive themselves and their locus in Peruvian society reveals multiple philosophical currents and ideological positions that circulate in Peru and that market women apprehend and make sense of in light of their economic practices. In this chapter I discuss the principal ideologies that seem to shape how market women think about themselves: the power of education in transforming their potential for upward mobility; the correlation between success and voluntarism that is often closely tied to assumptions built into their religious beliefs, such as a Puritan ethic or the need for self-sacrifice in order to achieve and be incorporated in mainstream Peruvian society; the donning of external markers, such as dress and hairstyle, to project a particular image; and elaborate notions of purity and pollution, a kind of hygienic model that correlates closely with an evaluation of their status.

Race lies just below the surface in Peru. Whereas in the past few had qualms about embracing the caste system overtly, today race is muffled and masked even as it continues to shape social relations. Almost all Peruvians have strongly held feelings about race, but they express them indirectly. Because territorial affiliation, the language one speaks, and even one's skin color are not criteria that define who is Indian and who is not, one critical concept that has come to dominate views of race is a scale of inferiority and superiority that depends heavily on an assessment of whether one is "cultured." One can become more cultured by becoming "educated." As one probes more deeply into this notion, however, one discovers that being "cultured" and being "educated" depend on with whom one socializes, how one behaves, the clothes one wears, the food one eats, where one lives, and one's occupation. These are not simply considered differences between people. These aspects of being "cultured" are viewed hierarchically, but one's place in the hierarchy depends greatly on who is interacting with whom. In addition, others may perceive a person as not cultured, whereas that person may perceive herself as "cultured." This disjuncture between self-perception and social perceptions has a long history in the Andes.[1]

For example, when I was working in the countryside, I came to have special relationships with the Pantoja-Zanabria family, whose compound I shared. Their child, Erlán, became my godson, and Demetrio and Victoria became my *compadres,* a fictive kinship relationship of co-parenthood. Erlán became very ill, and after treatments with several local healers were unsuccessful, I persuaded them to take Erlán to see a doctor in Cuzco. The whole family and one of the local healers reluctantly made the trip. I decided to treat them to tea and pastries at a little café I frequented. The room grew quiet when I walked in with them, and it was clear that I had committed a terrible transgression of Cuzqueño etiquette. My *compadres* were dressed well; both spoke Spanish, but Victoria wore her hair in braids, her skin is dark, and she had on multiple skirts. For all intents and purposes, she looked Indian, and regardless of her wealth or her education, she was treated as inferior. In contrast, in the market and countryside, Victoria is considered of high status and is treated with respect by her fellow community members and by the women whose stalls she frequents in the marketplace. She and Demetrio have been major sponsors of community fiestas, and Demetrio has held high office in the community. As a result of these slippery notions of attribution, no one is sure where they belong unless they make certain that others stay in their proper place; even less apparent and more insidious, people often come to feel as if they should stay in their place. From their reaction when we went to the café, I suspect that Demetrio and Victoria were uncomfortable and even angry at me for committing such a social faux pas. However, this was only a stumble. When we went to the doctor and radiologist, neither hesitated to shut the door on the parents (Demetrio and Victoria), and they attempted to direct their comments solely to me. The radiologist found the situation even more outrageous, assuming that because Erlán had very light-colored skin, I must be the mother and Demetrio the father. Although the behavior of these two professionals should not have surprised me, its tangibility made me feel shame and anger. A deep virulence characterizes race relations that cannot be watered down by being called "ethnic identity" or by being confined to notions of class and status that can be improved by means of a free market that promotes upward mobility.[2]

Many market women have internalized the dominant view of social Darwinism that holds sway in Peru. These women make efforts to avoid being perceived either as distinctive or as Indian. In 1991, I interviewed Lucila Chawar Ronda, who sold potatoes in the main market. She contrasted her position with that of her mother. Lucila, age twenty-seven, has a servant she pays to take care of her children, and she speaks mainly Spanish and very little Quechua. Her mother speaks only Quechua. They are from the countryside. She described the differences between them: "My mother and I are both mestizas, not *campesinas,* because we have moved up and are a little more than they are. My mother is improperly dressed though. She should be wearing her complete outfit: her apron, her skirts, her hat. She doesn't have her little jacket on either. She wears that outfit so that you will see her as a mestiza. I don't like dressing that way. It's very pretty but I don't like it. I don't like dressing differently. Other people see my mother as 'decent.' I see her as 'okay' [or acceptable—'regular']." Lucila, the daughter, is wearing typical western dress: a polyester sweater, short skirt, cropped hair, leather shoes, and nylon stockings. When I commented to a Peruvian friend who is a professor at a U.S. university how pretty the chartreuse color of the sweater she was wearing was, she told me that in Lima, urbanites disdain those who wear bright pink or magenta, calling it "*chola* pink," and that in the case of her chartreuse sweater, she would never wear it there because it would result in a similar reaction, and people would denigrate her and refer to her sweater as "*verde* [green] *cholapink.*" This notion of *chola* distinctiveness in clothing and the negativity with which it is greeted is a real thing, and market women recognize that it is projected onto them.[3]

Those who view their status as above that of market women in general find it unsettling that Peru's urban spaces are crammed with vendors who are educated, work hard, dress well, and understand the way markets function. Many politicians may view market women with distaste but nevertheless seek to garner their votes, and market women themselves are well aware that they are being used in neopopulist campaigns, in which they are depicted folklorically as "*cholas.*" These depictions may emphasize the erotic nature of *cholas* or their maternal qualities. The ironic result is that these images increasingly clash with the real lives and concerns of market women who, for reasons of racism and a desire for upward mobility, may no longer don the "*chola* costume" and may be nationally and transnationally mobile (see chapter 10 for more on this kind of manipulation).[4]

Once market women discover that obtaining education, working hard, dressing differently, and speaking Spanish—in short, imitating mestizo behavior—do not automatically gain them equal rights and treatment as Peruvian citizens, they may abandon the "alternative path," heralded by literary politicians and economist ideologues such as Mario Vargas Llosa and Hernando de Soto (1989), and turn to alternative, extralegal, and socially unacceptable forms of opposition to the prevailing social structure. Vargas Llosa and de Soto, among others, argue that this alternative path consists of eliminating bureaucratic obstacles that members of the informal sector confront and designing economic policies that include a more comprehensive tax structure; members of the informal sector will come to be the future middle class of Peruvian society. Of course, this is what most market women would prefer, but long experience has demonstrated that even when they achieve a degree of economic success, they continue to be the target of racial discrimination, a factor that many policymakers ignore. This experience may encourage them to form bonds of solidarity, especially in the face of unfair government policies or discrimination.

Likewise, *campesinos* who work and live in the countryside are caught in the net of race relations. Some of them, especially younger generations, think of nothing more than making it in the city and escaping the countryside. Others

Women in a market, talking and chewing coca, 1991. Notice the different hat and dress styles.

are immersed in a way of life that is distinctive and gives them pleasure and meaning, even as they are conscious of being exploited and discriminated against, including by market women, who may be their primary source for buying and selling goods in the city. Their cultural and economic practices set them apart from others.

The case of Dori Argondoña Martínez shows how issues of race are fused with the status markers of education, dress, religious beliefs, and hygienic models. Argondoña married a man of higher status and greater wealth. But her mother had been a market woman, and she wanted to continue in her footsteps. She was well educated, and as I explain in describing her success as a wholesaler in chapter 3, she was willing and able to take risks and innovate, partly because of her husband's capital. Sitting in her well-stocked store, proud of the education she has provided to her daughters and of the real estate she has acquired, she told me her view of race relations in response to my question, which I framed in a deliberately naive fashion:

> *Linda:* When I go to the market, I notice that people sometimes refer to others as mestizos, *cholos, campesinos.* What do they mean when they use these terms? Are there differences between these people?
>
> *Dori* (patiently but vehemently): From the *campesina,* the *chola* emerges. Because, look, the *campesina* wears clothes made out of homespun wool [*bayeta*]. Then, she changes, improves herself, by having a *pollera* [multiple full, gathered skirts], like that señora. That's a señora. That is, from the *chola* emerges a mestiza. The *chola* is that one who uses *bayeta,* with her traditional *montera* [flat hat].
>
> *Linda:* And the *campesina?*
>
> *Dori:* She *is* a *campesina.*
>
> *Linda:* But then why call the *campesina* a *chola?*
>
> *Dori:* Because she works the land. *She doesn't exist within society* [my italics]. She lives on plots of land.
>
> *Linda:* Then what's the difference between a *campesina* and a *chola?*
>
> *Dori: Chola, campesina.* We call them both things because she doesn't know how to read. She has a life that is too primitive, totally backwards. Thus, when she begins improving herself, then she's like that señora, a mestiza. And now, we are surpassing these people, becoming a little more refined. This is a person who's already a lady. She's overcoming, she's climbing. In my case, in her case [my research assistant, Teófila], we are already ladies. We are leaving everything behind. The traditions, native to our environment. Not just selling like this in the market. It might be a mestiza señora who has married an *hacendado* [landed estate owner]. Then she's at the *hacienda.* The gentleman likes to see his woman as he

has known her, but with more elegant clothes, with jewelry, with all that, with a watch, with her bracelets, to present her to his friends. Now, for example, in our case, in my case, in her case, she is working. To go out in the street, she has to make herself more elegant, if she goes to a gathering, she has to put on her jewelry. She has to know how to comport herself. This is the middle class, which we are.

Linda: Is it the same with men?

Dori: The native *campesino*, the Indian *campesino*, he knows what he does. He gets himself a woman. He marries from his parents. This man is completely responsible. Because woman and man, *campesinos,* have to work rock. From that they work, they obtain their sustenance. They raise their children. They make two sets of clothing a year, for Christmas in December or January, and for the Day of the Indian in June. His wife makes him his clothes. But he never accompanies her like a mestizo, by the arm, by the hand. Four or five steps ahead, the man, and behind, the woman. It's as if he didn't notice her.

You should go to some villages. The native Indian is very responsible as long as he is working the land. But his aspirations are minimal, his reach reduced, in accordance with his environment. His environment is very narrow, his training (capability), very limited. The mestiza looks, measures up a lady, wants to learn, modalities, well, she progresses a little. *Cholo, cholo, cholo,* is that one stretched out on the ground after drinking. Nothing matters to him. That's a *cholo.* He takes no responsibility for anything, not in society, not even in the environment that surrounds him.

In this exchange, dress is clearly perceived by Dori as an indicator of status. *Bayeta* skirts are made of homespun wool and associated with *campesinas;* many *polleras,* in contrast, are made of synthetic material and combed wool and indicate movement toward a higher status. The *montera* indicates proximity to native roots, whereas a tall, white stovepipe hat indicates occupational specialization and entry into the ranks of being the mestiza. Wearing Western clothes and either a straw hat or, better yet, no hat indicates the highest status of all. That these signs of status are actively manipulated by everyone and that there is a fluidity such that people escape from categories that others consider static contributes to the enormous ambiguity that surrounds the positioning of vendors in their varied skirts and hats, sometimes in pants, and always with their money purses hidden away.[5]

Mary Weismantel (2001:126), in her provocative book *Cholas and Pishtacos,* remarks that "like their tongue-in-cheek verbal performances, the market women's exuberant clothing styles perform race and sex as improvisational collages constantly subject to revision: they thus undermine the notion that the social order that exists, must be." It is this characteristic of market women that perplexes, angers, and sometimes attracts or arouses those who find it both tantalizing and discomfiting to encounter people who defy easy categorization in terms of their sex, race, or class.

Dori's statements also resonate philosophically with both nineteenth-century unilinear evolutionary theory and the Enlightenment notion that experience and environment have the capacity to transform to a more progressive or degenerate state. Her views incorporate voluntarism and emphasis on education: Willpower and proper training permit one to accept or reject tradition and the behaviors associated with it. There is also a subtle but definite ideal of patriarchy that runs throughout her account, at odds with her views of the emasculated *cholo*. A proper woman conforms to the expectations of her husband. Her entire account assumes and depends on her own position in the hierarchy of appropriate behaviors that correlate with being a *campesina, chola, cholo,* mestiza, or *dama*.

Domérica Hermoza also stresses education, but she rejects hypocrisy. In my long conversation with Domérica it became clear that she does not fuse class and race. Rather, she argues that one can be lower class, well educated, and therefore not consigned to an inferior race. Likewise, if one is lower class and poorly educated, one is simply being crass and sadly ignorant (not playful) in acting as if one is not a peasant: "The difference lies in education. Some people in Lima pretend that they are otherwise, not *cholas* or *campesinas*. They put on different clothes and makeup. But then, it turns out that they need help because they can't read anything. They are living a fantasy. And in the countryside, some women won't even use anything for their periods. They just have blood dripping down."

Virginia Lenes Tacuri runs a little dried goods stall. Her views are less common but reveal a growing recognition that there are no criteria that essentially distinguish Peruvians from one another. At the same time, the prevailing assumption is that being a *campesino* means a lack of education. Also, over and over again, economic class and ethnic identity are considered inseparable: "As far as social classes go, for me there's no difference between being a *chola* and a mestiza because today even the *campesinos* have risen by going to schools and high schools." The ambiguity in the observations of Virginia and Domérica is whether someone ceases to be a *campesina* or simply rises and becomes respectable within that category by mimicking the behavior and lifestyles of mestizos.

Another prevalent view of race relations among market women is that everyone is equal—they are all Peruvians or they are all mestizos—and that Peruvians throw around insulting labels when they do not get what they want. Often, this view is backed up by religious fervor, more often among Evangelicals than among Catholics. Marina Ordoña, the Evangelical wholesaler of used clothes, describes her position: "I can't really say what these terms mean . . . because we are all a mestiza race. We are a mixture. There are people who believe in trying to humiliate others with little knowledge, but it should not be that way. I do not like to insult people or treat them badly. The Bible says that we should not make differences among people, 'not even a bite of potato [of difference].' We should accept differences among people. These terms are the result of people who use them as insults because they consider themselves superior. But before God, we are all equal. Well, our ancestors spoke Quechua. They were Indians. Maybe they still have Quechua, their dress. Perhaps, that is why they use these terms if they themselves no longer speak Quechua or dress like that. But we should not treat people that way. We should treat them well."

Marta Hernández, a young woman who was selling manioc at a furious rate from a stall outside the central market, protested when I suggested that perhaps these labels had something to do with the way people dressed. Rather, she thought they had to do with people's behavior and occupation. "No, I consider myself mestiza because I work in the market. It has nothing to do with my dress. Who are *cholas*? No one should be made into a *chola*. All of us are equal. *Chola* is an insult. People call those who come from the highlands *cholas*. They are *campesinos,* but people try to talk about them this way. *Campesinos* are rebels. They act quickly, they have something to do, they come here quickly, they leave quickly, those from the highlands. Some of the people from Cuzco are bad. They want more manioc, they don't want the smaller ones and they pay no attention to the quality. If they can't get exactly what they want, they leave."

Given these views about race, class, and gender relations held by market women, it is important to remember that most of them are simply going about their everyday activities, making a living. They may see things more simply than those who observe them. It is important not to underestimate the extraordinary power that emanates from feeling socially comfortable. That is, the market women who sit near each other day after day, year after year, watching the traffic and people, have created an environment that is familiar to them and somewhat predictable. They know what to expect even when it is sometimes unpleasant. This kind of comforting structure often allows other kinds of potentially divisive attitudes and behaviors to remain submerged. When the environment itself is threatened, however, these potential fissures may become exacerbated or become even less significant, depending on the issue in question.

How market women perceive themselves, their dress, their activities, and their actions often differ from how others perceive them. This tension between education, an open society, and voluntarism on one hand and the essentialist nature of culture on the other hand is apparent among peasants as well. I had a long conversation with Leonarda Rimachi, a poor itinerant vendor who was selling small bunches of medicinal herbs on the ground along Ejército. When I asked her how she viewed herself, she said uncertainly, "We *campesinos* all work in the countryside, right? Maybe I am a *chola*. We have our traditional dress, right, that we wear at fiestas. When we are invited sometimes to come to the plaza in Cuzco wearing our traditional costumes, we come as *cholas*." This woman articulates clearly how perception has everything to do with what one is called and what one wears. She really does not know what to call herself and does not feel the need to call herself anything. She considers herself a *campesina* but knows that Cuzqueños consider her a folkloric and seductive *chola* when, decked out in her fancy clothes and jewelry, she is invited to participate in traditional dances in Cuzco's central Plaza de Armas, a custom that various mayors have encouraged, particularly during electoral campaigns. Her aspiration is simply to be unmarked, but she knows that in the society of which

Leonarda Rimachi, itinerant vendor of herbs in Cuzco, 1998. She considers herself a campesina.

she is a part, she is variably labeled according to her public presentation of self and how it is viewed.

Natalia Linares sells dogs, cats, birds, pigs, and rabbits as an itinerant vendor on Prolongación Pera, right above Polvos Celestes. She conflates territorial affiliation and education in her assessment of who is who: "I think that with respect to social classes, being a *chola* or a *campesina* is the same because both come from 'pueblos,' whereas the mestizo is someone who has knowledge and experience."

What is striking about the many variations on the race theme discussed here is the persistence of linking particular social statuses to territory and dress. In a similar vein, anthropologist Benjamin Orlove, in a perceptive article, "Down to Earth: Race and Substance in the Andes," reflects on the ways in which material substances, such as items made from dirt—roads, adobes, ceramic pots, and fields—are integral to how Andean people think about themselves and the racial categories in which others place them. Yet, as he points out, the relationships between human beings and earth substances are not always fixed, either, and the value judgments made about these relationships vary according to how people define production, exchange, citizenship, and nation building. In his words (1998:217–19),

> Since the earth has many attributes, it lends itself to different interpretations, much as racial ideologies, with their complex histories and contradictory political manifestations, tend toward different expressions. . . . Mestizos stress the low and contaminating qualities of the earth, the Indians its permanence and strength, different views of the same racial images. . . . These linkages between race and earth carry particular force in the altiplano because the earth is present in many ways. . . . In addition to knowing that fields lie near these towns, the mestizos can see from everywhere in town the bare surfaces of hills and mountains, greenish brown in the rainy season, yellowish brown at other times of year. The presence of the earth is made even more immediate by the importance of agriculture in the regional economy and by the importance of root crops, especially potatoes, in the diet.
>
> If the two groups agree on the greater proximity of Indians to the earth, they also agree on a complementary object. The mestizos are closer than the Indians to the nation. The adobe bricks made by a household contrast with purchased adobe bricks, purchased with money, with the national currency—connection with a national economy, interregional trade. For mestizos, roads are part of a single national network able to link (*comunicar*). To Indians, the same roads are a product of their labour, a part of the territory of the villages.

So what does this mean about those who are from the countryside but live in the city in the fragile concrete and adobe dwellings that creep up Cuzco's hillsides? What does it mean about the women of the markets, many of whom are bilingual and who invest in their children's education? The children of vendors who have been successful at the retail and wholesale levels often extend their reach internationally and become entrepreneurs and students in Argentina, Bolivia, Venezuela, the United States, and different parts of Europe, especially the northern countries. They acquire a valuable comparative perspective on race relations that they can then share with their parents. What does it mean about market women's willingness to give their relatives and paisanos from their natal villages a better deal, sometimes bartering with products but also striving to cultivate long-term relationships with lady housewives (who look down on them) through their servants, who place a premium on the exchange of currency because they have little else to offer?

Clean glasses and enamel dishes are the pride of market women who serve their *picante* and *chicha* in these containers to traveling *campesinos* in their rubber tire sandals and slick contraband dealers in their high heels. What does it mean when these women gradually experience the life of the street, the unwarranted abuses to which they are subjected by municipal authorities and come to recognize that politicians and labor unions alike cultivate their loyalty as pawns? And, finally, what does it mean as they struggle to make an economic go of it and learn to do it partly on the backs of other vendors who are less well established? The fluidity of which Orlove speaks and within which the market women live means that race relations and racial ideologies are exceedingly hard to pin down, yet they are obviously present as market women pick their way through mazes constructed from centuries of social engineering even as the exigencies of daily life constantly challenge these constructions.

It would not make sense to fix in concrete these race relations, as I discovered the hard way after observing life in the streets and conducting hundreds of interviews. Market women do not see themselves in a static position. Neither do *campesinos*. The only people who really see themselves in a static position are mestizos anxious to protect their social terrain from incursions. But they are in an impossible position. Although particular aspects of the demeanor, occupations, and phenotypes of some Peruvians may encourage racial prejudice that lies just below the surface, these signs are deceptive, hardly trustworthy or permanent indicators of someone's status or "race." In the realm of hardball politics, the rhetorical discourse of idealized *cholas* hardly corresponds to the images that market women have of themselves as entrepreneurs in the marketplace, struggling to make a living or to improve the future of their children. Nevertheless, market women may actively take advantage of publicly circulating images and perceptions of market women as *cholas* in order to get what they want, and Peruvians as a whole may buy into the image as a quintessential and distinctive indicator of what constitutes Peruvian culture. Certainly, the current president of Peru, Alejandro Toledo, used these images to his advantage as a World Bank economist who was the son of an Indian mother who spoke Quechua and a father who was a shoeshine vendor. It is an open question whether the disjuncture between images of *cholas* and their reality will ever become so great that the images no longer appeal within a language of cultural and political, gendered nationalism. In the meantime, racism thrives gingerly as more and more Peruvians do not stay where they belong. Rather, they are willing to take social and economic risks to defend their terrain, whether it is the right to occupy a stall and sell a small pile of potatoes, to speak Quechua and proudly wear their *bayeta* skirts or embroidered shawls in a café, or to demand what is their due as citizens, using education, the vote, the law, strikes, and demonstrations.

Notes

Portions of this chapter are paraphrased or reprinted from my article "To Be in Between: The Cholas as Market Women in Peru," *Comparative Studies in Society and History* 31:4 (1989): 694–721.

1. An interesting systematic example of this disjuncture between self-perception and social perception, both of which are partially shaped by the social and institutional history of race, can be found at the beginning of José María Arguedas's *Yawar Fiesta* (1985:vii–ix). Translator Frances Barraclough provides a rough schema of racial classifications as they are used in Arguedas's book, divided into how "the upper class," "mestizos," and "Indians" call themselves, respectively, and are called by others.

2. This notion, promoted by Hernando de Soto (1989) in his popular and controversial book *The Other Path*—that if Peru eliminates red tape and taps into the hundreds of thousands of "extralegal" entrepreneurs, making them legal, it will be well on its way to healthy economic development—does not address how race and racial perceptions play a role in social stratification.

3. Personal communication with Zoila Mendoza-Walker, November 2000.

4. Robert Albro (1997, 2000) has written several thoughtful pieces on how politicians in Bolivia have used rhetorical images and discourse to capture the votes of *cholas* in regional campaigns, conceptualizing them as the key to a coherent regional identity, whereas *cholas* themselves appear to be leaping out of these nostalgic and stereotypical images. See chapter 10 for more details on perceptions of *cholas* and populist rhetoric of politicians.

5. Gill (1994:104–6) explains how *cholas* don clothing, including *polleras,* which are gathered skirts, to distinguish themselves from Hispanicized mestizos and from rural *campesinos.* In her words, "The latest Aymara fashions are the contemporary manifestations of an ongoing historical process in which contending groups not only create new cultural forms, but also detach older styles from their original context, transplant them to new settings, and give them new or slightly different meanings. Many of the elements of a contemporary urban Aymara woman's wardrobe—a gathered skirt (*pollera*), shawl, derby hat, embroidered blouse, special jewelry, and shoes—are viewed by paceños of all social classes as being uniquely Aymara. Yet sixteenth-century provincial Spanish women were the first to wear the forerunners of these styles in the Americas."

9

Angels and Saints: Popular Religiosity

The pulsating world of popular religiosity in the Andes is apparent to any tourist who strolls the streets of Cuzco. Almost every day, one festival or another is under way, announced by parades, music, and dancing. For market vendors, religiosity occupies a space in which many different processes unfold that are set off but not separated from their daily affairs. In this chapter, I look at how the religiosity of market vendors explicitly involves the organization of their space and their understanding and use of the etiquette of exchange and its transgressive dimensions. The fiestas in which vendors participate replicate transnational dimensions of local marketing while they introduce potential paths for experimentation with new identities and challenges to existing ones. Commentaries on gendered ideologies through cross-dressing also weave in and out of these ritual occasions. Finally, a principal subtext of these fiestas is the tension between popular religiosity and institutionalized Catholicism.[1]

Michael Kearney (1996:62), an anthropologist who has been in the forefront of questioning the kinds of categories that Western social scientists have developed over the years to define peasants, notes that "informal economic activities are categorically subversive by defying official definitions of identity." The rich religious lives of the vendors with whom I became acquainted also subvert these official and often scholarly definitions. Market vendors do not seem to trouble themselves with wondering or worrying about the consistency and coherence of their religiosity. Their identities are manifold, and their religiosity incorporates "a veritable smorgasbord of cultural signs and values emanating from globally diverse sources" (Kearney 1996:62). This mix, far from being chaotic, as I try to show in this chapter, makes sense of the flows and rhythms, structures of stratification, institutional obstacles and possibilities, and pitfalls and windfalls that constitute the street lives of the market women of Cuzco.

Religiosity among market vendors includes several different genres, the most public of which are fiestas. Each section of the market celebrates its own saint day in festivities that last at least four days and often up to two weeks. In addition, many vendors actively collaborate with and participate in other urban fiestas. A few also play significant roles in fiestas that take place in their home towns. Wholesalers, especially the ones who deal in meat and potatoes, often are powerful sponsors of fiestas in the rural communities from which they obtain their products.

Another genre constitutes the highly individual decision of each vendor to designate a particular saint or virgin ("lady"), God, or Jesus as her protector to whom she can turn in need. This genre usually includes evidence of "miracles" that the protector has performed. Although it is somewhat different, I include here private acts of faith that draw from a native rural ritual complex that thrives with some transformations in the city.

A third genre, and here I run the risk of generalizing, consists of Protestant Evangelical faiths. Protestant Evangelicals place less emphasis on public, collective performances and reject the pantheon of saints and virgins. Instead, they place their faith fully and directly in God, Jesus, or the Virgin Mary and read the Bible in their homes as a family or in small group meetings in churches or houses of other Evangelicals. Many Evangelicals also participate in fiestas and individual forms of faith but in a somewhat different fashion, as we will see. For example, they abstain from drinking and dancing but may nevertheless walk in processions and assist in sponsoring fiestas. Although it is difficult to disentangle distinct motivations, the participation of Evangelicals in Catholic fiestas is more a social strategy rather than a religious act of faith.

Performances and Pragmatics: The Logic of Fiestas

There is a long tradition of studying religious faith, rituals, and fiestas in the Andean highlands. Catherine Allen (1988), Joseph Bastien (1978), and Inge Bolin (1998) have explored generally how rituals and celebrations perpetuate the distinctive identities of Andean highland dwellers, regenerating a cosmology and sacred geography that has its roots in pre-Inca practices. Although they do not pay much attention to changing social and political contexts—economic differentiation, migration, or the effects of colonialism—they nevertheless give us a sense of the complexity of Andean worldviews. Their work helps us recognize how more recently introduced beliefs and practices of Catholics (beginning in the colonial period) and Evangelical Protestants (beginning in the 1970s) have been interpreted or at times juxtaposed to an ideal native cosmological template.

David Guss (2000) offers a very different understanding of ritual in the Andes that allows us to grasp better the dynamic character of Andean religiosity. He shows how distinct fiestas in Venezuela, over time, are simultaneously viewed and used by participants and promoters for different purposes, some unintended, and may initially be experimented with spontaneously. Even when these purposes vary greatly, they often do not cause conflict. Occasionally, however, they generate debate and rancor. State agents may see fiestas as a sensible way to achieve a cohesive sense of nationalism; indigenous communities or intellectuals may view fiestas as sites of religiosity and as a way to revitalize native identities and reinvent traditions. Multinational corporations may encourage dance workshops and folkloric events to establish legitimacy and respect for their brand names in order to increase consumption. The beauty of Guss's treatment is that he shows how these striated and polysemic occasions, which change substantially over time, reveal a remarkable fluidity without becoming unrecognizable as particular fiestas or spectacles. These very qualities contribute to the power of fiestas.

Yet another view of Andean religiosity is provided by the contributors to a fine provocative special issue of the *Journal of Latin American Anthropology* (JLAA), "Performance, Identity and Historical Consciousness in the Andes," edited by Mark Rogers (1998). Like Guss, the contributors discuss how different kinds of ritual performances enact and comment on conflicted identities. To understand how ritual performance draws on, makes statements about, and constitutes different kinds of identities, context becomes critical. If the performance itself can be read as a text, that text can only be read well and carefully in light of context. As Stuart Rockefeller (1998:135, 136) puts it so well, "Context is what generates the possible meaning of a text. The context of a performance includes not only proximate events, but events in the past, previous performances, and possible expectations of the performance's outcome. . . . Context also has a tendency to efface itself. . . . Context is to a certain extent ineffable. . . . This ineffability is not an issue only for investigators . . . it is one of the key means by which folkloric representation gains its power over participants and audience. When a performance is moved from one kind of situation to another, it is easiest for all concerned to see what the represented practice and its representation have in common, while the differences, partly because they are so many and have such an uncertain relationship to what is being represented, tend to draw into the background, which makes it easy, almost unavoidable, to identify whatever messages the new context carries with the forefronted aspects of the representation."

Many a tourist or traveling student of religion in the Andes who participates in new age shamanic tours identifies this ineffability as spirituality, perhaps because of their own search for meaning in life. My interviews with vendors and my own participation in fiestas suggest almost (though not quite) the opposite: There is a weighty materiality to this ineffability. Movements, symbols, colors, music, costumes, and space itself speak loudly, sometimes directly, many times indirectly, to onlookers and participants at these events. At the same time, as Rockefeller found, context includes memories of how performances were done in the past, with whom participants celebrated, and personal markers of life cycles and life stages, such as the absence or death of people who had always been actively involved in the fiesta activities.

Fiesta performances and their attendant context are interactive, and their interpretation rests on the perspective and positioning of participants. Performances require participation, but the vantage points of the performers and participants or receptors vary greatly. Bringing together memories, activities, and meanings from different domains contributes to the potential that fiestas offer for experimentation. Rockefeller clarifies that no single individual, anthropologist or not, can completely analyze a fiesta performance. Where one is situated has everything to do with how one makes sense of a performance. Furthermore, the very materiality of ineffable context means that the newness of costumes, choreography, and music or of changing relationships between participants in the popular fiesta and the church hierarchy may hardly be evident to those who are younger or are newcomers. There is also usually too much going on for a person to take in everything that is happening. Fiestas themselves resemble open-ended systems, even as they remain patterned and recognizable.

Faith

For market vendors, faith is very much a part of context that generates the fiesta. To have faith is critical to the possibility of having a good year economically. Faith is embedded in the performance itself. One must have faith, or whatever fiesta one participates in or sponsors will not do one much good. Vendors who want to participate in or sponsor a fiesta must have a fount of social relations to activate the resources necessary to bring off a good show, but if they do not have faith, it is highly unlikely that they will reap economic and social rewards.

I stress this point because both publicly displayed and privately held religious faith is sometimes too simply understood as fatalism: If good things happen, God has willed it; if bad things happen, it is God's will that we endure it. However, in most of my conversations with market women, they never stated the second part of this definition. They did attribute good things to God's will or to the protection of the saint images they cared for especially. For example, Melchora Rayo's husband was killed in an accident. She explained, "When he was killed, I faced real problems and was very sorrowful. But I know we will never be lacking and our stomachs will always be filled with the blessing of *taytacha* ["the little father," referring to God]." Or take Victoria Quispe's view of her religious faith: "I believe in the Señor de Los Milagros ["Our Lord of Miracles," an important saint image who protects people from earthquakes, a common occurrence in the Andes]. I believe more in Jesus Christ. I have great faith in him. I ask him for things. I always have business. He never leaves me in the street." Bad luck and bad things happen to everyone, it seems, but faith in particular saints, God, or the Virgin Mary may protect Melchora Rayo or Victoria Quispe and even allow them to experience unexpected good fortune.

In another example of the link between the miracles of faith and fiestas, the principal sponsors (known as *mayordomos*) of Mamacha Asunta, the festival celebrating Our Lady of the Assumption on August 15, had been singled out because of their miraculous or healing powers. People who sponsor different aspects of a fiesta are said to "have a *cargo*." This *cargo* is considered both a burden and an honor. Principal sponsors are expected to provide the food and drink for a fiesta. Lesser sponsors may finance clothing for saint images, music, and costumes.[2] In this case, a woman who longed to have a daughter had twin girls after seventeen years of being barren, and her twins served as principal sponsors one year; the year before, she herself was the main sponsor. Amilcar, a man whose reputation has spread far and wide for his ability to cure diabetes using an herbal remedy rather than insulin, also served as the main sponsor for Mamacha one year. "Tener fe"—"to have faith"—is repeated frequently by market women as they encounter harsh life conditions, reap unexpected profits, are spared in violent robberies, or recover from near-death illnesses.

Most of the contributors to the JLAA volume veer between urban performances and rural performances, between "indios" and "mestizos" (or whites), between the matrices of rural and urban and of modern and traditional. They do not oppose them to one another but rather demonstrate the ambivalent, contradictory, and enriching ways in which identity unfolds. The religious practices of market vendors occupy the space knitting together these constructs

and racial ideologies. While participating in fiestas, I found written into the
urban landscape permutations of rural fiestas but also could see evidence of
transnational capital—symbolic, political, and economic—spilling over into
the streets, churches, and plazas.

Rockefeller (1998:121–22) sharply distinguishes between "fiesta" and "festi-

*Procession of Mamacha Asunta, 1998. Notice the fruit surrounding her
pedestal. Photograph by John R. Cooper.*

val." For him, fiestas are "celebrations, normally in some sense religious, organized by the campesinos." Festivals are "representations of what are taken to be the most significant performative elements of the fiestas. These representations are performed by the same people who would sing and dance in fiestas, but in the folklore festivals they do so in front of an audience." Market vendors' celebrations of saint days in urban areas combine elements of fiestas and festivals. They are neither traditional rural fiestas nor folkloric festivals that represent fiestas as public spectacles of performance. Their fiestas are potently religious, and there is little way to be "outside" the events that transpire over a two-week period. Many vendors and working-class people just watch the action; plenty of tourists find these festivals fascinating and enjoy themselves but understand little of their meaning. The mostly middle- and upper-middle-class Cuzqueños who look down on these popular spectacles of the street do their best to ignore or denigrate the entire event, although some take advantage of their ties to particular sponsors, supporting them in their sponsorship, because they have a personal relationship with them and know that they will receive favors in the form of lower prices or better produce in the future.

Saints

Mamacha Asunta (Our Lady of the Assumption)

I was asking Dori, one of the tomato queens who held a monopoly over the tomato market for so many years, how she had become so well established as a vendor when I heard the sound of a brass band. Dori, noting my distraction, ushered me out of her store. "Go, go," she said. "They are doing the *diana*." I asked her what the *diana* was and she patiently explained, "They will dress the Virgin for the mass tomorrow and decide who will take over the *cargo* [sponsorship] for next year." I hurried to join the procession, loving the thumping percussion and brass of the band. It reminded me of the pied piper. In front two raggedy porters carried an enormous wicker basket piled high with many kinds of fruit. Behind them followed the principal sponsor of this year's fiesta, along with many of the past *mayordomos* of the fiesta, most of whom were older women. They helped carry Mamacha ("Dear Little Mother") Asunta's clothes: her various velvet and thickly woven gold brocade capes and gowns. In their midst were the two twins, carrying the *demanda,* a small silver image of the Virgin. The twins had been offered the *demanda,* and their acceptance of it signaled that they had agreed to take on the burden of sponsorship for the next year. Behind the sponsors trailed the faithful, holding ornate, tall, flickering candles painted with gold leaf. Bringing up the rear were the stragglers like me who wanted to tag along. For me, it was a powerful sensation to walk through the normally congested streets and, without the presence of a single policeman, have all the vehicles stop to let us pass. Faithful spectators watched us in silence while hundreds of tourists snapped away with their cameras.

The dignified procession wended its way to the massive cathedral in the Plaza de Armas. At the cathedral, chaos erupted. The priest refused to allow the procession to enter the church, saying that it would disturb the tourists who were there. To each side of the cathedral are two smaller chapels. Finally, the priest let us into the smaller chapel, Triunfo, although he refused to allow the band inside. At that point, the ugly tension exploded. A nondescript woman dressed in typical market woman garb protested to all who would listen that the Virgin's clothes were not supposed to be changed until August 16. It was August 6, the beginning of the Novena for the Virgin. For nine days, masses were to be said for the Virgin. The woman belonged to the vegetable section, which shares the celebration of Mamacha with the potato, fruit, and onion sections. The fruit ladies section had been preparing to garb the Virgin in her new garments. The priest backed the vegetable lady. After many protests from the fruit ladies and their relatives, he finally relented and told the fruit ladies they could not dress the Virgin until 5 P.M., after the tourists left. The men and women argued with him, repeating that they had always done it this way and there was no reason they should have to wait. It was their Virgin. The vegetable lady intervened again, insisting that the candles from last year also not be removed. An uproar ensued, compounded by the priest's insistence that no candles at all be lit because they would blacken the ceiling and wax would drip onto the floor. The group tried in vain to reach a compromise with the priest by putting plastic under the huge stone candle holders, but the priest dismissed the suggestion, telling them they would have to use metal sheets. The argument intensified. One of the spokesmen for the group insisted, "We have done this for 450 years," and he queried, "Why doesn't the church have enough money from what they charge the tourists to provide a means for us to light the candles as we always have?" Things finally settled down. The vegetable lady left. The priest disappeared. The fruit women moved to an alcove in the recesses of the cathedral, where they began dressing a miniature Virgin image. They brought her out and set her down next to the huge Virgin. Then they all began dressing the huge image. They removed her outerwear until she was left in her underclothes. They proceeded to layer her again with new clothes, including a fine deep red velvet and gold brocade cape. Last year's towering candles were removed and replaced with new ones. They placed a sterling crown on Mamacha's head and adorned the entire area around her feet with the fruit that the porters had carried from the market. Everyone commented on how lovely the huge squash was. Strings of tangerines and oranges, bananas, custard fruit, melons, papayas, grapes, apples, and lemons draped the Virgin. Twelve tall vases of flowers, mostly lilies and light orange gladiolas, were placed around the images. The priest reappeared to complain that the fruit ladies were getting the floor filthy with all their confetti.

Their duties done, the sponsors gathered to discuss what had transpired. One argued, "We have remained silent too long and should speak out." Most of the others present seemed to agree with her. Another woman suggested, "We should compete with the vegetable section and show them that the fruit section can outdo them." Another woman responded, "That would not be a wise course of action. What counts is doing things with complete faith." Most of the women nodded their heads in agreement with her.

The overwhelming participation of women as sponsors for this fiesta differs from what happens generally in the countryside. There, mostly men hold sponsorships, and brotherhoods (*cofradías*) still exist that control different parcels of land. The crops from these lands fund the costs of sponsorship for the men. The exclusion of women from fiesta or ritual sponsorship is a substantial change imposed by the Spanish when they colonized the Quechua people. Gender and sexuality took a turn toward patriarchy, whereas under the Incas women had significant ritual responsibilities and held political offices, and native deities were male, female, and androgynous. The participation of women in the fruit or vegetable section as sponsors and bearers of the saint images is analogous to sisterhoods that hark back to Inca times. In these urban settings, just as is true of the brotherhoods in the countryside, faith and control over resources feed each other.[3]

When the caretaker began turning out the lights, we were forced to leave the church. The rocky beginning of the fiesta for Mamacha Asunta speaks directly to how a very local display of religiosity becomes inextricably entangled in the affairs of state and of an economy extending far beyond the control of the market vendors. The church as tourist attraction, revenue generator, and symbol of participation in the modern world directly confronts the veneration of Mamacha Asunta as a conduit of faith, status marking, and well-being, an anchor of decency, and hedonistic abandon through celebratory dance, food, and drink.

The next morning two masses, one at 6 and another at 6:30, at the cathedral ushered in the Novena of Mamacha Asunta. Each of the nine morning masses preceding the day of the fiesta itself had a sponsor, as did every single aspect of the fiesta. I got up very early the next morning to attend the 6 A.M.

mass. It was lovely walking to the cathedral with the rosy dawn glimmering over Cuzco. Many people were already gathered at the church. I am not Catholic but nervously went through the motions. The singing of the choir was ethereal. In such a peaceful setting, intermingled among the anguished images of the suffering of Christ and the unblemished, unperturbed Virgin images, faith made sense. The two candles that had replaced those from last year flickered brightly. The priest's commentary was punctuated by loud firecrackers being set off outside. After the priest's homily, the mood abruptly changed. The priest told the story of Saint Anthony of Padua, who, as a child, encountered another little boy who was a beggar. Antonio offered the beggar everything—food, clothing, and shelter—but the beggar said he did not want anything. Then the beggar opened his suitcase. Inside, it was filled with hearts. The beggar told him, "All I want is your heart." The priest berated the full church, telling them, "These external displays of paganism are worthless, pure garbage. What really counts is your inner faith. In other places, these external displays have been prohibited, but I have not yet prohibited them here. From this point on, there will be no fireworks set off from the ground. The image of Asunta will have to be moved to the Cathedral or you will not be able to light the candles. And what kind of faith do you have, coming late to the mass?" Over and over, he repeated his critique of their "pagan displays" and their "lack of faith," ending with a nasty, resounding commentary on the behavior of the fruit women: "You should be leaving gifts for the church. You never leave anything though you have always promised. The vegetable ladies, in contrast, have given to the church. They gave one of the pews and something else, I cannot remember."

I was sitting near the front of the church, and as the priest continued his strident remarks, I turned my head to see how many people had come to this mass. Despite how early it was and how disruptive attending a mass on a weekday is to people's work schedules in the markets, the entire church was filled with so-called pagans. In the early days of colonial battle by the Spanish priests for people's hearts and souls, there tended to be more tolerance for accepting indigenous practices as variants of the Catholic faith. Perhaps that was because the indigenous faithful were few in number. Today they are not obviously indigenous; they number in the hundreds of thousands in Cuzco alone and are among the most devout on their own terms. They also are not particularly fond of using money, whose power they understand full well, to shore up the church hierarchy, although they pay for the masses and keep the Virgin images well dressed.

When the mass ended, we walked outside, and the church quickly filled up for the second early morning mass. Outside huge cauldrons of alcoholic punch and soup were steaming away in the chilly dawn, stirred by the sponsors. We sat on long benches, someone sprinkled us with confetti, and the sponsors served us punch with sugar wafers, followed by a special soup called *adobo* and bread. This feast lasted hours. The sponsors served up enough food for the hundred or more people gathered in an organized display of power. All of the men were hefty and wore leather jackets. One had a motorcycle. Most of the women had abandoned their market clothes and wore suits and high heels instead. In a kind of wonderful defiance, they took the priest's admonishments literally yet obeyed him subversively, with some risk to themselves. Rather than lighting the firecrackers on the ground, they threw them, already lit, into the air, an act that produced a hugely loud, explosive display. I couldn't help but chuckle.

On August 14, the eve of the procession, the Virgin was garbed in a different outfit. A flashy and dangerous display of Catherine wheel fireworks in front of the cathedral took place: whirling wheels, a funny man that moved its arms and legs, airplanes, helicopters, shooting rockets, and shimmering splashes of gold, silver, blue, red, and yellow. The fireworks are considered to be a gift sent by devotees to Mamacha heavenward. It was a miracle that a fire didn't start or that someone was not seriously injured as some of the fireworks bounced off the roofs of buildings or landed near the gathered crowd. The band played European, Bolivian, and Peruvian music in front of the chapel where the sponsors stood.

A tall "market woman" watched over the beginning of the evening's pyrotechnics. She wore traditional dress—a tall stovepipe hat—with a carrying cloth around her shoulders. In fact, though, she was a man whose responsibility was to watch the crowd, keep order, usher in the fireworks, and perform like a clown. "Her" costume crystallized the bricolage that constitutes the identity of many market women as manly women and Indian *cholas* who assert themselves in a manner generally considered masculine, and in displays of ribald humor they buffer themselves from the hostility with which many of them are regarded. Mary Weismantel (2001) addresses the issue of transvestism and cross-dressing among market women at length, noting that rather than embracing virility because they wish they were men, thereby conforming to the patriarchal ideology that reigns in Peru, market women are doing something quite different.

She notes that market women are noted for transgressive behaviors equated with fertility, such as having children without husbands and, through their economic roles, contributing indirectly to fertility through the exchange of commodities rather than being commodities themselves, "there for the taking" by men for sexual purposes. In this particular instance, however, it was not a question of a woman dressing as a man but rather a man dressing up as a *chola* market woman. His behavior both satirized the behavior and costume of market women and challenged the dominant schema of socioracial and gender hierarchy that prevails in Peru. The medium of performance allows for political satire of the androgynous qualities of many market women and for this bricolage of cross-dressing and contradictory behavior to be enacted and explicitly acknowledged by participants and spectators alike.

For the next day's procession, both Virgin images were sprayed with perfume and sprinkled with rose petals and their faces carefully painted with makeup. They slowly exited the cathedral,[4] led by two groups of dancers. The first, made up of men dressed in silky blue shirts and pants, with bells on their calves, and of girls in miniskirts, danced the *tun tuna,* a modern splashy dance step that came to Cuzco from Puno, near the Bolivian border. The second dance group was the Qollachas from the Cuzco area. Among the Qollachas and Tun Tunas stomped the *ukukus,* half-bear, half-men, who occasionally blew on their ocarinas, and an *oso,* an enormous bear in sneakers.[5] Despite its enormous size, the bear was really a woman rather than a man, again drawing attention, perhaps, to how the vendors, as women in public places, constitute a threat because of their boundary crossings. The *ukukus* and the bear were responsible for controlling the crowd. The simultaneous association of the "uncivilized" with nonhuman and "civilized" with humans as a gendered gradient is apparent in these impersonations, where reversal is also part of the commentary projected: Those who are not fully human, whether men or women, impose and ensure order among humans by calling attention to "ideal" social structure.

A band of violins, trumpets, and drums followed the dancers. The past, present, and future *mayordomos* and the *demanda* preceded the small Virgin carried by women. The Virgin image, larger than life-size, standing on its pedestal, was carried by the men bringing up the rear. The procession moved slowly toward San Pedro, stopping periodically so that everyone could rest. The dedicated dancers had remarkable energy and stamina. Throughout the year, the dance groups watch videos of other dancers and practice. Some travel to other regions to watch other dancers perform. Many of them own their own costumes. All are fairly young, most the sons and daughters of fruit vendors. One has to be invited to join a dance group, so it is considered an honor. The dancers' participation in these groups for years constitutes a critical form of socialization.

Once we got to the market, we passed through makeshift arches, and the bystanders began throwing fruit, especially oranges and lemons, into the procession. These are intended as gifts to Mamacha and provide much-needed juice to quench the thirst of those in the procession. At almost noon, healer, former sponsor, and vendor Amilcar began distributing little plates of cheese and olives. The procession began moving again. At various points, the large Mamacha was sprinkled with rose petals and given gifts of carnations and fruit, for which she curtsied, leaning forward and then back, swaying as the sponsors holding her on her litter strained to keep their balance. A friend of mine noticed wryly, "Not a single ecclesiastical authority is present." The procession swelled with past and present sponsors, relatives, fictive kin, those who had contributed in large and small ways to making the fiesta successful, and the many faithful. The fiesta activates social networks, and I was impressed by the organizational skills needed to make it a success. In addition to drawing on social capital, the sponsors had to know exactly what kinds of goods were needed—candles, fireworks, bands, costumes, food, drink, clothes for the *mamachas,* carriers of the images, bread, sponsors for the masses—and all of these resources had to be supplied over a period of nine or ten days.

The procession continued past the San Pedro market. The sponsors, carrying slender yellow candles, made me feel protected, and they expressed their pleasure that I had joined the faithful. They asked whether this was my first time. I told them it was my first time in the city but that I had celebrated Mamacha Asunta's fiesta in the countryside. We continued all the way to the Belem Pampa bridge, under which Avenida Ejército stretches like a river of dust and fumes. I had rarely seen women serve as litter bearers. While those watching laughed and threw food, no one in the procession was laughing. Serious, focused on their faith, they prayed that Mamacha would hear them and protect them. Under the broiling sun, we stopped again. It was noon, and we had been walking for close to three hours. Plates of stewed chicken, carrots, cauliflower, lettuce, peas, tomatoes, and bread were distributed to everyone. *Chicha* and bottled beer were also distributed. Everyone was fed well. Devotion and faith are displayed through overexertion and overprovisioning. Catherine Allen (1988:150) notes that in the countryside on ritual occasions, such as feeding the dead or ensuring the fertility of llamas, everything is done to excess so that those who receive will be able to provide. The same philosophy prevails here in a different setting, where commodities and exchange value predominate in the market. The great circulatory system must be nourished fully and intensely so that Mamacha and therefore the market women who sell and the consumers who buy goods will be able to provide. In some way, all must be sated. This logic is certainly not what you would expect to find in a society that has fully embraced capitalism.

Sponsors of Mamacha Asunta, 1998. Photograph by John R. Cooper.

The sponsor's face was contorted with anxiety, and she was mostly scowl-ing. I had seen her often over the week. She carried a little piece of paper with notes scrawled on it reminding her of all the different things that different people had promised to provide for the festivities. Her husband, on the other hand, mostly smoked, drank, and talked with his friends, but he did not seem to be doing much of the hard work of serving his guests.

After lunch, the procession continued, stopping periodically, until finally it returned to the cathedral. Exhausted, I left the procession before it returned to the cathedral. Teófila told me that afterwards receptions were hosted in the homes of sponsors, and dancing and drinking continued until late into the night. Amilcar was furious that I had left. He had been expecting to host me, although he had not told me. I tried to assuage his irritation later by giving him copies of pictures I had taken of the procession.

The next day Mamacha's "Farewell" began, the responsibility of the potato vendors, who once again changed her clothes and adorned her with many different kinds of potatoes. The final day, the onion vendors did the same, and after bowing three times, Mamacha and her smaller image returned to the cathedral for another year.

This is only one kind of fiesta that market women participate in, but it is one of the most important. I have elucidated somewhat crudely some of the context that surrounds the events. Because I was such a rube, my exasperated market women friends and research assistant were forced to explain things in the most simplistic and straightforward manner possible. One of the most striking parts of the festival was the circuit the procession took. This circuit represented how the market is supposed to work, pulling together many of the different people and activities in different physical spaces that contribute to the circulation of goods.[6] It moved from the institutional heart of the city in the Plaza de Armas up toward the market of San Pedro, passing through the rows of *ambulantes,* then down toward the wholesalers and most itinerant vendors along the sidewalks and the railroad tracks of Avenida Ejército, below the bridge of Belem Pampa. Notably absent from this procession were the producers themselves. Instead of a direct connection between production and consumption in which producers fed to excess those who they hoped would provide for them, it was the vendors, those who capitalized on exchange, who enacted this aspect of fertility. Even the dances were not "traditional" indigenous fiesta dances.

Behind the circuits of exchange lies an elaborate system of *hurk'as,* the means by which principal sponsors request assistance for fiesta resources from their friends, relatives, and working companions. The *hurk'as* are one key to understanding fiestas and the close relationship they have to economic and social well-being. Literally translated, the *hurk'a* has two meanings. The first is associated with the labor of Indians on Spanish haciendas: Peons were given a *hurk'a* consisting of a symbolic offering of food, coca leaves, and liquor in exchange for their labor, instead of an appropriate wage. In the fiesta system, the major sponsors of the fiesta, long before the date of the fiesta, offer special breads and small glasses of liquor when they request assistance from their relatives, coworkers, and friends, and this request is called a *hurk'a.* Those who accept the *hurk'a* commit themselves to providing beer, costumes, the music, cost of the mass, food, or other items for some aspect of the fiesta for which the sponsor is responsible. Implicit in the consummation of these commitments is the Maussian notion that in the future the principal sponsor is obligated to provide for those who have supported her in her undertaking.[7]

La Almudena

Market women also participate in La Almudena, which celebrates the Virgin de Natividad (Our Lady of the Nativity). Almudena is remarkably different from Mamacha Asunta. Marisol de la Cadena (2000:231–71) offers a detailed description of Almudena, as it is known, and its history. Almudena is held on September 8, the same time as another Cuzco fiesta for the Virgin de los Remedios. It has created tension among Cuzqueños because Almudena attracts the working class and has been celebrated for far longer than Remedios, which is really for "*los profesionales*" ("the professionals"), as one woman put it, and she has been brought out only for the last ten years. When I asked Teófila to clarify who "the professionals" were, she said that they included some artisans, cattle dealers, bureaucrats from the Municipal Council and the university, and *personalidades grandes* (those who were known public figures in Cuzco).[8]

Almudena is a large fiesta. Barrionuevo (1980:60) writes that the Virgin of the Almudena is "an authentic chola virgin," a wonderful phrase that precisely describes not only why *cholas* at once disturb and tantalize the upper middle classes of Cuzco's provincial society but also how *cholas* may challenge existing categories, stereotypes, and definitions. The major participants are vendors who sell tourist artisanry in the Plaza de Armas and in the markets and merchants who sell contraband in the black market of Avenida Ejército. Many of the latter are from Puno originally but now live in Cuzco. The influence of Puno on the entire fiesta is substantial. Whereas in the past participants identified themselves as Puneños or traveled from Puno, now they identify themselves as Cuzqueños who have adopted the dances and clothes of Puneños. I always thought that a fiesta such as Mamacha Asunta was an expensive undertaking, but its cost pales before that of Almudena. At least sixty bands participate in the fiesta. The musicians and the costumes the dancers wear come from Puno. The dancers' costumes can cost anywhere from $150 to $200. To sponsor a band can run from $3,000 to $5,000. These are large brass bands of at least three cymbal players, three large drums, six snare drums, twenty horns, eight to ten saxophones, and fifteen trumpets.

One dancer, Flora Pompiya, is a black market vendor in Avenida Ejército. She started dancing the *morenada* in Almudena fourteen years ago. I asked her how she became a dancer and about her experiences as a dancer. "I decided to dance because I love it. The lieutenants invited me. They work here with me in the black market. I already knew how to dance because I used to practice. In the dance group we practice all year. Most of us are from Puno and Juliaca. A few of us live in Cuzco but are from Puno. I used to dance in Qoyllur Rit'i, but now I only dance Almudena.[9] It is extremely expensive to pay for all the food and drink. The band costs $3,000. The sponsors have to contribute cases of beer, three, five, cases for the whole group. There are about forty in the band and they drink about two hundred cases of beer in three days.[10] I have moved up through the ranks over the years. I began as a señorita, a *china* without a husband and children. Now I dance as a *chola,* as a couple, as a señora. I've only danced two years as a señora. I plan to continue dancing. It doesn't bring me commercial rewards. It is more for faith and it affirms my friendships and the communication among us: what kind of merchandise there is, what you can bring me."

Different dance groups perform dances with distinct origins.[11] And within each dance group, dancers often move up from one rank to another or laterally from one kind of position to another in accordance with their skills and their life stages. The terms used in dance group hierarchies draw from government and military bureaucracies at the same time so that leaders may be called kings (*reyes*) or chiefs (*caporales*), followed by lieutenants (*alferados*).

ENACTING EXCHANGE THROUGH DANCE   Zoila Mendoza, an anthropologist who specializes in ethnomusicology and different kinds of performance genres in the Andean highlands, has written extensively on how to read these dances and has delved into their history. She shows how much detailed knowledge people have absorbed and put to use as they participate in and watch these dances. In her study of two dance groups, the Majeños and Qollachas, for example, she found that both dances emerged out of growing tension between different kinds of transporters of goods in the Andes. Transport is a quintessential function of the market. The Qollachas depict those who used to accompany llama caravans, burdened with goods from the high reaches of the punas. They exchanged their wool and freeze-dried potatoes for lower-altitude products, such as corn, and essential resources, such as salt. The Majeños depict those who became part of the colonial mercantile economy and circuits of exchange as mule drivers hauling minerals, textiles, and other goods, especially to and from the mines and weaving sweatshops. Today, few llama caravans exist, but the different status attributions of these occupations have been reappropriated to refer to distinctions between those who own trucks and those who are only the chauffeurs, driving others' trucks. Both Qollachas and Majeños represent people who operate at primarily the wholesaler level of the market economy.[12] Originally, the differences between them were subtle, but they have grown.

Both groups of *transportistas* impersonate mobile merchants (*llameros,* or llama drivers, and *arrieros,* or mule drivers, respectively), choosing dances that connote their own roles as local entrepreneurs. Both the Majeños and the Qhapaq Qollas are regionally acknowledged as mestizo dancers. However, the Majeños embody powerful, wealthy, white, horse-riding mule drivers who come from a prosperous coastal valley and commercialize city goods, whereas the Qhapaq Qollas, despite their stylized form, embody the coarse, walking llama drivers from the punas who seek to barter their limited, rustic indigenous products. The Qollas have strived to show that they can compete with the Majeños by creating playful, engaging comic performances.

In addition to the dynamic Qollachas and Majeños, a slew of wonderful dancers hail from Puno and from the mining zones of Bolivia, especially Oruro, with its famous Carnival festivities. The *morenadas* are one of the biggest and most elaborate dance groups, made up of smaller groups: the *chinas,* the *cholas,* the leaders of these groups who are called *caporales* (among them an angel and a devil, who is considered the "king"), and *osos,* enormous clowning bears, some of whom have combined their furry costumes with black-faced masks in yet another commentary on and reflection of racial ideologies.

One of the most impressive *morenada* dance groups from Cuzco is called Gran Poder. Its name comes from a huge fiesta that takes place every year in La Paz, Bolivia and attracts hundreds of dance groups and enormous bands over a period of days. My research assistant, Teófila, was invited by a friend of hers to become a member of the group. Her friend is from Puno and sells in Cuzco's black market. Teófila danced in Gran Poder for eight years, beginning in 1982, and became a *caporal.* The group has a center in Puno where they keep all their different costumes. Teófila has fond memories of her dancing years. She and the other dancers traveled together to Puno and competed with other groups. Teófila considers her dancing days a time when she built strong and enduring relationships with her fellow dancers. She recounted to me how, in Puno, all the women slept in one room and the men in another. The thirty women pulled together their mattresses in a great circle. She said it was a way to make friends and gain experience. As we watched the dancers, whom Teófila greeted enthusiastically, I could see how much she longed to be out there with them.

I asked her why she stopped dancing. I thought I had gotten to know Teófila's life history, but I was wrong. She told me she had stopped dancing because if she had continued to dance she would have had to take on a sponsorship, which she was not sure she could afford. What she had not told me was that she had had a terrible accident in 1989 in which she almost lost her life. She was on a fieldtrip in a bus with the nursery school children with whom she worked, and the bus went over a cliff. She was completely paralyzed from her waist up and spent six months in the hospital. She tried to dance again in 1991, but the pain was too great. Of her original group, ten of the women have continued to dance and many more men have. Teófila added after telling me her story, "We express our faith through dance." Indeed, despite all the joviality and gay music, many of the dancers' faces conveyed a sober commitment and concentration. I wondered whether Teófila felt uneasy about her own faith because she could no longer display it or convey it through dance.

The performers in the *chola* dance groups work in the black market. Before they were married, they danced as *chinas,* but because the *chinas* are supposed to dance "with more movement" (their dances are more suggestive, even lascivious, and take much more energy), when these women marry they then dance as respectable *cholas.* It is interesting that they label themselves *cholas,* a term that I rarely heard in Cuzco except as an insult or as a term of endearment ("my little *chola*"). In Bolivia, in contrast, it is common to hear people referring to market women as *cholas.* In Cuzco, most market women who distinguish themselves through their dress and hat style call themselves mestizas. But this is one case in which they call themselves *cholas* and dress not as Cuzqueña mestizas but rather as Bolivian *cholas,* in copious silk skirts and capes, lace blouses, and rhinestone jewelry. As they dance, they swill large quantities of beer from bottles they share among themselves. It is also one of

Chola *dancers of Almudena, dressed Bolivian style, drinking beer, 1998. One is carrying a miniature saint image used to invite people to serve as sponsors for the next year.*

the few dance groups in which repeatedly the women sway, arm in arm, spontaneously, even when they are not formally dancing.

The *tun tuna*, also danced at Mamacha Asunta, is associated with the upper-middle-classes in Puno. These dancers use a Puno band, and the dancers themselves are merchants who bring in black market clothes from Bolivia through Juliaca. The *saya* is similar to the *tun tuna* but is danced by "the pueblo," vendors from Cuzco. The dance of the *saqras* (devils) also hails from Paucartambo. Rumor has it that the dance group is made up of many of the best pickpockets and thieves of Cuzco. Their costumes are a jarring combination of expensive jewels and cheap imitations sewed on rainbow-colored silks. Their hair is also dyed in rainbow colors. Like the *ukukus,* the *saqras* relish satirical and somewhat frightening antics that engage and repel the audience.

In earlier years, each of the dance groups competed in dressing the Virgin. Whichever group brought the most beautiful clothes would dress the Virgin. There is also a brotherhood of litter bearers, all of whom work in the market as porters. Their wives are responsible for providing them with food during the procession.

We walked up to Almudena, an unnerving journey because we were jammed shoulder to shoulder in a crowd, with drunks and pickpockets interspersed among the people. Almudena, to me, seems much more like a pilgrimage. Thousands feasted on fried pork, roasted guinea pig, beer, and *chicha* in the tents surrounding the church. The suffocatingly hot modern church (rebuilt after an earthquake) was difficult to enter because all available flat surfaces were covered with candles lit by the faithful. People were praying intensely, some weeping, hoping that their missives would reach the Virgin. Handkerchiefs, crutches, relics, a metonymous collection of what people dream of making whole again, surrounded each saint image: Saint Roque, Saint Isidro, Señor de Los Temblores.

Almudena is also far more of a transnational festival than Mamacha Asunta, and its structure encourages innovation and creativity. It resembles an immense circulatory system of possibilities that bring together all the various trajectories that commodities follow in the informal markets. Although an important role remains for retail vendors, many of Almudena's dancers are engaged in larger-scale marketing or transport ventures. In contrast, Mamacha Asunta is primarily the enactment of retail vendors, and they are the main participants. Almudena includes a far wider geographic range of participants from the neighborhoods of Cuzco, from Puno, Juliaca, Lima, various parts of Bolivia, and even Chile. Its principal devotees hail from Puno, and the sponsors of the festival tend to be Puneños, even when they live in Cuzco.

Participants in Almudena—performers and onlookers alike—took the action seriously. Wandering around, I heard various commentaries on the performances. One woman complained, "In past years the dancers were better. They were more active. They danced with more grace." Another woman added, "They dance now with modern steps, but not with as much grace." Several of my market women friends were upset because, for whatever reason, they omitted the *alabazo,* the benediction or greeting in front of the church. Dori explained that the *alabazo* usually called for the participation of a *chola* (impersonated by a man), a burro, and a *cachaco* (a military officer), dressed in black. A comic skit was performed in which various men fall in love with the *chola*. She flirts and responds, inciting the *cachaco* to fury. He then goes after the various suitors with his burro but fails to stop them. Again, this skit addresses the question of social order as the wholly masculine military officer fails to prevent men from falling in love with virile market women. It also enacts, ironically, how these very transgressive qualities may produce fertility, enjoyment, and laughter.

The various performances of the dancers reflect how they are always experimenting, and their challenges to the status quo are sometimes received positively, sometimes not. They do not experiment in a void, though. Even as they try out new dance steps, music, and costumes that may come from Europe, the United States, Bolivia, or Chile, other performers, musicians, and spectators offer a context for their creativity that is structured out of the historical strata of diverse memories of performance, stories, participants, and musical renditions.

Playing with sexuality and human, gendered, and racialized identities is integral to fiestas, whether they take place in highland rural communities or in urban settings. Often, these kinds of play incorporate commentaries on economic circuits and their insertion into the ways in which intercourse and fertility are impeded or encouraged. In rural communities, sexual play through performance is clearly linked to agricultural, livestock, and human fertility, threads that remain in urban festivities, but the playfulness is also a commentary on how exchange (in rural areas between humans, animals, and the supernatural) and commodity circuits (in urban areas within the market economy) produce profits. I saw one funny improvised skit among the thirsty *ukukus* who alternately scorned, mocked, and embraced Coca-Cola. Their ambivalence toward transnational capital—its tantalizing but hegemonic qualities—was easily communicated to the spectators but also allowed the dancers to express their own sentiments. The dancers, through multiple channels, represented market women as potently sexualized, almost promiscuous, but also

Gran Poder tun tuna *dancer with black-faced* oso *(bear), 1998.*

as wholly feminine and capable of defending their honor from evil men. The *china* and *chola* dancers and the cross-dressing *ukukus, cholas,* and bears challenge the views of women as madonna or whore, civilized or uncivilized, sexually feminine or masculine. They also call attention to the uneasiness with which men regard the power of market women.

Another significant difference between Almudena and Mamacha Asunta lies in how the *hurk'a* takes place. For Mamacha, a rough equivalence characterizes the *hurk'a:* If you contribute to my sponsorship, I will return the favor. Reciprocation might not necessarily occur when the giver has a sponsorship but rather in the course of daily affairs, providing information, products, or emergency needs. This kind of reciprocity does not entail a meticulous accounting sheet, but those who enter into such a contract have a sense of what is expected. Almudena's *hurk'as* function differently. Sponsors issue invitations, which they call *ayni.* In the Andean highlands, *ayni* refers to equivalent exchanges whereby if a man helps to plow his companion's field, down the road, his companion will do the same for him. However, in this urban commodity and black market milieu, *ayni* functions differently. A sponsor invites someone to the fiesta. If that person contributes ten cases of beer to the fiesta, the sponsor, in turn, would have to contribute fifteen or twenty cases of beer in return if the invitee as sponsor invited her in a subsequent year. This transaction resembles reciprocal exchange in form, but as Albro (1997:17–19) points out, the form itself is mutable and becomes hybrid. The action itself is appropriate, but there is no clear agreement about the content of the action. Rather, there is a "symbolic ambiguity" to the transaction, which Albro calls "intimate insincerity." An inflationary quality characterizes these sponsorship systems that correspond to the world of laundering drug money, working on the black market, and buying into commodity exchanges, especially at the wholesale level.

In these examples, the expression of religiosity and holding of faith do not correlate easily with the categories that social scientists use (e.g., race, gender, class). The very power of religiosity and faith emerges out of its vague definition. People who seem alike may hold quite different religious beliefs; people who seem different from each other may practice their faith in similar ways. I do not mean that faith and religion therefore become a fantastic Durkheimian cement that helps create social cohesion or that we do not find certain patterns or commonalities in how religiosity unfolds among market women. The following examples reveal how variation and individual interpretation contribute to the experiences of faith. In the conversations that Teófila and I had with market women, when we asked them whether they had any kind of religious faith, they often elaborated on their answers, making connections between the practice of faith and the survival of their households, the success of their marketing, the ability of faith to guide them in their treatment of others and in their judgments of how others behaved socially, and the memories of great fun they had at fiestas as dancers, musicians, or *cargo* holders.

Angels and Miracles

Public religiosity among market women occupies a site in which political tensions lie just below the surface, social networks are explored and exploited, gender and racial ideologies become raw material for playful commentary and biting satire, and the juxtaposition of economic survival and faith is illuminated. As these demonstrations of convertible economic, social, and political capital unfold in a defined field of religious celebration, they are hedged in by patron-client relationships, racial discrimination, circuits of transnational capital, a stagnant national economy, and oppressive gender relations within households. Fiestas do not lead to erasure of these conditions; rather, they frame and even draw attention to the sometimes sharp discrepancies between what can be imagined and what is reflected or represented on these occasions and to the daily rhythms of market women's lives. Another genre of religiosity serves as the site for at least some market women to process and give voice to these contradictions and discrepancies: the experience of miracles. These miracles contribute to market women's participation in public demonstrations and actions of faith, but the miracles themselves are highly personalized and often directly concern particular economic plights and household struggles.

Domérica Hermoza, who sells her sad piles of vegetables and colored yarns by the railroad tracks, listens to radio music, and dreams of being her namesake, the bold star of a soap opera (see chapters 2 and 3), clearly distinguishes between those who are saints, "He who is the father," and "She who is the Virgin Mary." For her, the Virgin as Mother of God is responsible for miracles. Because Domérica experiences miracles, this conceivably makes her a saint. Of all the women I talked to, she was the most articulate in explaining her personal religiosity.

> I'm Catholic, one hundred percent. I know that one God is our father and this father includes everyone and in the Virgin you see the exemplar mother as one single entity. They are multiplied in other parts so that people will see and believe that only one God exists. At times people doubt. They speak of a statue that they adore and they are carrying it, singing, dancing, but I see that in this statue of the Virgin that they are worshipping . . . they should have a little respect and fear [for the Virgin]. That is what you have to realize. That's what I realize. For example, they say, "Why do you carry a cross like I am carrying?" I say, "I too suffer, yes. No one is happy in the world. So, each of us has our cross and we carry that cross." And that's what I see. . . . Let's not confuse Saint Rosita with the Virgin Mary. . . . Saint Rosita is a saint, a woman, a person as we are and because she behaved well she became a saint. We should not confuse her with the Virgin Mary. The Virgin Mary is the mother of God. And wherever she suddenly appears, she performs a miracle, and then they give that miracle her name. So it is too with the Virgin Asunta, Virgin Rosario, Natividad. That's how I see it.

Juan Roa Apasa's understanding of the relationship between saints, God, and the Virgin Mary is similar to that of Domérica. He denies that he is either Catholic or Evangelical. "My faith is Jesus Christ. I only follow the word of God, analyzing it: What was the purpose of God for humankind? I read the Book in order to get to know it. Saints are those men who legally, from what I know, are men who have had faith in the Señor, the Creator. When they die, they stop being saints. They are remembered as those who served God. Of course, many people do celebrate saint days in the market."

For Domérica Hermoza and Juan Roa Apasa, saints are human manifestations of faith in God or the Virgin Mary. They are not superhuman, however, a belief that conforms to the orthodoxy that officials of the Catholic hierarchy strived to convey to Quechua people from the days of the Spanish conquest in order to wean them from their worship of *huacas* and *apus,* native shrines and mountain spirits, which they could then conflate easily with saint images. Interestingly, Evangelists have also tried to eliminate this faith in pagan images. Sabine MacCormack (1991:147) in *Religion in the Andes: Vision and Imagination in Colonial Peru* recounts how Andeans and missionaries perceived *huacas.* "In Andean eyes, the holy places or huacas . . . imbued as they were with divine presences, represented the history and the concerns of the community." However, according to missionaries, *huacas* were "common guardian(s) of the entire village . . . the eye of the village, the divine presence being manifest in a great stone standing in or next to each village of the region." MacCormack elaborates on the misunderstandings of *huacas* held by missionaries: "Some of these stones were endowed with protective power because they were deities or human beings transformed into stone, while others were associated with some event of transcendent importance. But these Andean characteristics of sacred stones remained unknown to the Augustinian friars, who instead found the stones standing outside the villages . . . to be reminiscent of the guardian angels of the nations, about whom they had read."

Domérica had already told me about her harsh childhood and home life and expounded on her business strategies. After drawing the distinction between the Virgin Mary and the lives of saints, she explained her own participation in the lives of the saints. Despite numerous interruptions for sales and conversations, she kept up her narrative wherever she left off, and I found myself mesmerized by her storytelling abilities, so much so that I didn't notice that my tape had run out just as she reached the climax of one of her miracle stories. Transcribing the tape later that evening, I couldn't help but wonder whether the hand of God had intervened. Note that when Domérica told me her story, she insisted on using the present tense, reliving what had happened a long time ago.[13]

> It's for this reason that always, night and day, I speak about, I think about, the beautiful things that have happened to me. When I gave birth to my last child, the fifth, I felt empty inside. I don't feel like I do now, with strength, but rather as if I am a piece of paper, and I say, "My God, what has happened to me, little beautiful God, what is going to happen, that I feel this way." I'm talking, thinking, how can these things be? I'm praying, I don't know how many mysteries it was, I really don't know. Many, many. I say to Him, "Look at my children, look, they are so little, they are all so little, I only have one older one, all of them are very little. Señor, you gave me these four children and with the one who is coming, they will be five. . . .

For these children, don't abandon me, don't leave me alone. I don't have a
mother or father or anyone in this world. I only have a sister, only ambi-
tious sisters who took the land of my mother and sold it, they took everything from me."

All these things I recount to Him. But I'm just talking nonsense. I don't
have any strength. I'm a piece of paper. At every minute the pain comes,
but nothing advances [describing her labor]. I continue in this way. And
I'm crying, kneeling, doing everything possible. And there's a lady they find
to help me give birth [a midwife] because in the hospital it costs too much.
So, this lady envelopes me in smoke, [saying] "with all the wind I have given
you, this, this, will be." Well, witchcraft it may be, I don't know. So I say,
"My God, there is no one more powerful than you [using the informal
'you'] in the world. So let it be. Your will, not the will of the people, but
Your will." And in that moment, I advance more and more but I still feel
empty, just empty. I don't have the strength to give birth, I don't have the
strength. And from one minute to the next, my son is born. And then, the
source, the placenta is delayed in coming out, and then so that it would
come out, they tied me with a rag, I think.

And from one minute to the next, it became thus, I see myself, and the
house, everything, is falling on top of me and then the earth opens and it
wants to bury me, it wants to eat me. I don't know what is happening to
me, I don't know what is happening, but I am feeling strange. At the moment that I am feeling this way, I lose consciousness. And when I ask, a
tall Señor rapidly approaches me, just when I have lost consciousness, with
his soft, large hands, his beautiful hands. He carries me and He rocks me
like a baby. I hold His neck and I am happy in His arms. And He continues to rock me, thus, thus, thus. He continues, continues, continues. I don't
know. A long time [bargaining interlude].

He carries me right until the moment when I respond. When I am re-
sponding I see clouds, just large bundles, and then I lose consciousness
again, and more and more and a little more, I see many people standing
and more and more and I am seeing something, I say, three or four people
I am seeing, more and more, and then it is clear. I look and now I see. The
people, that is, my children, my husband, the midwife who was accompanying me, they are kneeling. I look and the Señor is not there. I am stretched
out in bed. I say to them, "Where is the Señor who was carrying me? What
lovely hands, soft enormous hands he had, and he was carrying me." And
the lady says to me, "Oh, that must have been God, who carried you." I
was so full of joy, my God, I wept, "Thank you my God, you have given
me life, if it is only for my children."

Domérica recounts other miracles she has experienced: her skill in curing
people, the visions she has, and the flocks of white doves that circle around

her head from time to time. In the course of her stories, both the lady who served as her midwife and a little girl she has recently cured drop by her stall. She concludes, "It's for these reasons that I always say God exists, and if there were no God I know that the world would be smoke or something like that. That's why I go to mass, I pray, I confess. Sometimes one sins, saying, looking, telling, complaining, or sometimes eating too much, and we are always offending God, but I say, 'My God, pardon me, I believe that I am one worm more of the earth and that I bother You but You must pardon me and see that always I think about You and believe in You. This is what You must pay attention to, not my sins,' I speak to Him and thus, conversing with Him, I feel stronger, more animated."

In the colonial period, Spanish missionaries sought to extirpate native idolatries and impose proper Christian religiosity, but they became more and more alarmed at their inability to squelch native religiosity. Sabine MacCormack (1991:183–84) found in the narrative of one Spanish chronicler, Cristobal Molina, that despite the violent and persistent efforts of Spanish missionaries to destroy these pagan *huacas,* Andean "devils" seemed to be "growing in strength." During the Taqui Onqoy, one of the earliest uprisings of Andean people against colonial rule,

> Instead of entering embalmed bodies, rocks, and other material objects, as they [the *huacas*] had tended to do formerly, they now possessed living human beings and spoke through them. . . . Since the huacas spoke directly and explicitly in the words of the person into whom they had entered, that person represented the huaca and was revered as such. . . . Andean deities had long been accustomed to communicate or deliver oracles through the voices of human beings. . . . The Spaniards, on their side, had from the outset interpreted this phenomenon by recourse to the long-established Christian vocabulary of demonic possession. . . . Even so, the indwelling of gods in human beings . . . was not the same as it had been before the invasion, because it was in part conditioned by Christian notions of god dwelling in man that the missionaries had sought to inculcate for some thirty years.

It is not possible to pigeonhole the visions and miracles that Domérica describes, but similarities seem to exist between the speaking human *huacas* that swept the Andes during one of the earliest efforts of people to resist colonial rule and the way in which God speaks through her and uses her as his vehicle. These moments comfort and make her happy, and they feel familiar to her.

Some women experience good fortune as miracles. For them, these coincidences then engender faith. Eva Carhuarupay, among the poorest of vendors, tells me, "I was beside myself because I had no money for food, nothing for my children. I went to La Merced to pray to the Cross of Father Uraqa [Cruz del Padre Uraqa]. When I got home, my son, who was only nine at the time, was there. He told me he had found a wallet in the street, with money in it, including dollars. He was scared I would be angry at him. It was a lot of money at the time. It was a miracle and therefore I am a devotee of Padre Uraqa."

Other women are much like Eva in their understanding of saint images and miracles. They do not split hairs, wondering whether the saints are human or whether it is sinful to become a devotee of a saint rather than of God or the Virgin Mary. They take what the saints have to offer, a little unexpected money, recovery from illness, or fertility, and assume that they must make offerings to them in return. Those who are able to provide saints with more are recognized, and some women believe that if they provide the saints with more, there is greater likelihood that more will be returned to them in the form of miracles. Nevertheless, miracles can happen to the most impoverished, who may only be able to give the saint images a prayer or light a candle.

Evangelical Protestantism

The owner of the Caquetá stall who bought her [Pascuala's] children's dresses was a member of an Evangelical church. Between her faith and her business, Pascuala entered the church and discovered that religious fraternity could also multiply her clientele. (Salcedo 1993:113)

Evangelical Protestantism has swept through many Latin American countries since the 1970s. Again, it is a religiosity that is often mistakenly reduced to a few oversimplified precepts. The explanations for why many people in the cities and countryside of Latin America have converted to Evangelical Protestantism often focus on how the religion allows people to give up alcohol without being ostracized and to be accepted by mainstream middle-class society by adopting a Western work ethic and individualism. They also note that through their common religiosity and practices they create a community in the city that replaces what they left behind in the countryside. Yet the many market women and their spouses who consider themselves Evangelical Protestants do not fit this mold. Their religiosity is more subtle, made up of strands that do not allow a neat compartmentalization between Catholics and Evangelicals, and they do not necessarily abandon some of their values or beliefs that might be considered unacceptable to the middle class.

Many vendors, such as Dori, the powerful and successful wholesaler and tomato queen, have participated in the fiesta for Mamacha Asunta for years. I asked her why she participated in the fiesta if she was not Catholic and whether she had held a sponsorship for Asunta:

Dori: A sponsorship? No. No. But I have provided Mamacha Asunta's crown. I have provided her cape. I have provided her shawl, her hat, or a beautifully embroidered scapular, something, every year, because it is a custom. Those who work in the market have to comply with their commitments and I have never diverged from my plan. [Imitating what others say about her] "Look at Señora Dori, her cake, her *pisco* [a strong brandy-like liquor, made from white grapes], thank you." It's never had my name. I have never put my name on any gift that I have contributed. [Again, imitating what others say] "Little mother, why haven't you added your name?" Because those who give with this hand do not take with the other. I also gave San Pedro his cape without being asked. San Pedro is my neighborhood here [the market] and it is he who has given me this house.

Linda: Why don't you like fiestas?

Dori: It isn't that I don't like fiestas. I watch, I look, but I don't partake. Drinking, I don't like. I've never had the habit of drinking. . . . I have always practiced Catholicism. But my husband is Evangelical. I married as an Evangelical. My marriage godparents were two doctors, Mr. Willard and his wife, who was also a medical professor. They were from the U.S., from New York. They came as missionaries. In 1953, they were here in Monjaspata. From then on, never [no more drinking]. Sure, my mother, she knew how to drink, how to attend fiestas. But since I got married, I've submitted to obedience, to respect. . . . My brothers wouldn't have anything to do with him [her husband] because he was Evangelical. They told me, "No, he who doesn't drink is a savage whom we cannot invite to fiestas." So I didn't go either. If he didn't go, I didn't go. . . .

Every night, he reads me the Bible, to this day. "Look, I'm going to read you these paragraphs, these chapters." Every day in the morning, at noon, at night, we always pray, for everyone, for my daughter, for my granddaughter, for me. Even when my little girl was a baby, he read to both of us before we ate breakfast, before lunch. And in the morning, we had to give thanks to God for his blessings. We've never had a bad moment. . . . Beautiful days. He would say to me, "Everyday we have fiestas because we are in communion with God."

Later in the conversation, I asked Dori about her participation in politics. Long ago, she had held office in her union, and despite her husband's disapproval, she had helped to lead what became a violent uprising on the part of the market women. She came close to being arrested. I asked her whether she agreed with her husband's position. "Sure, I had to bite my tongue and ask for forgiveness. I said, 'I'm sorry but I didn't think this was going to happen.' Then he said, 'From now on, I don't want you to belong to anything. Politics, politics. Politics should be work. Our politics should be work, to show who we are. . . . What men should search for is peace, tranquility.'"

Although I encountered some poorer market vendors who were Protestant Evangelicals, the majority were better off. It is unlikely that their religious faith enhanced their upward mobility. A far more complex process underlies this correlation between Protestant Evangelicals and economic standing. One part of my interviews concerned race and ethnic labeling (see chapter 8). The responses of Protestant Evangelicals were quite interesting in what they seemed to reveal about how they viewed the correlation between their religiosity and their own racial ideologies. Some Evangelicals stress that labels such as *campesina, chola, mestiza, dama,* and *señora* are meaningless, and those who use them are ill-bred, poorly educated, and vulgar. Even very poor vendors subscribe to this viewpoint. Alejandrina, who sold piles of grass for guinea pigs on the ground along Avenida Ejército, said, "I bought a Bible in Quechua and Spanish from a priest in Yanaoca. People should follow what God says. People are equal even if they don't dress alike or don't speak Spanish, but the priest does not say this. Also, the priests, some of them, demand that we have *cargos* and fiestas. It shouldn't be like this because once people drink, they treat others badly."

Leonarda Rimachi, selling her medicinal herbs on the sidewalk, had sponsored several fiestas and danced in them in her home community in Paruro. She venerated the Virgin of Carmen, who she said "takes all our sins and weighs them in the balance. From the door of hell she separates us. . . . The Virgin also remembers us to God." However, she added, "They ask us if we are for the Evangelists. For Him only, we are all equal." Alejandrina and Leonarda Rimachi move between Evangelicalism and Catholicism. They consider themselves Catholic. They venerate particular saint images (a very Catholic practice), and Catholicism is hegemonically socially acceptable. On the other hand, they consider themselves Evangelical because they observe the injustice of many of the priests' practices and are attracted to the idea of a God who treats all equally. The better-off Evangelical vendors see this equal treatment as justification for their inclusion among middle-class Cuzqueños even though the latter are apt to reject and look down on them. They do not have difficulty maintaining contradictory beliefs: They espouse equality, but it is almost always equality within particular bounds. Although a hierarchy of racial superiority and inferiority is not clear-cut, and ethnic labeling is eschewed by almost all vendors, particular cultural practices create hierarchical distinctions. Those who are superior have been educated in these civilizing practices. Thus, the erasure of racial distinctions becomes equated with the attainment of education. Especially prevalent among Evangelicals who are better off, as well as some Catholics, is the idea that proper education will lead to a model middle-class demeanor, similar to that which they believe they themselves approximate.

When I asked Evangelicals about ethnic labeling, they acknowledged that people should be treated equally before God but that, indeed, there were differences between them—in the language they used, the dress they wore, particular negative personality characteristics they displayed, where they lived, and the occupations they had—but that these differences could be eliminated through education and a self-conscious awareness that using these distinguishing criteria as a means to justify racial discrimination was shameful. Although this understanding of ethnic labeling was particularly evident among Evangelicals, I also found it expressed among Catholics, especially those who wanted to be treated as "decent people," a self-respect they believe is accorded to members of Cuzco's middle class.

Market vendors who are Evangelical seem to be deploying what so long ago W. E. B. Du Bois called "double vision." He (1989:2–3) wrote of the position of "the American Negro" in 1903 as

> a sort of seventh son, born with a veil, and gifted with second-sight in this American world,—a world which yields him no true self-consciousness, but only lets him see himself through the revelation of the other world. It is a peculiar sensation, this double-consciousness, this sense of always looking at one's self through the eyes of others, of measuring one's soul by the tape of a world that looks on in amused contempt and pity. One ever feels his twoness,—an American, a Negro; two souls, two thoughts, two unreconciled strivings; two warring ideals in one dark body, whose dogged strength alone keeps it from being torn asunder. . . . The history of the American Negro is the history of this strife,—this longing to attain self-conscious manhood, to merge his double self into a better and truer self. In this merging, he wishes neither of the older selves to be lost. . . . He simply wishes to make it possible for a man to be both a Negro and an American, without being cursed and spit upon by his fellows, without having the doors of Opportunity closed roughly in his face.

Color itself is less a social and racial divide for market vendors than it is for African Americans. Yet the awareness among vendors of the consequences of institutional racism at work in Cuzco's provincial society has motivated some market women to embrace their religiosity as one weapon in their struggle to overcome their marginal racial, gender, and class status. It is ironic that Evangelicalism is a religion rarely embraced by Cuzco's elite, yet market vendors use it as an important way to achieve greater social justice and become accepted by the middle class. They see it as a way to be accepted as Peruvians, to retain pride in their occupation, and not to feel compelled to engage in self-hate or to stifle their roots and ties to their Quechua heritage.

Faith and Politics

As a person who is not particularly religious, I have always found it hard to understand the unquestioning faith that I witnessed as a part of daily life for so many in Cuzco. Talking with the women in the markets gave me a much better understanding of this dimension of their lives. They remain open to the miracles of faith because it is one of the most sustaining alternatives they can nourish. Unpredictable commodity circuits create the genuine recognition of lack of control. Lack of control, together with lack of resources, has always been a powerful incentive for faith. In addition, when market women hit rock bottom, this openness allows them to perceive and receive what others have to offer and assist them. These are not exactly miracles. Rather, they are the small practical and moral aids that make a difference in a hardscrabble life. Without faith, they might not recognize or seize upon these small aids. Faith creates indirectly the possibility of a support network on the streets, giving rise to a sustainable environment among those who have little. Giving people rides, lending them small amounts of money, feeding them a meal, providing them with temporary shelter—these are the deeds that faith makes possible. Marx long ago suggested that religion was the opiate of the masses. This is too easy a conclusion to draw, although it has a grain of truth to it. Religion may be an opiate, but it also helps market women to make the best of their dusty days.

Politics are far from absent in the unfolding of fiestas. As many a scholar has found, fiestas and rituals in general may create precisely the heightened tensions that cause politics to explode into violence. In the case of fiestas such as Mamacha Asunta, the fury of the church hierarchy, the transparent greed of the priests, the barely hidden racial ideologies that perceive market women as embarrassing and unacceptable aspirants to a middle-class way of life, the commentaries on the bold and potentially discomfiting transgression of gender categories that market women traverse as both women and entrepreneurs, the competition over recognition and market share on the part of different sections of the retail market, and the jockeying of corporations to gain commercial recognition through advertising and sponsorship reflect rather clearly the daily politics of city life. Also, although political action has some potential to improve market women's lot, something the market women themselves recognize, they also know that political action, like the faith of some among the Catholic church hierarchy, can be a enticing drug for the power hungry and opportunistic. Therefore, they gamble in both domains with strategic acumen.

The Catholic hierarchy and proselytizing Evangelicals have always sought to contain the identities of Peru's popular classes. Yet the religiosity of market vendors—their fiestas, their direct communication with God through the Bible, their conviction that miracles are possible—makes it utterly clear that their acts, deeds, and faith leap out of these boundaries as they forge a place for themselves squarely in the midst of all sorts of flows of commodities, ideas, beliefs, visions, and practices that neither the state nor religious officials can control.

Notes

1. Religious practices among market vendors involve both men and women, but the majority are women. In this chapter I refer to market women rather than vendors in general and specify occasions on which men play a significant role.

2. Anthropologists have debated heatedly whether the hierarchy of sponsorship in fiestas serves as a primary mechanism for some and not others to enhance their status and accumulate wealth and power. Those who support this position argue that to gain political power, people alternate climbing two ladders: that of the fiesta sponsorship hierarchy and that of political office. This was called the *cargo* system. Others argue that fiesta sponsorship actually serves as a leveling or redistributive mechanism that diminishes economic differentiation because sponsors must expend much of their material wealth to display their capacity to draw on and enhance their social status. Still others have pointed out how the dances, symbols, stages, and enactments that make up fiestas reveal a pure Andean identity or, alternatively, an intelligent coopting of "Indianness" to create folkloric performances that assert non-Indian dominance.

3. I am grateful to Kathleen Fine for suggesting this possibility with respect to women's high degree of participation in sponsorship of urban fiestas.

4. Sabine MacCormack (1991:180–81) notes the superficial resemblance of some Andean and Christian festivals during the colonial period. She makes the point that Spanish religious images themselves encouraged the ability of Andean peoples to appear as if they were venerating Christian saint images when they were really still paying homage to their native idols or *huacas:* "For their [the Spanish saint images'] sheer naturalism, their lifelike glass eyes, their blushing complexions, and their wardrobes filled with jeweled clothing, invited Andeans to perceive in them the huacas . . . of Christians." In the late twentieth century, it is unlikely that any deliberate or conscious effort is involved in the vendors' worship of and dedication to saint images as *huacas,* but their religiosity resonates with many agricultural rites of *campesinos* that are closely attuned to the lives of *huacas* and to the rhythms of harvesting, sowing, and irrigating that require careful attention and cultivation of the *huacas* and saint images associated

with these temporal periods. Market vendors retain a heightened consciousness of agricultural and herding cycles because they intervene directly in the circuits of commodities and in the supply and demand of the products they sell in the market. The materiality of the saint images, the distinctiveness of their physiognomies, and their personalities make more sense to Andeans than does God as an abstraction.

5. The *ukuku* is the son of a bear and a *campesina* stolen by the bear. According to Barrionuevo (1980:206), the story goes that the *ukuku's* first act is to kill his father. Then "society" tries to kill the *ukuku* by sending him to the jungle, where he will be devoured by wild animals, but he returns unscathed, with the skins of pumas wrapped around him. Finally, they send him to a distant highland village, where a bewitched man is terrorizing people. The *ukuku* succeeds in overcoming the man and saves his soul, receiving in return a great fortune. There are many variants of this story, but in all of them the *ukuku* ultimately is accepted by the society that first attempts to kill him. In a performance, the *ukuku* straddles these two dimensions of its being: the scary and unknown and the humorous and satirical.

6. Most of Cuzco's fiestas that celebrate saint images draw their crowd from particular neighborhoods that are devotees of that saint. Thus, the fiesta replicates in a different mode neighborhood relationships, feuding or competition between neighborhoods, while simultaneously moving these relationships out of the barrio to traverse periodically a larger circuit that incorporates other parts of the city and whose destination is the city's center, the cathedral. Autonomy, affiliation, and incorporation are all part of the metatext of fiesta circuits.

7. In *The Gift,* Marcel Mauss (1967) systematically explored reciprocal exchange relationships, demonstrating that they were rarely guided by simple altruism but rather were structured by cultural notions of obligation.

8. Remedios is celebrated at the convent of Santa Catalina. The nuns make the Virgin's clothes, and the principal sponsors are shoemakers. I have not pursued a study of Remedios, but it is probable that artisans have been major participants in the fiesta.

9. Qoyllur Rit'i is a pilgrimage that attracts hundreds of thousands of people who climb up to the glacial reaches of Mt. Ausangate bearing blocks of ice. Those who go as pilgrims are supposed to repeat their journey three years in a row in order to be blessed.

10. These are one-liter beers, twelve in a case.

11. For example, the *contradanza* (quadrille or country dance) is danced by those from "the barrio" (Cuzco), as are the Qollacha and the Majeño, but the latter dances hail from Paucartambo and are often danced in San Jerónimo, a market town of about 8,000 people located about twelve kilometers outside Cuzco.

12. Mendoza (1998:97) explains it this way: "In contrast to the *Majeños,* which became known as a *comparsa* of *dueños de carro* (dance group of car owners) because it had a high number of vehicle owners, the *Qollas* group became known as a comparsa of *choferes* (non-owner drivers) or *ruteros* (non-owner drivers who always cover a particular route)."

13. Domérica's miracle narrative, recounted to me in Spanish, very much retains Quechua syntax and Quechua markers indicating the passage of time and the use of repetition for emphasis. The original text makes this even more evident than the English translation and should be of interest to linguistic anthropologist seeking to understand the ways in which language and language change illuminate markers of ethnic identity and positioning. I have edited the translation slightly to help the reader to follow the dialogue but have attempted not to sacrifice the meaning or tone of the narrative.

10

Two-Way Streets: Political Action

In Andean rural society, negotiations over ethnic self-representa-
tions have been the stuff of everyday peasant politics since colonial
times. . . . Resurgent "Indianness" (that is, the juridical and dis-
cursive struggle to reclaim one's communal or indigenous identity
in order to recover lost colonial rights) was a weapon of the weak in
the postindependence period. Less understood, however, are the
changing social bases and politics of popular self-other distinctions
in everyday social practice—in the quotidian battlefields of rural
markets, city streets, government chambers, and peasant communi-
ties. . . . We still have much to study about the social sinews of
Andean regional economies: the swollen, overlapping sectors of in-
termediaries who emanated from, and tenuously connected, the dis-
parate cultural and economic fragments of Andean society.
(Larson 1991:36–37)

Lives in Motion

The politics of Cuzco's markets unfold quietly most of the time, a subterranean river of discontent not immediately evident to the casual stranger. Small
signs appear that signal conflict. Political rhetoric often wins out in the heat
of electoral campaigns when subtlety is abandoned. To understand the politics of the market requires us to understand the fullness of the lives of market
women and the history of the sometimes tempestuous battles they have
fought, mustering the courage to risk their livelihoods. In this chapter, I consider how market women take action politically. How do they succeed in
finding common ground? What are their motivations for taking what are
sometimes enormous risks, and what views do Cuzqueños hold of the political activities of market women?

Migration has been a long-standing phenomenon in the Andes, not only
across territorial divides but also across social and political ones. The course

of migration, together with four major historical moments, has gradually transformed Peru's racial and class topography and the political consciousness of
all Peruvians: the implementation of Peru's 1969 agrarian reform; the near
collapse of Peru's economy in the 1980s, followed by its restructuring and the
implementation of neoliberal economic measures; the belief that education is
a critical arm of upward mobility; and the ravages of the civil war in the 1980s
and early 1990s between the Peruvian state and the Shining Path guerrilla
movement, which displaced hundreds of thousands of *campesinos* from the
countryside to urban shantytowns. This last process was far more pronounced
in Lima and the central highlands than in the Cuzco region, although its effects were also felt there.

   These transformations have had dramatic consequences. The 1969 reform,
though not entirely successful, returned some economic resources to peasants, and in the course of reform proceedings, peasants became more sophisticated in their use of law and legal discourse. They learned how to lobby and
fight to defend their citizenship rights. The goal of educating their children
well, which so many in Peru hold dear, also helped increase the flow of people
to the cities. However, the economic and political events of the 1980s and early
1990s meant that as many people flocked to urban areas, unemployment
forced all sorts of Peruvians, including those who once considered themselves
middle-class, into informal service occupations in the streets, especially as taxi
drivers and vendors. Although domestic service had once been an alternative
source of employment that absorbed many migrants, the downturn of the
economy meant that fewer people could hire migrants as domestic servants
(see also Gill 1994). Therefore, more migrants had to find ways to make their
living on the streets. Castelike categories dissolved into the muddiness of
urban culture. This confusion of complex movements has had both salutary
and deleterious effects on the ways in which market vendors organize politically. The huge number of "in-between" people flooding the streets of the
cities, lumped under the rubric of the "popular classes," might seem to constitute a potential threat to existing racial and class structures, but the actual
composition of the popular classes is segmented and fragmented by distinctive relations of production and exchange and by gender ideologies at work
and in the home. At the same time, however, some among Peru's hispanicized
population have sought to defend the more castelike nature of the hierarchical and racial divisions of Peruvian society in order to ensure their own distinctiveness and superiority. Furthermore, the tectonics of constantly shifting economic and political alliances among the popular classes must also be
counterpoised to the common cultural flows that so many urban dwellers

share in the form of musical genres, religious festivities, spatial knowledge, food, language exchanges, and survival tactics.

Why do market women feel compelled to take political action? If one looks far back in the municipal records of Cuzco, it is apparent that market women, in particular, have been singled out as unladylike, dirty-mouthed, untrustworthy, usurious, and lascivious, even during times of relative peace between vendors, their clients, and local government officials. And at times of intense altercation, they are repeatedly described as insolent, ill-bred, delinquent, unpredictable, and vulgar women.[1] Yet if one strolls among the market stalls either inside or outside the permanent market, this characterization seems off the mark. Although market women want to make sales and will engage in creative subterfuges for that purpose, most of them want to have courteous and smooth relationships with their clients. Many are so dejected and depressed by the weight of life's burdens that the last thing they want is to be further harassed. Thus, market women generally do not mobilize politically because of daily tensions that result from being marginalized in terms of race, class, or gender. They are tough enough to weather these tensions through their support networks, knowledge of the streets, and skillful means of using bargaining to demand self-respect. Rather, they mobilize when their livelihood

Children with itinerant vendor, 1979.

is directly or indirectly threatened. On those occasions, they may organize to fight back against state officials seeking to relocate them, protest against policymakers who impose new laws and taxes that affect their income or employment, or rise up to challenge government economic measures that threaten their business and promise to grind them further into poverty.

Battling Machismo

The periodic political mobilizations of market women partially unmask the machismo that dominates gendered relations and gender ideologies, and the practices that result from them are central to actions taken against market women and their own political consciousness and mobilization. Neither virgin nor whore, market women create discomfort. Municipal and state officials respond to the protests and defiance of market women, which are aimed at economic and political policies, by portraying them as irresponsible, intransigent, and transgressors of their proper role as mothers; in short, they perceive them as whores. They view them as women in public spaces whose behavior is not submissive and dependent. This seesawing perception that both men and women have of ideal gender relations can lead to heightened danger for market women and for a great many other women who risk participating in politics and challenging established institutions, especially in public. Once state authorities become comfortable with the idea that market women (and others) are equivalent to whores, they feel little compulsion about harassing them sexually or even raping them.[2] The following conversation that I had with Lucre, once a vulnerable, itinerant vendor and now an elder and well-established political leader, is one example of the many subtle allusions and occasional explicit references to sexual harassment and rape that market women shared with me:

> Linda: When you began to sell outside, did you encounter problems with the authorities or municipal agents at first?
> *Lucrecia:* Yes.
> *Linda:* What kinds of things happened?
> *Lucrecia:* Because I sold in the streets, I would sit on a corner to rest sometimes. The municipal agent would come and make me leave, but I wouldn't agree to it. I fought with the agent, I fought hard, because as a young girl I had to make him respect me no matter what it took. Sometimes he would take my fruit. Sometimes, so I wouldn't have to leave, I would say, "Good, take them. It doesn't matter to me, but I am never going to beg for them nor am I going to say anything to them." When I

saw them, when they were coming, I was already fleeing. That's the way
my life was, but I always had confrontations with the municipal agents. I
think badly of, now he's getting old, one agent, Benavente, he was a boor.
Linda: And what did he do?
Lucrecia: He insulted us: "Those Indians, those filthy women, those dirty
women," he would say to us. Sometimes we would fight with him. Sometimes I would hit him with my basket. Then, since I was a girl, I would
run away.
Linda: Were there problems with sexual abuses?
Lucrecia: Some of them had problems, yes, some of them did, but since I
was a more knowledgeable child than they, I could negotiate better for
myself. I never said anything to them. I let them take my things away. I
never went to reclaim them because I knew very well that they would
take advantage of us. Not even married women escaped abuse.

Political Awareness and Action

Almost all of the market vendors inside and outside Cuzco's permanent markets are organized into unions, and most of the unions operate in a manner
similar to guilds, representing a particular product. People pay membership
to their union. The unions hold periodic meetings and elect officers who are
responsible for attending to their constituents' needs, which are quite limited.
Union leaders intervene in conflicts between municipal agents and vendors,
they raise money to help those who suffer tragedies, they lobby for better services for the vendors, and they mediate in conflicts among vendors themselves.
All of the unions made up of itinerant vendors (*ambulantes*) are federated into
one umbrella organization; the same is true of vendors in permanent markets
who are organized into sections that are then federated as a single unit representing each market. Finally, all the *ambulantes* are considered members of
the Federation of Ambulante Workers of Cuzco (FEDETAC).

Just along San Pedro Cascaparo Street outside the central market, there are
six unions. The most powerful is the union of *ambulantes* with about 250
members, established in 1975. It is highly respected, partly because it is so old.
It has endured. The members of this union, unlike many others, sell a wide
range of products. On the other side of the street are the five other unions that
were established about eight years ago. Inside the market, women are organized into "sections" that correlate with the product they sell; among them
the vegetable, fruit, potato, and bread sections are considered the most powerful. On occasions such as religious festivals, sellers of the same product,
whether they are *ambulantes* or *permanentes,* coordinate their activities.

One interesting question that scholars have asked about market women and that I was interested in trying to answer for myself is whether market women mobilize politically solely to defend their own self-interest or whether they have a political consciousness that is deeper and motivates them to coordinate with other sectors of the popular classes such as workers and peasants, thereby permitting them to mobilize in a more sustained fashion.[3] Political consciousness and mobilization constitute praxis, born of reflection and action together. Market women mobilize politically on the basis of what Donna Haraway (1988) calls "situated knowledge." This means that they do not necessarily share a collective ideology that emerges out of the same life experiences or class consciousness. Rather, they are heterogeneous, and their identities are multifaceted and dynamic. Lynn Stephen (1997), Florence Babb (1998), and Hans and Judith Marie Buechler (1992) have documented well the heterogeneity in economic relations among market women and the difficult and different paths toward political solidarity that exist among Andean vendors. In a society where machismo is pervasive, many women consider machismo appropriate and are proud of their sacrifices and submissiveness in one context but may feel compelled to abandon such a role when confronted with the reality of harassment and oppression. Furthermore, market women do not share the same relations of production and often are in intense economic competition with one another, making it very difficult for them to achieve political solidarity. Nevertheless, it is precisely through political processes that they may arrive at a common perspective and unite in their actions. However, it would be wrong to assume that collective solidarity necessitates homogeneity. As Stephen (1997:21, 22–23) concludes from her research with women in different kinds of social movements across Latin America, "The cases of women's organizing . . . suggest that, rather than assuming the natural existence of collective identities, we have to look contextually at how mobilization arises and how its meaning and interpretation may vary between individuals and over time. Groups of women who act together are often quite heterogeneous, and their ability to act comes from respecting difference while also forging a common argument through a shared set of questions. . . . Theories of collective action cannot be abstracted from the context within which they appear. . . . The blending of personal identity with political activism underscores how different and conflicting pieces of individual identity interact with structural conditions to influence the evolution of political commitment and strategy."

The political consciousness of many market women begins to develop, naturally enough, when they react to threats to their own self-interest. These may include imposition of price controls by the municipality, sexual harassment, seizure of goods, levying of fines, cutting off of basic services such as electricity and water, and, most common of all, being thrown out of their workplaces. In the course of reacting to these incidents, they gain a better sense of the meanings of authority and citizenship and of how they are being manipulated by political rhetoric and false campaign promises. Market vendors are also eminently practical. Therefore, they often strive to form alliances with labor unions. Labor unions do not necessarily welcome their participation, however, because of the very labor conditions of the vendors: Market vendors are difficult to organize, they do not necessarily stay in one place, they do not constitute a unified body, and they are overwhelmingly mothers with children. The latter turns out to be a critical obstacle when vendors' unions try to coordinate with labor unions, a subject to which I will return.

Every year, market vendors are expelled from their work sites or threatened with expulsion. It has almost become a ritual, and each year the women learn better how to resist the next time around. And few of them doubt that there will be a next time. Each time the market women confront the possibility of not being able to pursue their livelihood, they acquire more knowledge of how to fight back. Rarely are they entirely defeated, but theirs is a Sisyphean struggle.

Space and Political Resistance: The Battles of Spatial Order

> Money and commodities . . . were destined to bring with them not only a "culture" but also a space. The uniqueness of the marketplace, doubtless on account of the splendour of religious and political structures, has tended to be overlooked. We should therefore remind ourselves that antiquity looked upon trade and tradespeople as external to the city, as outside its political system, and so relegated them to the outskirts. The basis of wealth was still real property, ownership of the land. The medieval revolution brought commerce inside the town and lodged it at the centre of a transformed urban space. The marketplace differed from the forum as from the agora: access to it was free, and it opened up on every side onto the surrounding territory . . . and into the countryside's network of roads and lanes. [The market hall's] function was to shelter the transaction of business while permitting the authorities to control it. The cathedral church was certainly not far away, but its tower no longer bore the symbols of knowledge and power; instead the freestanding campanile now dominated space—and would soon, as clock-tower, come to dominate time too. . . . By the fourteenth century this space, known and recognized now, and hence representable, was able to gener-

ate purely symbolic towns, founded for the purposes of commerce in re-
gions which were still exclusively agropastoral, and where consequently
no commercial activity was as yet taking place. (Lefebvre 1991:265)

Space is a critical political resource in the conflicts that involve market women. Most market vendors have an astute understanding of how spatial relations operate. They also have a good grasp of how social space is organized and who is responsible for its design. They themselves contribute to the organization of social space or, more accurately, the disruption of that existing organization. Henri Lefebvre, in an effort to argue that Marxian approaches to relations of production too often have ignored the variable of space as a social and highly politicized dimension of economic relations, describes the transformation of religiopolitical centers into commercial hubs in Europe in the fourteenth century and with some irony traces how transformations in production coincided with the transformation of spatial organization and social functions, together with notions of temporality. These changes took place much later in the New World in the nineteenth century, yet their impact was similar. Even as the marketplace was marginalized, it came to dominate the center, causing discomfort and displeasure to the authorities who wanted to control it. The authorities wanted to control the form and functions of the marketplace—to obtain revenues from vendors, to assert their status as patrons, and to keep the marketplace in order, in accordance with their ideas about modernity and appropriate behavior. They also needed to keep the city's residents satisfied by keeping the price of commodities low.

These concerns have only become greater as the years have passed. Peru's economy cannot keep pace with the vision of modernity of its urban residents. The market is neither in the center nor at the margins of the imagined, well-ordered center of Cuzco. Instead, it is everywhere, making it impossible to control easily any of the aforementioned aspects. Looking back at the municipal archival record when debates were under way, first about whether the market should be relocated from the Central Plaza de Armas and then about where it should be relocated, residents and politicians referred repeatedly to the market as a focal point of infection.[4] Furthermore, the vendors are women who long ago ruptured the gender codes of gentility. They too find the market uncomfortable and unsatisfying, but it constitutes their livelihood, and they have learned how to use it and take advantage of the contradictions that lie within it in order to defend themselves. The very chaos can allow them to create order when they are assaulted by the authorities, seeking to clean up the streets. In fact, as Mitchell Duneier (1999) perceptively explains, despite the seeming disorder that a glimpse of the sidewalk offers, it is the market women them-

selves who serve as the eyes and ears of the streets, making them safe by en-
forcing informal rules of conduct and norms. The services and products that
vendors offer have a multiplier effect in that they need people to help them
move, store, or deliver their goods or to watch their stalls or informal spots
sometimes. These small jobs go to people who might otherwise have to turn
to panhandling or criminal activities. The services and products provided by
vendors also knit together a heterogeneous population on the streets in a social manner instead of isolating and segregating them. Finally, some vendors,
such as Lucre, become role models and mentors for more vulnerable women,
who then seek advice from her, drawing on her knowledge and experience,
and attempt to imitate her behavior. The disorder of the street vendors, in
reality, may prevent public space from becoming uninhabitable.

The use of space is always in flux, in accordance with national economic
dynamics. Some researchers have suggested that established enterprises have
deliberately created a reserve labor supply of women who, driven into the
informal sector, provide cheap goods to workers and often to formal enterprises in a chain of production that straddles the formal and informal sectors.
Certainly, the dynamics of Cuzco's markets reflect these conditions, but I do
not think that this is a deliberate policy, on the part of the government or of
Cuzco's few industries. The results are the same, nevertheless.

In arguing that space, place, and temporal rhythms and what they signify
can never be taken as given, Gupta and Ferguson (1992:17), explain that
"people . . . confound the established spatial orders, either through physical
movement, or through their own conceptual and political acts of
reimagination." Even in the conflicts that arise between different kinds of vendors, the unstable value attributed to different kinds of spaces in the market
becomes apparent. The organization of the social space of the marketplace pits
market woman against market woman, market women against municipal
authorities, and market women against urban residents. The struggles between
market women occur primarily between itinerant vendors outside established
markets and permanent vendors inside markets. To compete with permanent
vendors, the itinerant vendors often use rigged scales, switching them if they
receive word from their companions that the municipal inspectors are due on
the scene or if one of their *caseras* appears. One vendor explained to me, "We
only change it by about 100 grams or else the customer would know." The
ambulantes falsify the quality of their products, thereby receiving a few
centavos more than they should from naive customers. And there are plenty
of naive and harried customers.

The structure and rhythm of the permanent markets also give itinerant vendors an edge, even though conditions inside are cleaner and more peaceful. The permanent market officially closes at 5 P.M., whereas the itinerant vendors remain at their stalls until early evening. Finally, as the economy declines, even middle-class customers seek out cheaper products, assuming sometimes incorrectly that those outside the market are cheaper than inside. When I was doing my field research in 1998, the permanent vendors complained repeatedly that the market was *vacío* (empty) and that everyone was leaving, because they couldn't compete with the itinerant vendors. Indeed, many stalls were vacated by 3 P.M. Itinerant vendors also move through space, seeking better locations all the time. Permanent vendors attempt to combat the advantages of itinerant vendors by engaging in an underground economy of stall commerce, using their relatives and friends as a way to establish control over strategic stall sites, renting and even selling them, but always wary of being discovered by the municipal authorities.

Political Promises and Populist Parties

The strife between permanent and itinerant vendors is complicated by the political stratagems of enterprising politicians. Robert Albro has written extensively about the ways in which politicians across the spectrum in Bolivia use the metaphor of *cholaje* in their quest to represent themselves as men (and sometimes women) of "the people." Posters of proud *cholas,* many of whom are typed as market women, plaster the walls of La Paz. Barbecues take place with *chicha* music blaring. Politicians make a point to show up and make lavish expenditures at traditional *cholo* festivals. This kind of populist wielding of the *vox populi* in Bolivia, interestingly, has only recently been embraced by Peru's politicians. Until Toledo's successful run for the presidency, the Peruvian attitude toward *cholos,* whether in reality or metaphorically, remained generally negative, partly because those labeled as *cholas* and *cholos,* particularly market women, have not bought into this kind of rhetoric. They have already been sufficiently disenchanted by the numerous broken promises of politicians. In addition, Peru's racist ideology runs very deep, and unlike both Ecuador and Bolivia, where indigenous movements have gathered impressive momentum, Peru has no significant indigenous movement (see Montoya 1998).[5] Only in the 1920s, in the heyday of *indigenismo,* did intellectuals and politicians rhetorically consider the positive dimensions of Peru's Indian heritage.[6] Those positive dimensions were hedged in by notions of purity, an acceptance of "Indians," so long as they stayed in their place and did not "mix" with other races. *Cholos,* the quintessential product of cultural, racial, and political mixing, challenges the rhetoric of *indigenismo* as well as the provincial elite's aspirations to maintain its superiority. De la Cadena (1998:33) drives home this point in her study of *indigenismo* in the province of Cuzco: "A key indigenista cultural concern of the intellectual insurgents . . . was the premise that culture could transform race. They inverted reigning beliefs whereby race determined culture. Expanding upon its original premise, *indigenismo* was a political movement that had as its goal 'the revindication of the Indian.' Despite the renovation implied by the indigenista premise, however, the 'revindication of the Indian' accepted the prevailing assumption that the indigenous race needed improvement in order to be included as part of the nation . . . although the Peruvian and Mexican indigenistas were centrally concerned with the 'inferior races,' their nationalist solutions did not include a continuing process of bleaching through biological mixing with ostensibly 'superior' races."

Rotting Olives

Especially when presidential and mayoral campaigns are under way, market women become a central focus of politicians' platforms. Aspiring and incumbent mayors promise residents that itinerant vendors will be swept off the roadway. They simultaneously promise itinerant vendors that they will build them a "modern" market. In 1995, the municipal police ousted the 182 *ambulantes* who belonged to the union of San Pedro Cascaparo from the street and forced them inside the market. After six months of surveillance and bad business, one of the union's most respected leaders, Amilcar, became enraged and threw five vats of his olives out onto the street in front of the municipal agents. He challenged the other vendors to go back outside, protesting that there was no way he was going to continue working inside with all his goods rotting because of the lack of sales. The union members held *asambleas* (meetings) at night to decide what to do. Eventually, 120 of them risked going outside again. They occupied the street and established a new union. The mayor called them pimps and prostitutes (*majaderos*), and the struggle began anew. They stood their ground, but it was not easy. One woman explained to me that part of their success was that they were able to recruit a savvy legal advisor who had once worked for Federación Agraria Revolucionario Tupac Amaru del Cuzco, or the Revolutionary Tupac Amaru Agrarian Federation of Cuzco (FARTAC). For the first time, the union members drew on two principles: due process (*habeas corpus*) and the right to protection (*el recurso de amparo*). The litigation lasted a year, but this did not prevent the police from continuing to try to push them off the streets. While the litigation was ongoing, the vendors slept every night on the splintered and damp wooden platforms (*tarimas*) of the stalls where they normally displayed their goods. One day, the municipality told them that they had reached a settlement with the union. That night, they decided that they could finally return to their homes, sleep in their beds rather than out in the cold, and try to put their houses in order again. The same night, however, an army battalion, accompanied by the municipal police, began burning down the vendors' stalls. Once they heard what was happening, they frantically tried to get to their stalls but were blocked by the army and police. After this debacle, they decided they had "to study to get back our space." They met at night in small groups. Arming themselves with sticks, stones, and flags, they furtively reentered the street early one morning and reconstructed their makeshift stalls, using *tarimas* they had borrowed from other vendors. According to one union leader, at that point, the mayor decided it was too much trouble to harass them further, noting that they were *bien pleitos, tinterillos* (always litigating, little lawyers). When I pressed the union leader further, she added that to keep the peace, the vendors had had to buy off each of the municipal council members with millions of *intis* (the devalued currency of the time) and a basket of their best fruit. A few council members did not accept the bribe.

The story that the women tell of this confrontation is interesting because of the different kinds of tactics they use. Their bodies are an exceedingly important weapon in these battles and resemble effective pacifist actions taken by many grassroots movements. In the end they were duped by the police and, it appears, perhaps by their own union leadership, but for a long time they staved off attack by sleeping in their stalls, often with their children. They also relied on first- and second-hand knowledge of land invasions in the countryside and of the occupation of urban space for residential settlements. (In the 1960s peasant migrants staked out the hills surrounding cities and over the years transformed their makeshift shelters into permanent housing as cooperatives and *pueblos jovenes*.) They drew on the law with the help of their legal advisor, invoking the right to work and due process. Finally, they resorted to the usual *modus operandi* of using bribes to keep the peace.

Breaking Windshields, Pulling Hair, Making Space

In 1997, once again the vendors received written notification that they would be thrown out. As one woman described the events,

> At 4 A.M., the municipal police arrived, accompanied by the national police and bulldozers. We were all sleeping in our stalls so the police were prevented from tearing the stalls down. Three days later, at around 8 A.M., 150 well-armed police arrived and formed two columns on either side of the street. They destroyed one of our stalls. It belonged to the president of

the union so she was furious and grabbed one of the police. The rest of us pelted the police with sticks and stones. The leader, the mother of a family of a mestiza family ["una familia mestiza"] grabbed the mayor, shaking him by the shoulders and saying in Quechua, "Is this what you want? To make me die here? Is this what you want for our children?"[7] The MPs surrounded her, but we, her companions, broke through the circle. Then the national police arrived. Their job is to maintain public order. They tried to break up the fray. They accused the mayor of causing a scandal and they asked him to avoid violence.[8]

The second week, the municipal police again tried to oust us. For fifteen days, we slept on our tarimas. This time, we had inside information that the MPs were going to try to throw us out. The word spread from "base" to "base" so we were prepared when the invasion took place. The MPs came in tanks, trucks, bulldozers, and shields [tirapalos]. They destroyed ten tarimas. Our bases whistled to communicate to each other. Using sticks and stones, we began smashing the windshields of the column of trucks. There were about 200 MPs. The drivers of the trucks became flustered because they had no ability to maneuver in the narrow street.

The control of the very resource at issue that so angered the authorities was what the vendors used to their advantage as a weapon: the organization of the street's space. The national police observed but did not intervene. In addition to using their knowledge of the structure of urban space, the vendors also drew on the fears that so many urban residents secretly harbor that they are uncontrollable harpies. They surrounded ten MPs and the municipal director who at the time was a woman, Lizbet Yepes. One vendor screamed at her in Quechua, "Don't you have a mother? Where were you born to have to commit this abuse against us? Now, you'll see what happens when we strike you, pull your hair, trample you, so that you won't do this to us again. You may kill us but we'll go down together."[9]

As is true in so many parts of the world, the women deliberately occupied the front lines because they wanted to protect the men who were present, fearing that the latter would be more quickly seized as political agitators. In addition, the fury of the women reached new heights when four MPs captured two of their male comrades, one of whom was elderly. The women attacked the MPs, tearing off their clothes and leaving them practically naked.

The MPs, frustrated with the national police, surrounded them and accused them of not doing their job. The national police reiterated that there was no reason for them to intervene unless there were deaths. They reminded the MPs that the vendors were "madres de familia"—mothers. As the windshields began shattering, the trucks tried to back up, but in doing so they began smashing into each other. Once again, the market vendors succeeded in hanging onto their space, but their peace of mind was not to last long.

Two-Way Streets

On September 3, 1998, Cuzco's local paper, *El Comercio,* reported,

> "Despite the Intransigence of the Vendors, Intervention in Rerouting of Qasqaparo Street Is Immanent"—One of the works of great transcendence programmed by the Cuzco Municipality before its term expires is the total intervention in Qasqaparo Street, in order to connect it with the redesigned Tres Cruces de Oro artery and to optimize automobile transit in the Monumental Center of the city. Completion of studies and projects by the Office of Public Works demonstrate that it is possible to achieve this despite the intransigence of the ambulantes who have assumed ownership of this space for the last twenty years, ignoring the recommendations of the authorities that they move elsewhere to conduct their commercial transactions. . . . The eternal opposition, enemies of progress and development of this capital, have reared their heads again. . . . A delegation of these troublemakers visited the Municipal Palace, seeking dialogue with Mayor Raúl Salízar Saico who was happily acerbic in his appreciation of their visit. Represented by Teófila Huamán, and accompanied by the lawyer Gloria Charca Puente de la Vega, now an advisor to "the informals" they oppose the Mayor's plan because it is the only source of income for almost one hundred of their families. In response to their complaint, the mayor has been clear and adamant that the project is a given and will take place, no matter what. The mayor also clarified that of the hundred vendors that are posted along the street most of them belong to the same family and they've taken over various stalls, giving an impression that does not correspond to reality. The leader Teófila and the legal advisor left the Council, making threats against the Cuzqueño mayor, who was finally compelled to say that, despite the circumstances, and the moment of electoral excitement that the people are experiencing, one cannot mortgage the development of this city in exchange for a few votes.

The mayor's development project once again targeted the vendors lining both sides of San Pedro (also known as Qasqaparo), a one-way street. His planned eviction of the vendors followed similar actions that took place in Lima and Arequipa, with far more successful outcomes for politicians than in Cuzco. In both of those booming commercial centers, the vendors were ousted and relocated, clearing thoroughfares and pleasing many pedestrians and drivers. But in Cuzco, the mayor's actions met with mixed results.

In 1998, Cuzco's incumbent mayor, Raúl Salízar Saico, was up for reelection. When he first entered office, the vendors met with him and discussed moving to a new location, a piece of land that had been owned by Petro Peru. The budget for a new market for itinerant vendors was hammered out and the architectural design for a new market commissioned and completed. The new market would be light and airy, made up of three floors, with running water and bathrooms. All the *ambulantes* agreed that the location was suitable, just across from the permanent market of Wanchaq, which had benefited from Cuzco's expansion south of the city. Shortly thereafter, however, perhaps because the municipality needed revenues to pay its debts, the mayor sold the piece of land to a private company and claimed that no such agreement had ever been established. I was able to obtain a copy of the proposal, the budget, and the architectural plans.

Salízar Saico's party, the Pachacutec Movement, had been named after the ninth Inca, Pachacutec, who was responsible for transforming the nascent Inca state into a booming and vast empire, building roadways, storehouses, bridges, and temples and institutionalizing Inca imperial deities in order to consolidate the divine status of the ruling Incas. Salízar Saico was a sorry contrast to Inca Pachacutec, however, and political jokes abounded about this mayor who tore down one plaza after another, cut down the leafy trees that surrounded Cuzco's central plaza, and spent inordinate amounts of money employing people to dig up sidewalks and cobblestone streets. He was far more commonly known as the Destroyer of Cuzco. One of his favorite targets after his election to office was the itinerant market vendors. As elections for a new mayor fast approached, Salízar became more fervently fixed than ever on the *ambulantes*.

In August 1998, rumors began circulating that the San Pedro vendors were going to be thrown out. Although the rumors were not confirmed, the vendors became worried enough that once again they began sleeping in their stalls and holding union meetings under the auspices of FEDETAC. On Friday, August 27, they met and decided to form a front composed of two representatives from each of the six unions that lined the street. On Saturday, they decided to try to find out the mayor's intentions, without success. On Sunday, they held another meeting and decided to send their representatives to meet with the municipal authorities that Monday. The authorities confirmed that the vendors were going to be "evacuated" because of traffic congestion, competition, and the "messiness" they constituted. They had received many complaints from residents. In fact, a huge banner crosses over San Pedro, announcing "Yes, to a Monumental Zone, No, to Itinerant Vendors." In a second meeting on Monday between the union's legal advisor, Gloria Charca,

Banner raised by property owners and residents in Cuzco, which states, "Welcome! Monumental Zone. No to Itinerant Commerce!"

mayor Salízar, and the municipal director, Charca demanded that the mayor confirm his intention to throw out the vendors. He confirmed that this was his plan but promised not to throw them out until he could find a new place to relocate them. When Ms. Charca demanded that he sign a document to this effect, he refused.

Even holding these meetings was an enormous burden and trial for vendors. They lost out on sales while they were meeting. If they brought their small children and infants to the meeting, they were admonished to "shut up and leave," usually by union leaders, the majority of whom were men. Also, although there had been some improvement in holding the sessions in Spanish and Quechua, many of the women were unable to understand what was taking place because it was solely in Spanish, and once again, they were criticized by union leaders for not being bilingual or literate. Despite these shortcomings, the meetings were remarkably well attended each time by 150 to 200 people, most of them women.

On Tuesday, August 31, the women gathered for another meeting at FEDETAC's headquarters. The atmosphere was tense. Late the night before, the municipal police had attempted to paint a bright yellow line down San Pedro. The line symbolically and literally meant that the *ambulantes* would be thrown out to make way for two-way traffic. The women harassed the painters to such an extent, shaking their paint buckets and pushing and shoving them, that they could not finish the job.

The meeting of the vendors with their leaders exploded because the vendors had learned that in their meeting with the municipal director and mayor, their own union leaders had consented to "regularize" their members, that is, make sure that their members had paid their licenses and that each member had only one stall. A number of problems beset the efforts of union leaders to rationalize their members' uses of space. Some members had not paid for their licenses. Others had two stalls, a situation prohibited if husband and wife were running them. If some other combination of family members rented the stall, it was considered distant enough not to matter. Finally, some members had paid for membership in more than one union and had a stall that belonged to each union.

These conflicts reveal that a whole economy of space is at work in the market. Intense debate ensued, with some arguing that all the vendors should be protected and others that they needed to act in the interest of political pragmatism. The political pragmatists won the day, with some compromises. Older vendors (*ancianos*) who had not paid for their licenses would be protected. But the *buitres* (vultures) would be thrown out. It was agreed that vendors could not have membership in two unions but that couples could occupy two spaces in the same union. (The secretary general himself fell into the latter category.) Everywhere, the *ambulantes* were trying to think about alternatives to remaining informal, and everywhere they were trying creatively to maximize their use of space.

On September 2, 1998, Cuzco's newspaper *El Sol* reported on negotiations between the market women and the mayor:

> Around 400 ambulantes from Tres Cruces de Oro raised their voice in protest yesterday against Raúl Salízar Saico, who they said was making fun of them, not fulfilling his promises to them, and that they would have to take matters into their own hands by adopting forceful measures. "We have been without work for four months, and our children no longer have anything to eat—this doesn't interest the mayor, but it makes us desperate. For that reason, we've convened a meeting for next Friday to try to resolve this problem for once and for all. We will take measures that we agree upon in the meeting. The Attorney General [La Fiscal de Prevención del Delito] has told me that because I am defending our right to work, they will send me to prison, but if we have to defend the bread of our children, it doesn't matter if I have to go to jail," said Paulina Rojas de Serrano, Secretary General of the ambulantes of Tres Cruces de Oro.

This is another problem generated by the mayor Raúl Salízar, who now wants to convert Ccasccaparo into a two-way street even though the vendors have said they won't give an inch. . . .

In a meeting between the mayor and the leaders of FEDETAC, he promised to hold another meeting with FEDETAC, at which he would form a Mixed Technical Commission in order to find a solution to the problems of the ambulantes. But yesterday when the ambulantes met at the municipal palace for the meeting, the mayor paid no attention to them. He spent more time talking with the ambulantes of Ccasccaparo, making them the same proposal he had made to Tres Cruces de Oro, telling them he would form a Mixed Commission to reach a solution to their problem. But the mayor will probably pay no attention to them and forget what he promised them yesterday, just as he did with the ambulantes of Tres Cruces de Oro.

The vendors were told that the secretary general of the union and municipal director would meet with the vendors to measure their stalls in the evening. Everyone was scared to death that this was simply a pretext for throwing them out. The meeting was to begin at 8 P.M., late enough that most people would be in their houses. The secretary general announced that he did not plan to be at the meeting because he had to go to Arequipa to pick up fruit. This catalyzed the call to replace the current leadership of the front and replace it with a new one called a commission. Those who called for new leadership wanted well-seasoned leaders who had gone into battle before. Many of them believed that the current secretary general had sold out to the municipal authorities and the mayor. Picking up fruit was just a pretext. Although many gathered were furious at the secretary general, they were not willing to challenge him. Two women who had leadership experience and were well respected, Paulina Rojas and Aidé Garces, had received threats for two weeks running that they would be arrested as political agitators and tried in a military court if they persisted in their actions. The debate continued, with some wanting to follow a legalistic path toward dialog while others thought they should be preparing for political struggle. They finally decided that they would sleep in their stalls, make banners and flags, and paint over the yellow line with black paint that is difficult to remove. They would also get a legal advisor to help them to draft a restraining order. The meeting lasted from 3 P.M. to 8 P.M.

When I was sitting with some of the women discussing the impending expulsion, one of them snorted and observed that the municipality didn't even seem to be considering Avenida Ejército, which was "a time bomb, waiting to happen. What they were doing was like cleaning the house by sweeping the dust under the bed." Another woman noted that at the Wanchaq market, they

had tried to control the problem of the itinerant vendors by completely fenc-
ing in the market, encircling all the itinerant vendors. But, of course, new vendors situated themselves outside the fence. Many of the women voiced their
complete distrust of the mayor who had promised so much to the 500
ambulantes of Tres Cruces de Oro and then thrown them out, as the newspaper article in *El Sol* confirmed. A few of the women, especially those who had
not paid their licenses, were resigned to the possibility of abandoning their stalls
permanently. I asked Eva Carhuarupay, who attended all the union meetings,
what she would do if the *ambulantes* were ousted from San Pedro. She replied,
"I'll just go from market to market, wandering [*ambulando*]." I asked her which
markets she would go to, and she mentioned a whole circuit of markets in the
Sacred Valley of Urubamba, so she didn't mean confining herself to being an
itinerant vendor in Cuzco, but rather going on the road. She concluded, "I don't
really care about politics at all. I am too busy trying to survive."

Mob Tactics

Tuesday at 9 P.M. I returned to the market, ambivalent and nervous about being
there late at night. But if something was going to happen, I wanted to be
present. I traveled to the market by taxi, my shopping bag at my side, but
instead of fruit and cheese, inside it were my tape recorder and camera. When
I got there, I went straight to Justina's fruit stall. There was a large crowd across
the way at the train station, but I was a little scared about going over there by
myself. Justina didn't want me to go over there at all. Her eyes were filled with
sadness. She had already lost her oldest daughter to the politics of the market, not because she was killed by the police but because during one of the
assaults on the vendors, she refused to go to the doctor even though she was
in great pain, and she died of a ruptured appendix. Teófila, my research assistant, was one of Justina's two remaining daughters. She was a member of the
union leadership, serving as their secretary, and was perceived as a firebrand.
She said she had to act to honor the memory of her sister.

Reluctantly, Justina's husband took me over to the crowd. In the middle
stood the municipal director of the market, surrounded by municipal police.
Surrounding the municipal police were rings of market vendors, mostly
women, but some young and old men had joined the crowd as well. They were
surrounded by yet another circle of police, then several rings of vendors, then
another ring of police. It was a volatile situation, and I was not at all sure what
I should do or what my role should be. I had my tape recorder ready to tape,
but it was hard to hear above the screams and shouts and traffic. I started taping anyway. The vendors were demanding to be left alone. They accused the

director of having sold them out. Intermittently, there were shrieks and whistles and people shouting, "We are only trying to make a living, for God's sake. The mayor will betray us, just as he betrayed the vendors of Tres Cruces." Chanting followed that made little sense unless one understood the context— "Let it rain, let it rain"—the idea being that the police and director would not be able to measure off people's stalls if it started to pour. And no one wanted the measuring to take place even though they had yet to figure out an alternative. They were stalling, waiting for a restraining order that they hoped to have in hand by the next day. They had not had time to paint the yellow line black. Gradually, the whole crowd (and I) moved to the other side of the street, which was usually occupied by vendors of the San Pedro union. The crowd's anger was growing. I was literally pushed on top of the *tarimas* and commanded by the vendors to photograph the director as he began to attempt to measure the space that would be allocated to each stall. What first greeted the director when he reached the other side of the road was a plastic sack covering a homeless man in rags, sleeping. Several people pointed at the sack, jeering, "This is what happens if people do not have work."

People started to jostle and yell at me to take pictures. I was being made the center of attention even though it was the last thing I wanted. Things got even worse when everyone started clamoring that I should tape what was happening. I was already taping, but people did not realize how powerful the microphone was, and they wanted me to get closer and closer. I was not sure whether I was being more endangered by the attention and protection of the pressing crowd or less. The police narrowed their eyes, began whispering, and then began to focus their attention on me. One periodically mouthed, "Qué feo, qué feo" ("how ugly, how ugly"). I kept hoping they would think I was a local journalist, and then I remembered that freedom of the press was shaky in Peru. I began worrying about being targeted as a political agitator because, at the time, agitators were either booted out of the country or tried by a military court. This was worse than anything I had experienced during the civil war. Things got even more heated. One of the police tried to block my recording by turning on his walkie-talkie. The crowd surged and roared. By then, there were several hundred vendors on the scene. I could do nothing to control the situation, caught between the vendors' reasonable demands and my fear of the authorities. Fortunately, the director turned to the police officer and told him to turn off his walkie-talkie. The crowd demanded that I speak on their behalf. I kept telling them they could speak very well for themselves.

The confrontation lasted long into the night, and much of it concerned who had the right to a stall and the distinctions to be drawn between stalls "above," which were wider and more established, and those "below," which deserved a different treatment because the street funnels and becomes narrower. Over and over, the vendors called the mayor a traitor, reminding him that he had promised to relocate the 500 vendors of Tres Cruces he had ousted last year. The municipal director tried to control the crowd, saying he was a mediator between the mayor and the union. But the women claimed their own leaders had been bought off and were corrupt. Finally, the director gave up and invited everyone to attend a meeting with the mayor the next morning. He insisted that he would not throw the vendors out if they regulated themselves. Aidé, one of the so-called political agitators, communicated to the director that they were willing to speak with the mayor. She assured the director that they would be respectful because they were "bien educadas" (well-educated and, by implication, well-mannered), but they would fight for their rights. Shortly thereafter the meeting began to end, but just at that point, a crowd formed around me. The press of bodies pushed me past the *tarimas*. A stick fell past my face. People were shouting, almost in unison, that I had to get into a taxi immediately before the police took away my tape and tape recorder. I felt scared as more and more bodies pressed against me. The women pushed me into a cab and even wanted to accompany me, but I persuaded them that I would be around the next day and would give the tape to "La Paloma" ("The Dove"), as Teófila is called by her union comrades.

I did not go to the meeting with the mayor the next morning. I was worried that my credibility had been destroyed. Teófila told me the mayor was apoplectic during the meeting, throwing chairs and notebooks, accusing the vendors of not supporting his political party, and complimenting the municipal director for taking the right path. The union's legal advisor again tried to get the mayor to confirm that he was "reordering" the vendors. He affirmed it was the case and then tried to persuade the vendors that the total change in width would be only five meters. The vendors realized that this was absurd because diminishing the width of the *tarimas* by five meters would never leave enough room for the stalls, the pedestrians, and two-way traffic. They told him he was "deceiving" them, and they did not want to be used as he had used the vendors of Tres Cruces. He responded that it was disgraceful the way they were selling things outside, contaminating the bread, contaminating the olives. The union's legal advisor had planned to use a restraining order (*acción de ámparo*) to keep the mayor from ousting them. The *acción de ámparo* is similar to a right-to-work law and does not allow people to be prevented from working without cause. However, the new constitution no longer honored the law, and the mayor argued that, of course, the *ambulantes* could continue working.

They would just have to work somewhere else. He ended the meeting with an ultimatum: If they did not agree to arrange themselves in two lines with each *tarima* measuring 1.5 meters by 1.2 meters, then he would "call out his trucks, his tractors, the military and the police and wipe them out because society was demanding that he eradicate them" (personal communication, Téofila Huáman). The *ambulantes* pleaded for "a Solomonic solution," but it was not forthcoming. The mayor retorted that he "no longer had any time for them." He didn't care about garnering their support for the upcoming election. He was "the only pachacutec" and wanted "to satisfy the *vecinos* [urban elite]." Two articles appeared in the local press, both sympathetic to the plight of the *ambulantes.*

Signing Off

Resignation, a grim appraisal of reality, fear, barely concealed anger, and the experience of years of packing and unpacking characterized the scene I came upon the following evening as the women of the market began storing their merchandise in crates, measuring their *tarimas,* and apprehensively waiting for the arrival of the municipal workers. The truck finally arrived. As the vendors' goods disappeared, the rats and rat droppings appeared. The union members huddled in a group. The scene was a sharp contrast to the other nights, when people still had hope even though they were worried that things could get much worse. Now, the statements were subdued: "Let us hope we can continue to work. Let us hope they do not take advantage of us. How cold and how late will it get?"

The municipal workers took out a long sliding ladder, raised it, and hoisted a two-way street sign high on a telephone pole. They posted one on each side of the street. Garbage burned, the detritus of the makeshift workplaces of the poor. Familiar cabbies slowly went by, commenting to the vendors with black humor, "The next place we'll see you is Huancaro." (Huancaro is on the outskirts of the city.) One of the market women retorted, "Not even in San Jerónimo." (San Jerónimo is a large open air regional market about twenty miles from Cuzco.)

Discussion

The next day, I walked to the market. Everything was eerily peaceful along San Pedro. All the *tarimas* were properly aligned within white painted stripes. The traffic moved in both directions. Ironically, there was still not enough room for the cars, pedestrians, and stalls, but the mayor had made his point. I noticed that several women who had not paid for their licenses had not been forced to leave. Eva and her half-sister, Lucre, were still there. Some of the stalls, such as Justina's, were still longer than they were supposed to be. This was a problem for the women further down as the street narrows. Teófila said that the vendors had negotiated unsuccessfully until 3 A.M. with the women below. Solidarity goes only so far.

As for me, the fallout from "the mob" had indeed compromised my credibility. The municipal director sent out feelers, inquiring who "that trouble-maker journalist" was. But things were worse. The FEDETAC's secretary general, whose membership had considered throwing him out, began calling me a "communist agitator" and would not speak with me even though just a week before he had enthusiastically agreed to let me interview him. And there was enough bad blood between the *ambulantes* lining San Pedro and the vendors inside the market that I began having trouble getting some of the *dirigentes* (leaders) of the formal market to talk with me. I had learned long ago in Peru that in such a snake's pit, field research requires that all doors stay open and that one talk with as many different players as possible. This practice had always given me credibility, and it had also allowed me constantly to reweave and juxtapose the narratives and dialogs I participated in and to reflect on the interactions themselves, making connections that I never could have made otherwise. For the next several weeks, I did most of my work along Avenida Ejército and spent hours reviewing the history of the market and municipality in the municipal archives. I was lucky that these archives were no longer housed in the Municipal Palace, where I might be recognized; they had been relocated to the Municipal Library, where I was welcomed warmly.

When I left Peru, San Pedro was a two-way street, although traffic flowed less smoothly than before the failed uprising, and pedestrians were at a greater risk than ever before of being run over or crushed between a *tarima* and a bus. The market vendors were still staking out their space. Although they had temporarily acceded to the white striped lines, I have no doubt they will gradually expand, inciting yet another incursion by the authorities down the road.[10]

The incidents I have described in this chapter cannot be defined as victories or defeats, and they have different meanings for the women who participated in them. They demonstrate the complexity of citizenship rights in the context of marketplace culture, economies, and politics. The everyday kinds of resistance that vendors use are peculiar to the position in which they are situated and which, in many cases, they have been forced to occupy. They resort to using space and spatial relations as weapons and resources with which they can challenge authoritative discourse and urban designs. And their knowledge of spatial relations is not limited to urban environments and therefore is not easily accessible to all urban residents. Many of the tactics they use are replicated in the countryside in land invasions, and more than a few of the vendors got their first experience in staking out space when they came as migrants and took over the hillsides to build their shacks. They know how to occupy space. They also take advantage of socially acceptable strategies—the vote, the law, and the media—to make their case.

These kinds of resistance are not distinct from more extensive kinds of mobilization. Rather, the tactics culled from knowledge of how space is organized, manipulation of weights and measures, use of language, and deployment of the physical body itself and of gendered identities become critical when, organized into unions, they confront en masse the armed authorities. In other words, economic relations of production alone do not satisfactorily explain how or why market women are able to sustain their struggles against state agents and urban residents who find their presence a constant reminder of the failure of modernity. The culturally grounded knowledge that circulates among market women about how to read and decode spatial relations assists them greatly in their political actions and in their ability to make a living.

At the same time, skillful as they are in manipulating spatial codes and occupying space, the vendors cannot surmount their ambivalent position. Their struggles are hemmed in as they warily assess how much social standing they want to risk and whose wrath they can afford to incite, whether it is the wholesalers, *campesinos,* their clients, or other market women who are differently situated. They are hardly naive. Most of them do not hold one or another sector of market women ultimately responsible for the fractiousness among them. They know it comes from afar, from the "dictatorship," as many called the government of Alberto Fujimori, which oversaw neoliberalism, floods of imports, narrowly channeled economic growth, and soaring unemployment. These economic policies were accompanied by particular social attitudes and a kind of social engineering linked to spatial design. Despite the awareness among many Peruvians of the growing income disparity between rich and poor and greater desperation among lower-class urban residents and peasants in the countryside about how they and their children will survive, many better-off Peruvians and politicians discount the validity of such despair. The age-old tenets of modernization theory, together with deeply rooted racism, have been internalized to such an extent that the assumption among politicians and prosperous urban residents is that if people are experiencing economic failure, it is their fault, and they are not following the proper model of development.

Vendors recognize that these attitudes permeate Peruvian society. They also know that the divisiveness among them and the violence they experience cannot be easily remedied by the surging yet factitious populism of local political parties that have proliferated, with names such as "Let's Go Neighbor," "We Are Peru," "My Peru," or "Peru, the Possible," attempting to persuade the popular classes that they can be a single harmonious entity.

Finally, unlike many among Peru's poor, they are willing to act on the rhetorical discourse that constitutes ideal Peruvian citizenship and demand their rights rather than resign themselves to paternalism. Although they were not entirely successful, they attempted to sanction their own leadership for resorting to shady deals rather than principled opposition. Once again, they stood in the middle, however, not capable of demanding their citizenship rights solely by using the rule of law.

One of the first acts of the new mayor, Carlos Valencia, elected at the end of 1998, was to address the National Congress of Ambulantes in Cuzco, promising the itinerant vendors that he would build them a new market.

Notes

Portions of this chapter are paraphrased or reprinted from my article "Market Places, Social Spaces in Cuzco, Peru," *Urban Anthropology* 29:1 (April 2000): 1–68.

1. The municipal record is full of such adjectives. See also de la Cadena (2000) and Weismantel (2001).

2. Lynn Stephen (1997:35–36) elaborates on the "links between Catholic images of femininity and their use by repressive states to control women." In her words,

> Images of the Virgin Mary portray an idealized woman who is an obedient, self-sacrificing mother, subordinating her needs to those of her children. . . . The counterpart to the image of the Virgin Mary is that of the Whore, as manifested in the story of Mary Magdalene, the prostitute who is counseled by Christ. As a Virgin Mary opposite, the Whore is seen as aggressive, impure, disconnected from motherhood, and a male sexual object. Her sexuality is constructed to service men, and her personhood (if she is granted any) is focused through this role.
>
> Women as citizens are projected as being under the care and supervision of the state. . . . In this extension of Catholic imagery, the various offices of the state—whether they are heads of state, generals, or police authorities—are extensions of male family members. Women who deviate from the characteristics associated with the Virgin Mary by disobeying state authority and assuming an active role in society can be cast into the opposite role of symbolic whore.

3. See Florence Babb's (1989) superb and pioneering *Between Field and Cooking Pot*, in which she documents the struggles vendors face in organizing politically and overcoming ambivalence about their class identities.

4. See, for example, AHM Leg. 90, 1929–30, a letter dated November 12, 1930 to Cuzco's mayor from the market inspector, or another letter, AHM Leg. 98, 1935, dated

April 17, 1935, from the Abbess of the Convent of Santa Clara and other property owners, regarding the horribly unhygienic conditions of the market.

5. Peru has a history of peasant organizing in formal political parties and federations.
They attempt to combat racist ideologies by making economic demands for land and
citizen rights, but these demands are rarely couched in terms of a recognition of indigenous culture or values, and they are rarely explicit condemnations of Peru's racist
heritage.

6. Mirko Lauer (1997) has written a series of insightful essays discussing the history of the concept of *indigenismo* in Peru between the 1920s and 1950s, distinguishing between a nativism that directly entailed returning to Peru's native "Indian" roots
and what he calls "*indigenismo-2*" in which "Indians" are used, manipulated, represented and co-opted by different sectors of Peru's criollo society. He also explores
the gap that exists between how indigenism has been constructed politically and
culturally. Marisol de la Cadena (1998) also addresses the political and regional cultural movement of *indigenismo,* painting a detailed picture of its proponents and its
evolution in Cuzco itself.

7. Original Quechua: "Kaypi wañuchiway munaspaykiywa. Qan kaniwanki waway-
kunata."

8. According to what I heard, the national police are more supportive of the vendors than the municipal police. I find that this division has more to do with the rivalry
that has long existed between the different police forces than it has to do with any sympathy for the plight of the vendors.

9. Original Quechua: "Manachu mamaykiqan. Maymanta naciramunki qan kay
abusuta ruwaranaykikupaq. Kunanmi rik'unki takaykimanta hap'ispa allinta sarusaykitu
huk kutinpi mana kayta ruwawanaykikupaq. Wañuchinakusunpas piru kuskamanta!"

10. The following wry commentary from Salcedo's (1993:110) saga of heroic vendor
become magnate captures the futility of municipal measures and infrastructures intended to stanch the flow of vendors on the streets:

> With Independence and the formation of the Republic, a veritable . . . flood
> of municipal ordinances tried to block the work of itinerant vendors while, at
> the same time, artists like the painter Pancho Fierro and the writer Manuel
> Asencio Segura were inspired by their actions to create a folkloric genre of paint-
> ing and theater.
>
> But each new municipal ordinance also signified a small advance for the ven-
> dors. Each prohibition also concealed some concession. Every prohibition was
> also a recognition of the existence of their activities.
>
> In 1915, an ordinance was passed prohibiting the sale of food in the street and
> denying itinerant vendors the right to use public thoroughfares, but it also es-
> tablished some hygienic control, allowed the use of tricycles, and provided for
> the registration and payment of municipal licenses. In 1959, a new municipal
> ordinance recognized the right to "transitory standing" in public thoroughfares
> and limited the capital of itinerant vendors to a maximum of 2,000 soles. As has
> occurred with so many Peruvian laws, this municipal disposition would promptly

become "a dead letter." An old colonial tradition established that in Peru, "the law is respected but not complied with." In fact, for that immense wave of provincial immigrants, to comply with the law was equivalent to death. As was true since colonization, the country continued legislating for minorities despite the government's own recognition that the life of the street transpired via other paths.

Conclusion: What's in Store?

Peru has captured the imagination of people the world over because of its Inca monumental heritage, typified by the grandeur of Machu Picchu, quaint customs, haunting Andean music, mummified Inca ice queens, the ocean currents of El Niño, and massive earthquakes. These romantic images are balanced by the violence of the years of Peru's civil war, reported almost daily in the international media, and by the cowboy-and-Indian drug wars, which in large part have been scripted, if inadvertently at times, by U.S. anti–drug trafficking policies.[1]

Far less flashy perhaps are the lives of the numerous men and women making their living in the cities of Peru, often with little to begin with other than a few oranges and bananas, one or two contacts, the clothes on their back, and the knowledge they have acquired in the countryside and in the course of making their way to the city. They are contributing to the character of today's Peru. This image is rarely spoken of in international circles, and within Peru it is viewed by many middle- and upper-class Peruvians, and by some politicians, as a problem to be solved or as a festering sore. For some Peruvians, the reality of Peruvian street lives has been transformed miraculously into a gay and festive folkloric image as a projection of the essence of Peru.

In his tale of the life of a poor vendor from the countryside who makes good in Lima, Salcedo drives home the following demographic facts about the changing face of Peru's capital. Over twenty years, between 1957 and 1977,

> two out of every three Peruvians lived in cities, exactly the opposite of the way things were in 1940. During those 40 years [from 1940 to 1977], the urban population grew more than three percent per year; the rural population grew at less than one percent. Between 1940 and 1981, the number of migrants increased more than six times. . . . Twenty years later, two thirds of Lima's population was comprised of migrants or the children of migrants.

*My research assistant, Teófila Huaman Tito, her sister, Cleófila, and her mother, Justina,
at their fruit stand along San Pedro Street, 1998.*

> Between 1976 and 1981, a second migratory wave took place. . . . While
> in the traditional district of Barranco, six persons a day were born; in Co-
> mas [a migrant neighborhood], more than 35 were born per day. In aristo-
> cratic San Isidro, the statistics estimate that 1.5 new San Isidrinos were born
> per day; in tumultuous Lurigancho, almost 40 births took place every 24
> hours. (Salcedo 1993:105–6)

I am not invoking these demographic statistics to suggest that the struggles
involving Andean market women result from overpopulation but rather to
highlight the dramatic transformations that have taken place in Peru's social
geography. Cuzco, with a population of 300,000 and the capital of a highland
department, hardly holds the same magnetism for migrants as does the national capital of Lima, with a population of 13 million, but it too has been the
site of unprecedented migratory movement and population shifts, and these
movements have had substantive consequences for Peruvians and for the ways
Peru is thought about in international circles.

Diving In

Whenever I return to Cuzco, one of the first things I have to do is go to the market. In my early trips there, I went mainly to purchase things I needed to take with me to the countryside for two weeks at a time or to have handy while I was working in the city. After I started working on this project, I went to various markets, not only for my research but also to visit the women I had gradually gotten to know. Sometimes, I accompanied them, walking along dusty paths, from the market to their houses high on the hillsides surrounding the city—compounds still under construction, furniture tightly encased in thick plastic, guinea pigs darting back and forth on a mud floor, a second story just under way, a propane stove, television, stereo system, and refrigerator proudly displayed in the living room, books neatly shelved next to documents wrapped in yellowing newspaper—and slurped a delicious soup while worrying about the snarling dog that guarded the entryway.

Despite my many trips back and forth to the market, I always found it a difficult undertaking, fraught with a degree of fear and confusion. I had to brace myself for my market days. It felt like diving in and being blinded by murky and turbulent water. Even now, when the patterns of the market are less opaque and I can see through the chaos to human beings, economic laws, and cultural models at work that transform or challenge those laws, a fairly clear psychological divide separates the cafés, plazas, circuits of traffic, serpentine flows of pedestrians, and variety of neighborhoods, from the open air and central indoor markets of the city. It is this sensation that in part compelled me to write *Peruvian Street Lives*. I wanted to try to understand why that border persists and to bring the lives of market women into the center from the margins that they occupy in the public imagination. An even more compelling reason for me to write this account was the paradoxical reality of Cuzco that challenged so forcefully the existence of the border itself. Not only in Cuzco but throughout Peru, this divide has been dissolved by the gradual transformation of the cities themselves, which are inhabited primarily by people very much like the women of the markets I have described. Their clothes, folkloric images on billboards, music, and cuisine have come to constitute the identity of Peruvian urban life, even as market women themselves are too often treated as if they do not exist or are a scourge on decency by a shrinking yet powerful minority. Even as some Peruvians seek to shore up the border and the women of the market fight among themselves; conform or reject the status quo of decency, sexual norms, and gender stereotyping; sell their wares and hang onto their stalls; and place their faith in the saints who watch over them, their children, the land, and their business, the face of Peru continues slowly and surely to change.

As I worked on this book, the reasons why it was such a big step for me to dive in became clear: Put simply, the ease of living with clearly defined categories—wealth and poverty, Indian and mestizo, educated and illiterate, male and female, rural and urban—was shattered in the informal markets of Cuzco. The markets were hardly mixing bowls or melting pots, but the women who worked in them could not be neatly placed. Practically speaking and sociologically, they defied being delimited, and for me as for so many people, this was unsettling.

The open air markets may some day be a peculiarity of the past, replaced by regulated supermarkets. For a moment I imagine, nostalgically, that the culture of the markets and the paradoxes and struggles of the women who work in them will gradually become part of the history of the city. The women will recount to their children their personal stories of going from rags to riches, and they will elaborate their life histories with the flourishes they have absorbed from the soap operas that so many of them watch on television. As dangerous as it is to make predictions, however, I think it far more likely that even as the demographic trends Salcedo notes continue, even as the border ceases to exist as a checkpoint that can operate with any kind of efficacy, and even as politicians recognize that polarized images and policies will no longer capture many votes, the border will persist. The watermarks of race, gender ideologies, and culture will indelibly affect the ability of market women to achieve upward mobility, have their citizenship rights respected, protect their persons from abuse, and gain acceptance socially. Of course, some will succeed, but many more will not. Of those who succeed, the majority will reject their roots. Their children may re-embrace them, perhaps, following the age-old pattern of generations of immigrants to foreign lands. Still, the street lives of Cuzco's market women have their own momentum. Eyes that watch and ears that listen from the sidewalks and stalls take in the secrets of the street and gain power from knowing they have stories to tell, music to dance to, people to meet, families to nurture, and places to go. They also know how to convert that knowledge into what people cannot do without.

Note

1. U.S. anti–drug trafficking policies in Latin America have focused primarily on eradicating coca, the leaf from which cocaine is processed, and on destroying processing plants that transform coca leaves into paste and then into cocaine powder. Cultivation has taken place primarily in Peru and Bolivia, whereas processing and export to the United States and Europe occur primarily in Colombia. The United States has

periodically invested millions of dollars (and most recently more than a billion dollars in the form of Plan Colombia) in equipment and militaries in these countries to fight the drug war and has sometimes intervened directly, providing agents from the Drug Enforcement Agency to support the war. In both Peru and Colombia, these investments have taken place concurrently with civil wars. It has been well documented that U.S. funds intended for fighting drugs are channeled into purchase of weapons by militaries engaged in civil wars, drug traffickers and guerrillas use coca growers as pawns from whom they can extract taxes, and the military itself becomes caught in the net of corruption, benefiting from the lucrative drug economy. The herbicides used to destroy coca bushes harm human health and the environment, and it is very easy to recommence coca cultivation. Coca leaves grow in poor soil and provide a harvest three times a year, something that very few other cultigens can provide. Finally, coca has been part of the social etiquette and ritual life of Quechua people for centuries, and the stigma now associated with using it and the exorbitant tax on coca leaves are threatening a central aspect of Quechua identity. Gootenberg (1999), Pacini and Franquemont (1986), Morales (1989), and the Washington Office on Latin America (1991) provide excellent coverage of this complex topic.

References Cited

Abercrombie, Thomas. 1991. "To Be Indian, to Be Bolivian: 'Ethnic' and 'National' Discourses of Identity." In *Nation-States and Indians in Latin America*. Ed. Greg Urban and Joel Sherzer. 95–130. Austin: University of Texas Press.

Alberti, Giorgio and Enrique Mayer, eds. 1974. *Reciprocidad e Intercambio en los Andes Peruanos*. Lima: Instituto de Estudios Peruanos.

Albo, Xavier. 1991. *Pueblos Andinos, Siglo XX*. Unpublished manuscript. La Paz, Bolivia.

Albro, Robert. 1997. "Virtual Patriliny: Image Mutability and Populist Politics in Quillacollo, Bolivia." *Political and Legal Anthropology Review* 20 (1): 73–92.

———. 2000. "The Populist Chola: Cultural Mediation and the Political Imagination in Quillacollo, Bolivia." *The Journal of Latin American Anthropology* 5 (2): 30–88.

Allen, Catherine. 1988. *The Hold Life Has*. Washington, D.C.: Smithsonian Institution Press.

The American Heritage Dictionary of the English Language. 1992. 3rd ed. Boston: Houghton Mifflin.

Angles Vargas, Victor. 1983. *Historia del Cusco (Cusco Colonial)*. vol. 2, book 1. Lima: Industrial Gráfica.

Archivo Histórico Municipal (AHM), Cuzco. 1860–1869. Leg. 2, June 18, 1858.

———. 1860–1869. Leg. 2, September 17, 1858.

———. 1860–1869. Leg. 2, November 12, 1858.

———. 1860–1869. Leg. 2, February 7, 1859.

———. 1860–1869. Leg. 2, February 28, 1859.

———. 1924. Leg. 84, February 21, 1924.

———. 1924. Leg. 84, September 10, 1924.

———. 1924. Leg. 84, October 16, 1924.

———. 1924. Leg. 84, October 18, 1924.

———. 1925. Leg. 85, May 26, 1925.

———. 1929–30. Leg. 90, November 12, 1930.

———. 1930. Leg. 91, March 14, 1930.

———. 1935. Leg. 98, April 17, 1935.

——. 1945. Leg. 124, March 26, 1945.

——. 1950. Leg. 144, April 1, 1950.

——. 1950. Leg. 144, April 27, 1950.

——. 1950. Leg. 144, September 25, 1950.

——. 1950. Leg. 144, November 13, 1950.

Arguedas, José María. 1985 [1941]. *Yawar Fiesta*. Austin: University of Texas Press.

Arnillas Laffert, Federico. 1996. "Ekeko, alacitas y calvarios: La fiesta de Santa Cruz en Juliaca." *Allpanchis* 47: 119–35.

Babb, Florence. 1998 [1989]. *Between Field and Cooking Pot*. Austin: University of Texas Press.

Barrionuevo, Alfonsina. 1980. *Cusco Mágico*. Lima: Editorial Universo.

Bastien, Joseph. 1978. *Mountain of the Condor: Metaphor and Ritual in an Andean Ayllu*. St. Paul, Minn.: West Publishing. (Reissued by Waveland Press, 1985.)

Bolin, Inge. 1998. *Rituals of Respect: The Secret of Survival in the High Peruvian Andes*. Austin: University of Texas Press.

Buechler, Hans and Judith Marie Buechler. 1992. *Manufacturing against the Odds: Small-Scale Producers in an Andean City*. Boulder, Colo.: Westview Press.

Bunster, Ximena and Elsa M. Chaney. 1985. *Sellers and Servants: Working Women in Lima, Peru*. New York: Praeger.

Burns, Kathryn. 1999. *Colonial Habits: Convents and the Spiritual Economy of Cuzco, Peru*. Durham, N.C.: Duke University Press.

Chartier, Roger. 1979. "La 'Monarchie d'Argot' entre le mythe et l'histoire." In *Les Marginaux et les Exclus dans l'Histoire*. Ed. Bernard Vincent. Paris: Union Generale d'Editions.

Chauvin, Lucien D. 1998. *Latinamerica Press* 30 (48), Lima, December 24, 1998.

Colloredo-Mansfeld, Rudi. 1999. *The Native Leisure Class: Consumption and Cultural Creativity in the Andes*. Chicago: University of Chicago Press.

de Azevedo, Paulo O. D. 1982. *Cusco Ciudad Histórica: Continuidad y Cambio*. Lima: Proyecto Regional de Patrimonio Cultural PNUD/UNESCO y Ediciones PEISA.

de la Cadena, Marisol. 1996. *Race, Ethnicity, and the Struggle for Indigenous Self-Representation: De-Indianization in Cuzco, Peru, 1919–1992*. Doctoral dissertation, University of Wisconsin, Madison.

——. 1998. "From Race to Class: Insurgent Intellectuals *de Provincia* in Peru, 1910–1970. In *Shining and Other Paths: War and Society in Peru, 1980–1995*. Ed. Steve Stern. 22–59. Durham, N.C.: Duke University Press.

——. 2000. *Indigenous Mestizos: The Politics of Race and Culture in Cuzco, Peru, 1919–1991*. Durham, N.C.: Duke University Press.

de Soto, Hernando. 1989. *The Other Path: The Invisible Revolution in the Third World*. Foreword by Mario Vargas Llosa. Trans. June Abbott. New York: Harper and Row.

Du Bois, W. E. B. 1989 [1903]. "Double Consciousness and the Veil." In *The Souls of Black Folk*. 1–19. New York: Bantam.

Duneier, Mitchell. 1999. *Sidewalk*. New York: Ferrer, Strauss and Giroux.

El Comercio, 1998. "Intervención de la calle Qasqaparo es inminente." Cuzco, September 3, 1998, p. 3.

El Comercio, 1998. "Unos ochocientos comerciantes ambulantes dejarán la avenida Grau." Lima, August 24, 1998, p. A9.

El Comercio, 1998. "Vendedores ambulantes abandonan las calles centrales de Cañete." Lima, November 16, 1998.

El Comercio, 2001. April 4, 2001.

El Sol, 1998. "Comerciantes de Tres Cruces de Oro protestan contra burla del Alcalde." Cuzco, September 2, 1998, p. 3.

Espinoza Soriano, Waldemar. 1987. *Artesanos, Transacciones, Monedas y Formas de Pago en el Mundo Andino, Siglos, XV y XVI*, vol. 1. Lima: Banco Central de Reserva del Perú.

Fuller, Norma. 1997. "Fronteras y retos: varones de clase media del Perú." In *Masculinidad/es: Poder y Crisis*. Ed. Teresa Valdés and José Olavarría. 139–52. ISLA, Ediciones de Las Mujeres. Santiago: FLACSO.

Garmendia, Roberto F. 1968. *El Progreso del Cuzco, 1900–1977*. Lima, n.p.

Giddens, Anthony. 1984. *The Constitution of Society: Outline of the Theory of Structuration*. Cambridge, England: Polity Press.

Gill, Lesley. 1994. *Precarious Dependencies: Gender, Class and Domestic Service in Bolivia*. New York: Columbia University Press.

———. 1997. "Relocating Class: Ex-Miners and Neoliberalism in Bolivia." *Critique of Anthropology* 17 (3): 293–312.

Gootenberg, Paul, ed. 1999. *Cocaine: Global Histories*. London: Routledge.

Gupta, Akhil and James Ferguson. 1992. "Beyond 'Culture': Space, Identity, and the Politics of Difference." *Cultural Anthropology* 7 (1): 1–23.

Guss, David. 2000. *The Festive State: Race, Ethnicity, and Nationalism as Cultural Performance*. Berkeley: University of California Press.

Haraway, Donna J. 1988. "Situated Knowledges: The Science Question in Feminism as a Site of Discourse on the Privilege of Partial Perspective." *Feminist Studies* 14 (3): 575–600.

Hardoy, Jorge, ed. 1983. *El Centro Histórico del Cusco*. Lima: Banco Industrial del Peru.

Harris, Olivia. 1995. "The Sources and Meanings of Money: Beyond the Market Paradigm in an *Ayllu* of Northern Potosí." In *Ethnicity, Markets, and Migration in the Andes: At the Crossroads of History and Anthropology*. Ed. Brooke Larson and Olivia Harris. 297–328. Durham, N.C.: Duke University Press.

Harrison, Faye. 1998. "Introduction: Expanding the Discourse on Race." *American Anthropologist* 100 (3): 609–31.

Hartman, Roswith. 1971. "Mercados y ferias prehispánicos en el área andina." *Boletín de la Academia Nacional de Historia* (Quito) 54 (118): 214–35.

Kearney, Michael. 1996. *Reconceptualizing the Peasantry: Anthropology in Global Perspective*. Boulder, Colo.: Westview Press.

Klarén, Peter. 2000. *Peru: Society and Nationhood in the Andes*. Oxford: Oxford University Press.

Krauss, Clifford. 2001. "To Weather Recession, Argentines Revert to Barter." *The New York Times,* May 6, 2001.

La República, 1998. "Municipalidad habría pagado campaña a Raúl Salízar Saico." October 17, 1998, p. 7.

Lahr, John. 2002. "Whirlwind." *The New Yorker,* December 9, 2002, pp. 100–109.

Langer, Erick. 2002. "Spatial Analysis and Ethnic Economies in the Andes, 1780–1980." Paper presented at the Southern Historical Association Meetings, Baltimore, Maryland, November 2002.

Larson, Brooke. 1991. "Andean Communities, Political Cultures, and Markets: The Changing Contours of a Field." In *Ethnicity, Markets, and Migration in the Andes: At the Crossroads of History and Anthropology*. Ed. Brooke Larson and Olivia Harris. 4–53. Durham, N.C.: Duke University Press.

Larson, Brooke, Olivia Harris, and Enrique Tandeter, eds. 1995. *Ethnicity, Markets, and Migration in the Andes*. Durham, N.C.: Duke University Press.

Larson, Brooke and Rosario León. 1995. "Markets, Power, and the Politics of Exchange in Tapacarí, c. 1780 and 1980." In *Ethnicity, Markets, and Migration in the Andes*. Ed. Brooke Larson, Olivia Harris, and Enrique Tandeter. 224–56. Durham, N.C.: Duke University Press.

Lauer, Mirko. 1997. *Andes Imaginarios: Discursos del Indigenísmo 2*. Lima: SUR and CBC.

Lefebvre, Henri. 1991. *The Production of Space*. Trans. Donald Nicholson-Smith. Oxford: Blackwell.

MacCormack, Sabine. 1991. *Religion in the Andes: Vision and Imagination in Colonial Peru*. Princeton, N.J.: Princeton University Press.

Mannheim, Bruce and Krista van Vleet, 1998. "The Dialogics of Southern Quechua Narrative." *American Anthropologist* 100 (2): 326–46.

Marcus, George. 1998. *Ethnography through Thick and Thin*. Princeton, N.J.: Princeton University Press.

Massey, Doreen. 1992. "Politics and Space/Time." *New Left Review* 196:65–84.

Matos Mar, José. 1988. *Desborde Popular y Crisis del Estado: El Nuevo Rostro del Perú en la Decada de 1980*. Lima: CONCYTEC.

Mauss, Marcel. 1967. *The Gift: Forms and Functions of Exchange in Archaic Societies*. New York: Norton.

Mayer, Enrique. 2002. *The Articulated Peasant: Household Economies in the Andes*. Boulder, Colo.: Westview Press.

Medina, Leandro. 1991. *Interacción Verbal en un Centro de Abstos de Puno*. Unpublished manuscript.

Mendoza, Zoila. 1998. "Genuine but Marginal: Exploring and Reworking Social Contradictions through Ritual Dance Performance." *Journal of Latin American Anthropology* 3 (2): 86–117.

Mintz, Sidney. 1964. "The Employment of Capital by Market Women in Haiti." In *Capital, Saving and Credit in Peasant Societies*. Ed. Raymond Firth and B. S. Yamey. 256–86. London: George Allen and Unwin.

———. 1996. *Tasting Food, Tasting Freedom: Excursions into Eating, Culture, and the Past*. Boston: Beacon Press.

Montoya, Rodrigo. 1998. *Multiculturalidad y Política: Derechos Indígenas, Ciudadanos y Humanos*. Lima: SUR, Casa de Estudios del Socialismo.

Morales, Edmundo. 1989. *Cocaine: White Gold Rush in Peru*. Tucson: University of Arizona Press.

Municipalidad del Cuzco. 1993. *Plan de Gobierno Municipal Qosqo, 1993–1995: Programa de Acondicionamiento Teritorial Desarrollo Urbano*. Cuzco: Municipalidad del Cuzco.

Nash, June. 1979. *We Eat the Mines and the Mines Eat Us: Dependency and Exploitation in Bolivian Tin Mines*. New York: Columbia University Press.

The New York Times. 2003. "Peru: 20-Year Conflict Claimed 69,000." Aug. 29, 2003, p. A3.

Orlove, Benjamin. 1998. "Down to Earth: Race and Substance in the Andes." *Bulletin of Latin American Research* 17 (2): 202–22.

Pacini, Deborah and Christine Franquemont, eds. 1986. *Coca and Cocaine: Effects on People and Policy in Latin America*. Cultural Survival Report, No. 23. Cambridge, Mass.: Cultural Survival and Latin American Studies Program, Cornell University.

Plattner, Stuart. 1989. *Economic Anthropology*. Stanford, Calif.: Stanford University Press.

Radcliffe, Sarah. 1997. "The Geographies of Indigenous Self-representation in Ecuador: Hybridity, Gender and Resistance." *European Review of Latin American and Caribbean Studies* 63:9–27.

Rockefeller, Stuart. 1998. "'There Is Culture Here': Spectacle and the Inculcation of Folklore in Highland Bolivia." *Journal of Latin American Anthropology* 3 (2): 118–49.

Rogers, Mark, Special Issue Guest Editor. 1998. "Performance, Identity and Historical Consciousness in the Andes." *Journal of Latin American Anthropology* 3 (2).

Romero Neyra, Fernando. 1993. *Estudio Socio-Económico del Gremio de Trabajdores Ambulantes FEDETAC*. Cuzco: Centro de Estudios Regionales Andinos "Bartolomé de Las Casas."

Rostworowski, María. 1970. "Mercaderes del Valle de Chincha en la época prehispánica: un documento y unos comentarios." *Revista Española de Antropología Americana* (Madrid) 5:135–78.

———. 1977. *Etnía y Sociedad Costa Peruana Prehispánica*. Lima: Instituto de Estudios Peruanos.

Salcedo, José María. 1993. *El Jefe: De Ambulante a Magnate*. Lima: FIMART.

Salomon, Frank. 1978. *Ethnic Lords of Quito in the Age of the Incas: The Political Economy of North-Andean Chiefdoms*. Doctoral dissertation, Cornell University.

Samanez Argumedo, Roberto. 1992. "Ciudad de Cusco." *Revista Medio Ambiente y Urbanización* (Buenos Aires) 9:38.

Seligmann, Linda J. 1989. "To Be in Between: The Cholas as Market Women in Peru." *Comparative Studies in Society and History* 31 (4): 694–721.

———. 1993. "Between Worlds of Exchange: Ethnicity among Peruvian Market Women." *Cultural Anthropology* 8 (2): 187–213.

———. 1995. *Between Reform and Revolution: Political Struggles in the Peruvian Andes, 1969–1991.* Stanford, Calif.: Stanford University Press.

———. 1998. "Survival Politics and the Movements of Market Women in Peru in the Age of Neoliberalism." In *The Third Wave of Modernization in Latin America: Cultural Perspectives on Neoliberalism.* Ed. Lynne Phillips. 65–82. Wilmington, Del.: Scholarly Resources.

———. 2000. "Market Places, Social Spaces in Cuzco, Peru." *Urban Anthropology* 29 (1): 1–68.

———. In press. "The Art of Expressive Exchange: The Mediation of Quechua Identity in the Marketplace." In *Inscribing Andean Voices: Quechua Verbal Artistry.* Ed. John Schechter and Guillermo Delgado. Bonn: BAS.

Shanklin, Eugenia. 1998. "The Profession of the Color Blind: Sociocultural Anthropology and Racism in the 21st Century." *American Anthropologist* 100 (3): 669–79.

Sikkink, Lynn. 2001. "Traditional Medicines in the Marketplace: Identity and Ethnicity among Female Vendors." In *Women Traders in Cross-Cultural Perspective: Mediating Identities, Marketing Wares.* Ed. Linda J. Seligmann. 209–25. Stanford, Calif.: Stanford University Press.

Silverman, Helaine. 2002. "Touring Ancient Times: The Present and Presented Past in Contemporary Peru." *American Anthropologist* 104 (3): 881–902.

Smith, Margo. 1973. "Domestic Service as a Channel of Upward Mobility for the Lower-Class Woman: The Lima Case." In *Female and Male in Latin America.* Ed. Ann Pescatello. 191–207. Pittsburgh: University of Pittsburgh Press.

Soja, Edward. 1989. *Postmodern Geographies: The Reassertion of Space in Critical Social Theory.* London: Verso.

Stepan, Nancy Leys. 1990. "Race and Gender: The Role of Analogy in Science." In *Anatomy of Racism.* Ed. David Theo Goldberg. 38–57. Minneapolis: University of Minnesota Press.

Stephen, Lynn. 1997. *Women and Social Movements in Latin America.* Austin: University of Texas Press.

Stephenson, Marcia. 1999. *Gender and Modernity in Andean Bolivia.* Austin: University of Texas Press.

Tamayo Herrera, José. 1981. *Historia Social del Cuzco Republicano.* Lima: Editorial Universo.

Vilas, Carlos. 1999. "The Decline of the Steady Job in Latin America." NACLA, *Report on the Americas* 32 (4): 15–20.

Walker, Charles. 1999. *Smoldering Ashes: Cuzco and the Creation of Republican Peru, 1780–1840*. Durham, N.C.: Duke University Press.

Washington Office on Latin America (WOLA). 1991. *Clear and Present Dangers: The U.S. Military and the War on Drugs in the Andes.* Washington, D.C.: WOLA.

Weismantel, Mary. 2001. *Cholas and Pishtacos: Stories of Sex and Race in the Andes.* Chicago: University of Chicago Press.

Weismantel, Mary and Steven Eisenman. 1998. "Race in the Andes: Global Movements and Popular Ontologies." *Bulletin of Latin American Research* 17 (2): 121–42.

Whitten, Norman E., ed. 1981. *Cultural Transformations and Ethnicity in Modern Ecuador.* Urbana: University of Illinois Press.

Willis, Paul. 1977. *Learning to Labor: How Working Class Kids Get Working Class Jobs.* New York: Columbia University Press.

Zelizer, Viviana. In press. "Circuits of Commerce." In *Self, Social Structure and Beliefs: Explorations in the Sociological Thought of Neil Smelser.* Ed. Jeffrey Alexander, Gary T. Marx, and Christine Williams. Berkeley: University of California Press.

Index

53, 176; as dancers, 179–80; as negative label, 129–30, 131, 138–40, 155, 205–6; in politicians' rhetoric, 150, 159n4, 205–7; reality vs. image of, 159; sexuality of, 147n10

circuits: capitalist and non-capitalist, 45, 81; of colonial economy, 177; of commodities, 81, 180, 192, 194n4; of debits and credits, 49; of industrial and finance capital, 14; of markets, 31, 39, 175, 214; of religious processions, 175, 194n6; of tourists and markets, 30, 39, 101; of transnational capital, 180, 181, 183

citizenship rights: complexity of implementing, 218–19; demand for, 216–17, 220; of Quechua people, 7; understanding and use of, 197–98, 202; union's use of, 206–7

civic pride, 24

civil war (Peru): as context, 8, 197

class: anxieties based in, 22–23; dances and, 180; defense of system, 197–98; discrimination based in, 15, 70; fiesta preferences and, 176; race and perceptions of, 154–59; religiosity and, 188, 190–92. *See also* gender ideologies; racial ideologies; social status

clothing: of *campesinas,* 44; of *cholas,* 129–30, 150, 160n5; as marker, 150–57; for saint figures, 167–69, 171, 174, 180, 189, 194n8; as self-conscious choice, 145–46, 147n9, 155; sources of fiesta, 180, 181; territory and social status linked to, 157–58; transvestism and, 171–72

Clubes de Madres (Mothers' Clubs): role of supply and demand in, 114

Coca-Cola: as commentary on transnational capital, 181–82

coca leaves and chewing: attempt to eradicate, 226–27n1; example of, *151;* exchanges and offerings of, 46, 81, 126, 175; selling techniques and, 143; uses of, 18n3

Colloredo-Mansfeld, Rudi, 6

colonialism: alcohol use under, 18n3; Andean and Christian rituals under, 193–94n4; gender under, 5, 32, 169; legacy of, 221–22n10; modernity desired in, 22–23; native religiosity under, 187; racial categories under, 129; women's roles under, 32. *See also*

Catholicism and Catholic Church; Spanish invasion and conquest; Spanish language

commerce and trade: barter distinguished from, 146n1; environmental and marketing model and, 29–30; in fiesta/festival markets, 119; as market subsidiary, 21; role in countryside, 80; types of, 40n1; typical U.S. compared with informal Cuzco, 71–72. *See also* market

compadrazgo (fictive kinship): of author, 149; of cattle dealers and peasants, 137; in language of selling, 122; risk reduction and, 97; role of, 78–79, 80–84

competition: absence of, 3; as context of sociability, 38–39; in credit system, 109; decline of wholesaler-retailer, 100–102; of neighborhoods, 194n6; of permanent vs. itinerant vendors, 204–5; political mobilization in context of, 201; respect juxtaposed to, 83; skills in balancing, 45; solidarity juxtaposed to, 45–46, 48–49, 53; vendors' communication with consumers and, 120–21, 135

consumers: butchers' exchanges with, 137–40; hostility of, toward wholesalers, 88; impersonal relationships of, 87; language of, 133–34, 139–40, 150–51; meat desired by, 136, 137; organizing by, 91; perceptions of, 12, 95; regulations requested by, 90–91; social status of, 130–36; vendors' communication with, 120–23, 130–32, 135. *See also* mestizos/mestizas

contradanza (dance), 194n11

Convent of La Merced, 22

convents, 22, 194n8

credit: dependence on, 84–85; record keeping of, 47, 50, 109, 110; types of, 107; vendor's description of, 49–50; wholesalers' role in, 81, 82, 95–97; wholesale system of, 108–10; words for, 85, 86n11. *See also* banks; loans

credit associations, rotating, 107, 116–17

creditos (scrip or barter money), 46, 109

crime, 25, 26, 72, 204

Cuzco: Catholic patroness of, 142; description of, 1, 17n1; development project in, 209–11; market report and proposal for, 101–2; as multilayered hierarchy of space,

14; official market in, 22–23; Plaza of San
Francisco in, 22, 128; population of, 21–22,
24, 41n4, 224; psychological borders dis-
solved/defended in, 225–26; Tacna compared with, 127. *See also* Plaza de Armas
(Cuzco)
Cuzco Municipal Council, 61

dances and dancers: *cholas* as, 179–80; as expression of faith, 178–79; in fiesta activities,
172, 174, 175, 176–77; origins of, 177, 194n11;
sexual and identity play of, 181–82; transportation differences in development of,
177–78
Day of the Dead, 126
debt, 85, 86n11. *See also* credit
decente and decency, 23, 122
de la Cadena, Marisol: on Almudena, 175–76;
on *cholas*, 117–18n1; on *indigenismo*, 206,
221n6; as influence, 6
demonstrations: against relocation, 206–17;
street theater as, 105–7; against taxes and
SUNAT, *98,* 102
de Soto, Hernando, 151, 159n2
diana, 167
disease, 23, 203–4
domestic servitude: less demand for, 197;
market purchases and, 139–40; as means of
survival in economy, 32, 64; struggles in,
70n1
Dori. *See* Argondoña Martínez de Gutierrez,
Doris ("Dori")
"double vision" concept, 60, 191
drug trafficking, 113, 223, 226–27n1
dualities concept, 12
Du Bois, W. E. B., 60, 191
Duneier, Mitchell, 69–70, 203–4
Durkheim, Émile, 183

earth: value judgments and, 157
earthquakes, 37, 165
ecology: marketing models based in, 29, 81
Economic Commission on Latin America
and the Caribbean, 28
economic models: assumptions in, 45; ecol-
ogy/agricultural cycles as basis for, 29, 81;
in Quechua context, 146n5

economies: decline of, 97–100, 107–8; diverse
circuits in, 45; effects of monetary, 85–
86n5; environment's control and, 29–30;
respect juxtaposed to, 83, 86n10; subsistence and import linkages in, 41n3. *See also*
employment; informal sector; money;
neoliberal economic measures
Ecuador: central market nodes in, 40n1;
hybridity in, 145; indigenous movement in,
205
education: desire for, 66, 67, 108; as marker,
55, 150–51, 154; territorial affiliation linked
to, 157; upward mobility possible via, 129,
148–49, 191, 197
Eisenman, Steven, 124
ekeko (good-luck man/statue), 46, 53n1
El Chinito (supermarket), 30
El Comercio (Lima), 100, 103n6, 209
electricity, 23
El Sol (Cuzco), 212–13, 214
employment: formal sector, 48; informal
sector, 28; instability of, 55–56; losses of,
108, 112, 116, 197; sexual division of labor
in, 56–57; by vendors, 204
environment: social/economic control of,
29–30
equality: beliefs in, 154–55, 190. *See also* citizenship rights
Espinoza Soriano, Waldemar, 40n1
ethnic status: complexities of, 124–25; labeling and, 191–92; self-representation of, 196.
See also cholos/cholas (half breeds); indigenous people; mestizos/mestizas; racial
ideologies
ethnography, 9–13, 218
Evangelical Protestantism: alcohol rejected
in, 59–60; economic standing and, 190–91;
equality as ideal of, 155; ethnic labeling and,
191–92; family ideal of, 56; fiesta participation and, 162, 188–89; introduction of, 163
evolutionary theory, 150, 154
exchange: business use of (wholesalers), 73–
77; context of, 122, 146n4; enacted
through dance, 181–83; fiesta procession as
reflective of, 175; ritualized use of, 81. *See
also ayni* (reciprocal exchanges); language
of selling; market chain; reciprocity

Linda J. Seligmann is a professor of anthropology and coordinator of the anthropology program at George Mason University. Her publications include *Women Traders in Cross-cultural Perspective: Mediating Identities, Marketing Wares; Between Reform and Revolution: Political Struggles in the Peruvian Andes, 1969–1991;* and numerous articles in such journals as *Cultural Anthropology, American Ethnologist,* and *Ethnohistory.* She also occasionally publishes political analyses in local and national newspapers and journals, including the *Washington Post* and *Latin American Studies Association Forum.*

Define + cite examples of "popular religiosity" in Cuzco. How does religion influence the market economy and the specific economic lives of women?

The University of Illinois Press
is a founding member of the
Association of American University Presses.

Composed in 10/13 Galliard
with Galliard display
by Jim Proefrock
at the University of Illinois Press
Designed by Dennis Roberts
Manufactured by Thomson-Shore, Inc.

University of Illinois Press
1325 South Oak Street
Champaign, IL 61820-6903
www.press.uillinois.edu